P9-ASJ-152

MOTHERS AND DAUGHTERS
IN THE TWENTIETH CENTURY

MOTHERS AND DAUGHTERS IN THE TWENTIETH CENTURY

A LITERARY ANTHOLOGY

EDITED AND INTRODUCED BY
HEATHER INGMAN

Edinburgh University Press

© Selection and Introduction Heather Ingman, 1999

Edinburgh University Press Ltd
22 George Square, Edinburgh

Typeset in Weiss
by Hewer Text Ltd, Edinburgh, and
printed and bound in Great Britain by
MPG Books Ltd, Bodmin

A CIP record for this book is available
from the British Library

ISBN 0 7486 1175 4 (paperback)

The right of the contributors to be
identified as authors of this work has
been asserted in accordance with the
Copyright, Designs and Patents Act 1988.

For my mother-in-law,
Irene von Prondzynski

CONTENTS

Acknowledgements   ix
Prefatory note   xiii
Introduction   1

Charlotte Mew (1869–1928)   43
The Quiet House   46

May Sinclair (1863–1946)   49
From *Mary Olivier: A Life* (1919)   51

Anna Wickham (1884–1947)   57
The Angry Woman (1916)   60

Anzia Yezierska (?1880–1970)   64
From *Bread Givers* (1925)   67

Winifred Holtby (1898–1935)   73
From *South Riding* (1936)   75

Virginia Woolf (1882–1941)   86
From *A Sketch of the Past* (1939–40)   90

Jean Rhys (1890–1979)   96
From *Wide Sargasso Sea* (1966)   99

Tillie Olsen (?1913–)   110
I Stand Here Ironing (1956)   113

CONTENTS

Sylvia Plath (1932–1963)   122
Balloons (1963)   125

Margaret Drabble (1939–)   127
From *The Millstone* (1965)   129

Adrienne Rich (1929–)   146
Mother-in-Law (1980)   149

Storm Jameson (1891–1986)   151
From *Journey from the North* (1969)   154

Kathleen Raine (1908–)   164
Heirloom (1971)   166

Alice Walker (1944–)   168
From *In Search of Our Mothers' Gardens* (1974)   171

Maya Angelou (1928–)   183
From *I Know Why the Caged Bird Sings* (1969)   186

Toni Morrison (1931–)   200
From *Beloved* (1987)   203

Eavan Boland (1944–)   217
Night Feed (1982)   219

Zee Edgell (1940–)   221
From *Beka Lamb* (1982)   223

Amy Tan (1952–)   230
From *The Joy Luck Club* (1989)   232

Angela Carter (1940–1992)   240
Ashputtle *or* The Mother's Ghost (1987)   243

Margaret Atwood (1939–)   253
Giving Birth (1982)   255

Michèle Roberts (1949–)   272
God's House (1993)   274

Bibliography   293

ACKNOWLEDGEMENTS

I would like to thank everyone at Edinburgh University Press for their support for this project, especially my editor, Jackie Jones, and her assistant, Carol Duncan. They have been unfailingly available to give assistance and advice. I would particularly like to thank Patsy Stoneman for sparing the time to read an early draft of the introduction. Any errors that remain are of course my own. I would also like to thank the following for their support and advice: Angela Leighton, Marion Shaw and especially Ferdinand von Prondzynski. Lastly I would like to thank colleagues and students in the English Department at the University of Hull for providing a stimulating and pleasurable environment in which to write and teach.

Grateful acknowledgement is made to the following sources for permission to reproduce material in this book that has previously been published elsewhere. Every effort has been made to trace copyright holders but if any have inadvertently been overlooked, the editor and publishers will be pleased to make the necessary arrangements at the first opportunity.

Charlotte Mew: 'The Quiet House' from *Collected Poems and Prose* V. Warner (ed.), Carcanet in association with Virago, 1981, Manchester, reproduced by permission of Carcanet © the Estate of Charlotte Mew; May Sinclair: excerpt from *Mary Olivier. A Life*, published by Virago, 1980, London, reproduced with permission of Curtis Brown Ltd., London, on behalf of the Estate of May Sinclair © May Sinclair; Anna Wickham: 'The Angry Woman' from *The Writings of Anna Wickham, Free Woman and Poet*, edited and introduced by R. D. Smith, Virago, 1984, London, reproduced by permission of George Hepburn © George Hepburn and Margaret Hepburn; Anzia Yezierska: excerpt from *Bread Givers*, Persea Books, 1975, New York © Louise Levitas Henriksen 1970, reprinted by permission of Persea Books; Winifred Holtby: excerpt from *South Riding*, Virago, 1988, London, reprinted by permission of Little, Brown; Virginia Woolf: excerpt from 'A Sketch of the Past' from *Moments of Being* by Virginia Woolf, revised and enlarged edition published by The Hogarth Press, 1985, London, copyright © 1976 by Quentin Bell and Angelica Garnett, reprinted by permission of the executors of the Virginia Woolf Estate and by Harcourt Brace & Company; Jean Rhys: excerpt from *Wide Sargasso Sea*, published by Penguin, 1968, copyright © Jean Rhys 1966, reprinted by permission of Penguin Books and by W. W. Norton & Company, Inc.; Tillie Olsen: 'I Stand Here Ironing' published in *Tell Me A Riddle and Yonnondio*, Virago, 1990, London, reproduced by permission of the *Pacific Spectator* © 1956 by the

ACKNOWLEDGEMENTS

Pacific Coast Committee for the Humanities of the American Council of Learned Societies, in *Pacific Spectator*; Sylvia Plath: 'Balloons' from Sylvia Plath, *Collected Poems* edited by Ted Hughes, Faber & Faber, London, 1981, reproduced by permission of Faber and Faber Ltd. and HarperCollins, © Ted Hughes 1965; Margaret Drabble: excerpt from *The Millstone*, Penguin, 1968, Harmondsworth, originally published by Weidenfeld & Nicolson (1965), reproduced by permission of the Orion Publishing Group Ltd. and The Peters Fraser and Dunlop Group Limited on behalf of © Margaret Drabble 1965; Adrienne Rich: 'Mother-in-Law' from Adrienne Rich, *The Fact of a Doorframe. Poems Selected and New 1950–1984*, W. W. Norton & Company, Inc., 1984, New York, reprinted by permission of W. W. Norton & Company, Inc., © 1981, 1984 by Adrienne Rich © 1975, 1978 by W. W. Norton & Company, Inc.; Storm Jameson: extract from *Journey from the North Vol. 1*, Virago, 1984, London, reprinted by permission of The Peters Fraser and Dunlop Group Limited on behalf of The Estate of Storm Jameson © Storm Jameson 1969; Kathleen Raine: 'The Heirloom' from *Collected Poems*, Hamish Hamilton 1956, London, reproduced by permission of Kathleen Raine © Kathleen Raine; Alice Walker: for the excerpt from 'In Search of Our Mothers' Gardens' from *In Search of Our Mothers' Gardens: Womanist Prose* © 1974 by Alice Walker published in Great Britain by The Women's Press Ltd., 1984, 34 Great Sutton Street, London EC1V ODX, reprinted by permission of David Higham Associates and Harcourt Brace & Company; Maya Angelou: excerpt from *I Know Why the Caged Bird Sings*, Virago, 1984, London, reproduced by permission of Little, Brown and Random House USA © Maya Angelou 1969; Toni Morrison: excerpt from *Beloved*, published by Picador, 1988, London, reprinted by permission of International Creative Management, Inc. © Toni Morrison 1987; Eavan Boland: 'Night Feed' from Eavan Boland, *Collected Poems*, Carcanet, 1995, Manchester, reproduced by permission of Carcanet and W. W. Norton & Company, Inc. © Eavan Boland 1995; Zee Edgell: excerpt from *Beka Lamb*, Heinemann,

1982, Oxford, reprinted by permission of Heinemann Educational Publishers, a division of Reed Educational & Professional Publishing Ltd., © Zee Edgell 1982; Amy Tan: excerpt from *The Joy Luck Club*, Minerva, 1994, London, reproduced by permission of Abner Stein © Amy Tan 1989; Angela Carter: 'Ashputtle *or* The Mother's Ghost' from *Burning Your Boats* by Angela Carter, Chatto and Windus, 1995, reproduced by permission of the estate of the author c/o Rogers, Coleridge & White Ltd., 20 Powis Mews, London W11 1JN, copyright: The Estate of Angela Carter © 1995; Margaret Atwood: 'Giving Birth' from *Dancing Girls and Other Stories*, Virago 1984, London, first published in Great Britain by Jonathan Cape Ltd. 1982, reprinted by permission of Random House UK Ltd., and McClelland & Stewart, Inc., the Canadian publishers © 1977, 1982 by O. W. Toad, Ltd.; Michèle Roberts: 'God's House' from Michèle Roberts, *During Mother's Absence*, Virago, 1994, London, reprinted by permission of Little, Brown and Company (UK) © Michèle Roberts 1993.

PREFATORY NOTE

In this introduction I try to find links in the mother-daughter story across cultures and across decades. This does not mean that I regard motherhood as a fixed, universalised concept. On the contrary, as these extracts show, it is affected by many factors including race, class and history. In the headnotes I have endeavoured to provide each excerpt with its own social and cultural context.

'Year, if you have no Mother's day present planned,
reach back and bring me the firmness of her hand.'
(Judith Wright, 'Request to a Year')

INTRODUCTION

Amongst the immense flowering of women's writing this century the mother-daughter story takes pre-eminence. All women who write or read are daughters and some of them are mothers. During the course of the twentieth century the mother-daughter relationship has increasingly fascinated women writers who have seen in the bond with the mother the beginnings of their own story. Writing about their mothers they come to understand themselves.

'The loss of the daughter to the mother, the mother to the daughter, is the essential female tragedy' wrote Adrienne Rich in

Of Woman Born. Motherhood as Experience and Institution (1976). The recovery of that relationship with the mother is the subject of this anthology. Its beginnings, in the early part of this century, are muted. Charlotte Mew's poem, 'The Quiet House', presents a household robbed of its maternal presence by death. It echoes a situation common in nineteenth-century novels by women where mothers are largely absent, ailing, dead or devalued. Though not directly autobiographical (it was written before the death of Mew's mother), the poem nevertheless draws on the losses Mew suffered in her personal life, her feeling of extreme isolation and her longing for death and the dissolution of personality. In a letter dated 1913 Mew wrote that of all her poems 'The Quiet House' was the most subjective (Mew 1953: ix). The poem connects lack of a mother with lack of a strong identity on the part of the daughter.

When mothers do appear in fiction written by women at this date they are frequently the focus of their daughters' hostility, as in the extract from May Sinclair's novel, *Mary Olivier: A Life* (1919) where the daughter struggles against her mother's rigid definition of femininity. Mrs Olivier expects her sons to learn Greek but finds it inappropriate for a girl. She expects her sons to go away from her but she cannot tolerate any expression of independence on the part of her daughter. She is able, as this extract demonstrates, to bring the entire weight of society and its underpinning of patriarchal (which favours the male) religion to bolster her authority. In the course of the novel Mary has to learn to fight society, her mother, her heredity and her upbringing in order to develop herself as a poet. The portrait of her growth has been seen as the female counterpart to Joyce's *A Portrait of the Artist as a Young Man*.

May Sinclair was greatly interested in and influenced by Freud's psychoanalytical theories. In his early work Freud judged hostility to be characteristic of the bond between mother and daughter; however, towards the end of his life, he came round to the view that he had underestimated the strength of the mother-daughter bond. In his

1933 lecture on 'Femininity' he saw attachment to the mother as more prolonged for girls than for boys and crucial to the development of female identity.

In May Sinclair's novel, Mary Olivier's struggles are complicated by the fact that she is never able to break the tie with her mother. Sinclair goes beyond Freud in showing the bond between mother and daughter extended well into adulthood. In its portrayal of an unhealthy mutual dependence between mother and daughter *Mary Olivier* may be compared with Sinclair's later work, *The Life and Death of Harriett Frean* (1922), with its powerful analysis of the destructive and infantilising effects of Victorian ideas of self-sacrificing womanhood and the part mothers play in transmitting those ideas.

If so far we have only considered the daughter's angle that is because the mother's voice is fairly silent in this period. One exception is Anna Wickham's poem 'The Angry Woman' (1916). Although Wickham was the mother of sons, her poem has been included here as a remarkably early example of a mother speaking in her own voice and demanding not to be trapped in the mothering role. 'The Angry Woman' arose out of Wickham's experience of marriage to a husband who passionately resented her literary activities as diverting attention from himself. It may be compared with other poems where Wickham protests against the essentialising of mothers, for example 'Woman Determines to Take Her Own Advice', published in the same volume as 'The Angry Woman'. Wickham's demand for mothers to be recognised as subjects in their own right foreshadows the work of feminist theorists of the 1970s and 80s such as Adrienne Rich and Jessica Benjamin.

During the inter-war period in Britain the mother's voice is increasingly heard in fiction written by women. A number of factors contributed to the emerging discourse on motherhood in this period. One was the New Feminist concern for mothers in the home as opposed to Old Feminism's concentration on equal rights and women in the workplace. There was, too, an increased focus on mothers in a number of laws passed during the inter-war period, for example, the 1918 Maternity and Child Welfare Act, the 1922 Married Women (Maintenance) Act, the 1922 Law of Property Act and the 1925 Guardianship of Infants Act giving mothers equal right with fathers to appoint guardians for their children. There was a proliferation of advice to mothers in women's magazines and childcare manuals by medical experts. In particular in the inter-war period Frederick Truby King's ideas on childcare (strict routine, breastfeeding every four hours, early toilet training, not too much kissing and cuddling) became very influential. Devised partly to combat high infant mortality especially among the poor, King developed the notion of mothering as a craft in which mothers needed training and supervision by professionals (Richardson 1993: 32–7). With King, motherhood became institutionalised. This, in turn, placed tremendous pressure on mothers. Inter-war novelists as different as Rosamond Lehmann and E.M. Delafield write frankly about the difficulties of mothering. In Lehmann's novel *A Note in Music* (1930), Norah reflects that 'motherhood had proved in anticipation chiefly a physical process; in realization – not overwhelmingly glorious: an enormous worry and responsibility, an enormous hindrance to liberty' (Lehmann 1930/1982: 139). In *The Way Things Are* (1927) Delafield's heroine, Laura Temple, finds the advice in childcare manuals idealistic and unhelpful when she is confronted with the brute realities of childrearing.

Anthropologists like Jane Harrison (1850–1928) contributed to the emerging discourse on motherhood with their explorations of ancient matriarchal civilisations. In *Mythology* (1924) and in her earlier *Prolegomena to the Study of Greek Religion* (1903), Harrison argued that in the Homeric Olympus the mother, Demeter, came to be separated from the daughter, Kore, and robbed of her attributes which were then distributed amongst various maiden goddesses (Athene, Aphrodite and Artemis among others). Harrison clearly locates the power of the patriarchy in this separation of the mother from the daughter and the suppression of the mother's voice. 'Zeus the Father will have no great Earth-goddess, Mother and Maid in one, in his man-fashioned Olympus' she writes (Harrison 1922: 285).

Anzia Yezierska's novel, *Bread Givers* (1925), illustrates the burden of patriarchal religions on women's lives and the marginalisation of the mother they entail. Sara Smolinsky, the heroine of Anzia Yezierska's novel, is a Jew born in Russian Poland. Her family, like Yezierska's, has fled to the United States to escape persecution. *Bread Givers* is the story of Sara's rebellion against the Orthodox faith of her father. For Reb Smolinksy women are the servants of men: he expects his wife and daughters to provide financial support while he devotes his life to study of the Torah. 'It says in the Torah, only through a man has a woman an existence' he tells Sara (Yezierska 1925/1975: 137). But Sara has grown up in America: she rejects the Old World and its traditions, and leaves home determined to live her own life.

Although the mother figure is necessarily marginalised in this portrayal of a daughter struggling against a patriarchal religion, Sara's mother nevertheless plays an interesting role in the novel. Though her life has been one of self-sacrifice to the husband whom she hero-worships, Mrs Smolinsky gives Sara money to escape and, as this extract shows, aids her daughter in her chosen path. Sara feels guilty before her mother's example of sacrifice but she is unable to leave off pursuing the American dream of education and freedom. Studying at night to be a schoolteacher and working ten hours in a laundry by day, Sara has no time to visit her mother. She almost leaves it too late.

Despite her loyalty to her husband, it is Sara's mother who affirms her daughter in her chosen profession and, though she too worries about Sara's unmarried state, defends Sara against her sisters' sneers that she has become an old maid. The mother's memories of her girlhood in Poland and her brilliantly coloured hand-crocheted tablecloth evoke a spirit that has not been entirely crushed. In her autobiography *Red Ribbon a White Horse* (1950), Yezierska wrote of her own mother: 'Mother, who could outcurse the Devil when worried for bread, and who could outwail all the mourners at a funeral, could also outshine all the young girls dancing the *kazatzka* at a wedding when she was happy' (Yezierska 1950: 50). Covertly, Mrs Smolinsky aids her daughter in her rebellion against the father and his 'Torah-made world that's only for men' (Yezierska 1925/1975: 95).

Yezierska's novel shows the way in which a patriarchal society shapes the mother-daughter relationship and the extra burdens carried by working-class mothers and daughters. These themes are evident too in the extract from Winifred Holtby's novel *South Riding* (1936). In *South Riding* Sarah Burton, the headmistress of Kiplington High School, fights in the face of indifference from governors and the local authority to provide a decent education for her girls. She hopes to imbue her pupils – for the most part daughters of local tradespeople – with her own belief in life's possibilities. This excerpt reveals the extent to which Sarah underestimates the obstacles placed in the way of working-class girls like Lydia Holly even where, as in the case of Mrs Holly, the mother is supportive of her daughter's attempts to get an education. At the age of eleven, Lydia won a scholarship to Kiplington High but was unable to take it up until three years later because she was needed at home to look after her younger brothers and sisters. Now, with Mrs Holly pregnant again and having been told by her doctor that another pregnancy might be fatal, it seems as though Lydia will once again be forced to relinquish her education for domestic commitments. The grinding drudgery of the working-class mother's life is realistically evoked by Holtby. And the extract reminds us that at a time when mortality in general was falling rapidly maternal mortality actually increased during the inter-war period – a statistic that highlights government hypocrisy in proclaiming the value of mothers to the nation. Vera Brittain wrote in 1930 of 'the savagery of this country's contemptuous indifference towards the needs of maternity' (Berry and Bishop 1985: 133).

The suppression of the mother's voice in the patriarchy, high-lighted by Jane Harrison, was a problem that haunted Virginia Woolf for much of her life. Indeed it can be argued that the whole of Woolf's *oeuvre* may be seen as an attempt to recover the maternal principle as a counterweight to the patriarchy in which she lived (Ingman 1998: 125–44). Woolf's early daughter figures – Rachel Vinrace, Katharine Hilbery, Clara Durrant – all experience difficulty establishing themselves securely as adults partly through a reluctance to break with their mothers. In *Mrs Dalloway* (1925), embattled as she is in a patriarchal society, Clarissa Dalloway nevertheless expresses her maternal impulses to create and connect by giving parties which are for her a work of art, 'an offering' (Woolf 1925/1981: 109). And in *To the Lighthouse* (1927), Mrs Ramsay's ability to give shape to the moment presiding over a dinner party remains in Lily Briscoe's mind as a creative act. Lily realises that Mrs Ramsay's qualities of mothering are qualities she herself needs as an artist. She becomes the first of Woolf's daughter figures to inscribe herself into the symbolic without betraying the mother.

The ability of Mrs Dalloway and Mrs Ramsay to give shape to the moment recall Woolf's comment on her own mother, Julia Stephen, in the autobiographical sketch 'Reminiscences' written in 1908: 'All lives directly she crossed them seemed to form themselves into a pattern and while she stayed each one was of the utmost importance' (Woolf 1990: 42). In the extract from 'A Sketch of the Past' (written between April 1939 and November 1940) Woolf resurrects her mother, going behind the idealisations of her father's *Mausoleum Book* in an attempt to find the real woman, much as Rachel Vinrace in *The Voyage Out* (1915) has to lift the veil off her dead mother who has been presented to her as the Victorian model of how a woman should be, 'very sad and very good' (Woolf 1915/1981: 187).

Despite Woolf's efforts there is something in Julia Stephen which eludes her daughter, as there is something in Mrs Ramsay which eludes Lily Briscoe. In a patriarchy the mother's presence is not so easily retrieved. Yet others besides fiction writers were endeavouring to do so: the inter-war period was also a time when female psychoanalysts – Hélène Deutsch, Karen Horney, Anna Freud, Melanie Klein – were revising Freud's father-dominated theories in favour of a more mother-centred psychoanalysis.

Between 1924 and the early 1930s Karen Horney (1885–1952) spelled out her critique of Freud in a series of papers which insisted that the psychology of women had hitherto only been described from the male point of view. She drew attention to men's envy of women's mothering and argued that 'female identity was determined through identification with the mother rather than disappointed identification with the father' (Sayers 1991: 92).

In 1945 volume 2 of Hélène Deutsch's work *The Psychology of Women* was published, focusing on motherhood. In it she argues, as Julia Kristeva, Luce Irigaray and Sara Ruddick were later to continue, that mothering need not be limited to the reproductive function. Women, she says, can put their maternal qualities to use in the wider spheres of art and science 'by drawing indirectly upon the active aspirations of motherhood and the emotional warmth of motherliness' (Deutsch 1945: 487). Deutsch also states, against the climate created by the media in the inter-war period, that mothering does not possess a fixed universal essence but means different things to different women depending on such factors as a woman's emotional life, her economic situation, her personal ambitions, and so on (Deutsch 1945: 54–5). Partly as a result of her own experience of combining motherhood with the demands of a professional career, Deutsch was aware of the difficulties of mothering as well as of the fact that not all women engaged in a career might welcome the interruption of a child. Her emphasis on the difficulties facing mothers has parallels with the inter-war novels of Rosamond Lehmann and E.M. Delafield mentioned above.

During the inter-war period Melanie Klein's play therapy with children found that the child first identifies not with the father, as in Freud, but with the mother who thus becomes central in the infant's early development (see Klein's 'Early Stages of the Oedipal Conflict'

1928 in Mitchell 1991). Object-relations theory is generally held to derive from Klein's work. In 'The Origins of Transference' (1951: in Mitchell 1991) Klein argues that in the first few months of life the infant deals with internal anxieties by splitting herself and the object on which she vents her rage (the breast that goes away and frustrates her) into a good part and a bad part, directing feelings of love and gratification towards the 'good' breast and destructive impulses towards the 'bad' breast. This process occurs during the first three or four months of life and Klein terms it the paranoid-schizoid position. Gradually the ego's growing capacity for integration leads to states in which love and hatred are synthesised. This brings the infant into the depressive position, for Klein the central position in a child's development. The infant's aggressive impulses towards the bad breast are now felt to be a danger to the good breast as well, as increasingly the infant perceives and accepts the mother as a person. The infant's depressive anxiety is intensified as she feels she is destroying a whole object by her aggression.

According to Klein, this anxiety reaches its height by about the middle of the first year. The infant works through the depressive position as the ego becomes more unified and there is a growing perception of reality and adaptation to it. At this point, good experiences of being mothered allay the infant's anxiety and lead to an increase of love and trust. However, in the absence of adequate mothering the infant may have difficulty negotiating the depressive position and her future mental health may be put at risk.

Klein's theories may be usefully applied to the excerpt from Jean Rhys's novel *Wide Sargasso Sea*, published in 1966 but begun some time in the late 1930s. Rhys's novel shows the effect on a daughter of the absence of adequate mothering. As an impoverished white West Indian, despised by both wealthy Europeans and blacks, Annette Cosway lacks a positive identity to transmit to her daughter. Antoinette, her mother and her sick brother live in isolation and fear on their decaying estate. The beginning of Antoinette's life foreshadows her end when she will be trapped in Rochester's attic, robbed of her identity by the new name (Bertha) he has foisted on her.

Annette Cosway's failure to provide sufficient maternal nurturance leaves Antoinette forever haunted by memories of the lost maternal bond. The excerpt shows Christophine acting as a surrogate mother, rescuing Antoinette from her loneliness and providing her with a playmate. But Christophine is separated from Antoinette by race and class. She is powerless to help her survive in white patriarchal society: when Rochester invokes the twin arms of the patriarchy, the law and the police, Christophine is unable to defend Antoinette.

Like many of Rhys's heroines Antoinette, lacking a secure sense of self, drifts in a hostile society, trying to bolster her fragile identity with the aid of drink, perfume and fashionable clothes, all ways of conforming to a patriarchal society's construct of femininity. She looks to Rochester for the nurturance she was unable to gain from her mother but he fails her. At the end of the novel, in one mad, liberating gesture, Antoinette recovers the lost mother-daughter bond as she recreates the fire that engulfed her childhood home.

Rhys's novel illustrates Melanie Klein's view that the depressive position is never really worked through. Loss in later life can reawaken our fear of losing the good internal object. Klein's theory of art (outlined in 'Infantile Anxiety Situations Reflected in a Work of Art and in the Creative Impulse' 1929) as flowing not from a Freudian sublimation of the instinct but from a wish to repair relations with others and in the first place with the mother, is also useful in understanding some of the extracts in this anthology. In Rhys's own life her troubled relationship with her mother and with her mother country, Dominica, left her with a perpetual feeling of emptiness which was assuaged only by writing.

Rhys's failed relationship with her mother also left her unable to be an adequate mother herself. Her son died as a baby, possibly as a result of neglect (Angier 1990: 112–3). When her daughter, Maryvonne, was born in 1922 Rhys found herself unable to provide for her either emotionally or financially, and Maryvonne was largely brought up by other people. Rhys was not alone in this among our authors. Anzia Yezierska gave birth to a daughter, Louise, in 1912 but was unable to combine writing with motherhood and the four-year-old Louise was sent to live with her father. Another writer of the period, Antonia White, whose daughters were born in 1929 and 1931, frequently expresses in her journals her feeling of being burdened by them: 'I *must* consider the children though I often feel I would like to walk right out and start a new life by myself' she wrote in 1937 when her daughters were eight and six respectively (Chitty 1991: 98).

These writers' difficulties with mothering highlight the unreality of the advice they were being given by childcare professionals. In the 1940s and 50s the focus of childcare manuals switched from giving authoritarian advice to mothers to dwelling on the child's physical and emotional needs. Melanie Klein's British followers – Fairtrip, Guntrip, Winnicott – placed emphasis on the self as constructed in social relationships rather than through instinctual drives. This downplaying of Klein's emphasis on instinctual drives shifted attention to the environment provided by the mother. She became entirely responsible for her child's intellectual and emotional well-being and was portrayed as naturally merging her own needs with those of her child: in his essay 'The Mirror-Role of Mother and Family in Child Development' Donald Winnicott speaks of 'the mother's role of giving back to the baby the baby's own self' (Winnicott 1971: 118). The mother is central to her child's development but simply as an object for her child's needs. She must mirror the child's moods, not reveal her own. In his immensely popular book, *Child Care and the Growth of Love* (originally published as *Maternal Care and Mental Health*, 1951), John Bowlby stresses the damage caused to the child if deprived of the maternal presence and paints a picture of the mother devoting herself entirely to the care of her child while the father works to support them. That the mother should not go out to work, or indeed have any interests outside her child, is explicit in the writings of both Winnicott and Bowlby.

'I Stand Here Ironing', Tillie Olsen's extraordinarily moving short story, points up the idealisation of mothering present in these middle-class male theorists as well as their glossing over of the political and economic realities of mothers' lives. Published in 1956, 'I Stand Here Ironing' looks back to the Depression and the war years in America as the narrator-mother recalls their effect on her raising of her eldest daughter. The iron becomes a metaphor for the external circumstances which deform the mothering task: poverty, lack of support, the treatises on feeding to schedule, the interference by outside agencies. As in all of Tillie Olsen's work 'I Stand Here Ironing' portrays the social, political and economic structures that weigh on the lives of working-class mothers and daughters, restricting them from achieving their full potential. Yet in the end there may be hope for Emily as, almost instinctively, she rises above her circumstances and transforms her unpromising life into art, first in her games with Susan and then on the stage. Emily's choices are limited and she may never achieve her full potential, but her mother hopes there will be 'enough left to live by'.

'I Stand Here Ironing' may be compared with the title story of the collection in which it was published, 'Tell Me a Riddle', where the mother's voice, silenced by years of poverty and caring for others, breaks through at the end in anger as Eva reclaims her selfhood and her radical youth. Olsen's novel *Yonnondio* (1974), also explores working-class motherhood as Anna struggles to rise above the twin oppressions of class and gender and give her children an education. Her struggle is mirrored in that of her daughter, Mazie, who tries unsuccessfully to resist being drawn into her mother's life of drudgery, fighting to retain her creativity and intelligence. Olsen finds art and beauty and occasional moments of redemption in the daily lives of this mother and daughter while at the same time depicting the tragic waste of lives that have failed to reach their potential. It is too late for Anna and Mazie, but at the end of the novel there is hope for the future as baby Bess discovers her power.

In all her writings Tillie Olsen explores motherhood as the core of working-class women's oppression. In her groundbreaking work *Silences* (1978), she lists motherhood as one of the forces that historically has silenced women writers and she points out the loss to literature of the insights a woman writer who has experience of mothering might bring. One critic has said of Olsen: 'Her writings about mothering, about the complex, painful, and redemptive inter-actions between mother and child, have helped a new generation of women writers to treat that subject with a fullness and honesty never before possible in American literature' (Rosenfelt 1981: 397).

In *Silences*, Olsen attributes Sylvia Plath's suicide to the tragic conflict between her art and her responsibility to her two small children. Although financially more secure than Olsen's working-class mothers, Plath was still tied to the unvarying routine of caring for her children against the background of the 1950s and early 60s ideology of women as homemakers who were meant to assume total responsibility for their children. In childrearing, as in everything else, Plath set herself high standards: friends have testified to the care she took over her children. After Ted Hughes's desertion she would get up at four in the morning in order to fit in her writing with caring for them.

If Plath the daughter has been extensively discussed, Plath the mother has perhaps been less exhaustively trawled over. There has been an understandable tendency to interpret her later poems in the light of her death but, taken by itself, 'Balloons' is a wry, gentle poem. Addressed to her small daughter in February 1963, just over a week before Plath's death, it is full of perfectly observed detail which opens up to suggest universal themes of innocence, joy, change and loss. It may be compared with 'Candles' and 'Magi' written in 1960 and inspired by Frieda's birth, and also with Plath's late poems to her son, 'By Candlelight', 'Nick and the Candlestick' and 'Child'.

Motherhood in fact plays a large part in Plath's later poems. In 'Barren Women' her motherhood is brandished as a weapon against childless women, particularly Hughes's women friends. Her own miscarriage is remembered in 'Parliament Hill Fields' and 'Three Women', a verse play she wrote in 1962. In this play through her portrayal of three women on a maternity ward – one who gives birth to a son, one who suffers a miscarriage and a third who gives up her new-born daughter for adoption – Plath covers a remarkable range of women's feelings about childbirth. Her biographer, Anne Stevenson, calls it 'the first great poem of childbirth in the language' (Stevenson 1989: 234).

Al Alvarez has said of Plath: 'The *real* poems began in 1960, after the birth of her daughter, Frieda. It is as though the child were a proof of her identity, as though it [sic] liberated her into her real self' (Newman 1971: 58). Plath's tender, last poems to her children have been overshadowed by those savage poems casting off mother, father and husband, but they suggest she was finding a sort of redemption from suffering through her children. They make that failure even more tragic.

The ideology of the exclusive mother-child bond weighs heavily on Margaret Drabble's early 1960s novels. Drabble's novels stress the difficulties of mothering in a society where to abandon oneself to the needs of one's infant is seen as natural behaviour on the mother's part and they depict the problems encountered when highly educated young women find themselves trapped in the roles of wives and mothers. In *The Garrick Year* (1964) Emma discovers that with a baby on her knee she has suddenly become socially invisible, though previously she has been a successful model. This is a society which pays lip-service to idealisations of motherhood while in practice mothers are discounted even by other women. Emma reflects: 'Motherhood has of course infinite compensations, though I can well believe that some people are driven to a point where they cannot feel them' (Drabble 1964/1966: 10).

In *The Millstone* (1965), the birth of Rosamund's daughter provides a moral turning point in her life. Until now Rosamund, brought up by liberal middle-class parents to be independent and restrained, has evolved an evasive and self-protective lifestyle which allows no one to get close to her. She cannot bring herself to the intimacy of making love except once with the unthreatening George. She becomes pregnant and makes clumsy attempts at an abortion before deciding that it will be possible for her to have a baby without interrupting her academic career. Though brought into contact with another reality when she attends the National Health Service antenatal clinic with its patronising doctors and unfeeling treatment of pregnant women, Rosamund experiences a remarkably easy and joyful childbirth. She organises part-time childcare so that she can continue with her thesis, but her carefully arranged life starts to spin out of control when her daughter, Olivia, is discovered to have a congenital heart defect.

The excerpt shows Rosamund breaking out of her inherited puritan restraint. Refusing any longer to be self-effacing and considerate of others, she places her own needs and those of her daughter first. The institutionalisation of mothering which she had not resisted in childbirth she resists now as she screams hysterically to see her daughter against all the hospital rules.

Like many of Drabble's early heroines, Rosamund's self-discovery comes through maternity rather than sexuality but there is no easy sentimentalising of motherhood in Drabble's work. Emma knows that motherhood 'can sour and pervert the character beyond all recovery' (Drabble 1964/1966: 10), as indeed many of Drabble's older genera-tion of mothers in these novels have been soured. Drabble's novels are early examples of portrayals of the tensions of motherhood without the theorising that was to come later. Drabble writes out of her own experience of mothering rather than from any theoretical standpoint, though she has acknowledged the influence of Simone de Beauvoir's *The Second Sex* which she read at Cambridge (Rose 1980: 1–2). By looking at the effect of mothering in women's daily lives Drabble prepared the ground for the more theoretical discussions of the 1970s and 80s. 'There are undercurrents of rage' she has said, 'but those are veiled protests compared to the 80s' (Kenyon 1988: 89).

In these early novels Drabble often highlights the split between her heroines, minds and bodies. In *The Waterfall* (1969), Jane feels: 'My ability to kiss and care for and feed and amuse a small child merely reinforced my sense of division – I felt split between the anxious intelligent woman and the healthy and efficient mother – or perhaps less split than divided. I felt that I lived on two levels, simultaneously, and that there was no contact, no interaction between them' (Drabble 1969/1971: 103–4). This sense of a split between women's intellectual aspirations and the lives they were expected to lead as wives and mothers was angrily articulated in Betty Friedan's influential book *The Feminine Mystique* (1963) investigating the growing discontent among middle-class American wives and mothers at being confined to the home – the feminist movement was starting to get under way in America and Europe.

In the 1960s and early 70s, feminism tended to be dismissive of mothers, seeing them as having capitulated to the patriarchy's construct of femininity. In order for a daughter to achieve selfhood, they proclaimed, she had to cut herself off from her mother. The emphasis was on sisterhood rather than motherhood or daughterhood. Simone de Beauvoir's negative views on motherhood and the mother-daughter relationship in *The Second Sex* (1949) were still highly influential. 'Maternity' wrote de Beauvoir 'is usually a strange mixture of narcissism, altruism, idle day-dreaming, sincerity, bad faith, devotion and cynicism' (De Beauvoir 1949/1972: 528).

Then came Adrienne Rich's groundbreaking book *Of Woman Born. Motherhood as Experience and Institution* (1976) in which she draws on her own experience of motherhood as well as anthropology, medicine, psychology, literature and history in order to examine the patriarchal ideology of motherhood. She looks at the ways in which the patriarchy distorts both the relationship between mother and child and the practices surrounding childbirth. Rich calls upon women to reclaim their experiences of pregnancy, childbirth and motherhood. She strips bare the myths of the 'natural' mother, the maternal instinct and unconditional mother love as she describes her struggle after her sons' births to regain her sense of autonomy and continue writing poetry. 'I knew I was fighting for my life through, against, and with the lives of my children' she writes (Rich 1976/1977: 29). In her chapter on 'Motherhood and Daughterhood' describing her relationship with her own mother, Rich calls the mother-daughter relationship 'the great unwritten story' (Rich 1976/1977: 225) and examines the way in which that relationship has been distorted and trivialised by living under a patriarchy. She calls upon mothers to give daughters a sense of the possibilities of their lives and expands the term 'mothering' to include any woman who nurtures other women.

Rich's poem 'Mother-in-Law' picks up on themes in *Of Woman Born* by looking at the way in which women's identity is easily crushed in a male-dominated society and the mother-daughter relationship occluded, particularly when the daughter is a lesbian. In the early part of the twentieth century there had been a silence surrounding the mother and her lesbian daughter. In Radclyffe Hall's novel *The Unlit Lamp* (1924), the daughter's lesbianism is never openly named between Mrs Ogden and Joan, indeed Joan does not clearly define it to herself. In Rose Macaulay's novel *Dangerous Ages* (1921), the only time Mrs Hilary mentions her daughter Pamela's relationship with Frances is when she worries that too much involvement with another woman might prevent her from marrying. In Radclyffe Hall's novel *The Well of Loneliness* (1928), the daughter's lesbianism is named, provoking an outburst of anger and disgust from the mother. This hostility between mother and lesbian daughter continues through the century to Rita Mae Brown's *Rubyfruit Jungle* (1973) and Jeanette Winterson's *Oranges are Not the Only Fruit* (1985). In part it is a consequence of living in a society where women are seen as needing a man for economic security: ' "Now see, it don't make sense for you to want women. No woman's gonna keep you" ' Carrie tells her adopted daughter, Mollie. ' "You go out there and marry some man and he'll keep you. You'll have money then. You'll be sorry. There's no security with a woman." ' (Brown 1973/1977: 240).

Rich's poem 'Mother-in-Law' was published in *A Wild Patience Has Taken Me This Far* (1981) and may be glossed with the poem 'Grand-mothers' in the same volume. In the latter poem, Rich evokes the thwarted lives of her two grandmothers, particularly her maternal grandmother who in different circumstances might have become a writer. In her poem 'Snapshots of a Daughter-in-Law' published in the volume of that name Rich again shows how heavily patriarchal ideology weighs on mother-daughter relations.

Of Woman Born was immensely influential and led to an explosion of feminist writing on mother-daughter relationships in the late 1970s and 80s. At the same time sociologists and psychoanalysts were exploring the mother-daughter bond, revising Freud and locating female identity in fluidity and connectedness rather than autonomy and separation. In *The Reproduction of Mothering. Psychoanalysis and the Sociology of Gender* (1978), Nancy Chodorow argues that women's monopoly of childcare in the early years of a child's life leads to a dangerous polarisation of gender positions whereby women are encouraged to display skills of empathy and nurturing and men are socialised to be aggressive, non-empathetic and emotionally repressed. Because mothers have to prepare their children for life outside in the patriarchy, Chodorow writes, mothers treat their sons as separate and independent but merge their own identity with that of their daughters so that girls emerge from being mothered with a capacity for empathy built into their definition of self in a way that boys do not. In other words, women are psychologically prepared for mothering by being mothered by women. They come to define and experience themselves as continuous with others whereas boys do not. Chodorow's solution to breaking the cycle is to advocate shared parenting by women and men.

One other consequence of this pattern of development, according to Chodorow, is that women crave more intimacy in their relationships than men can provide and thus they seek to recreate with their babies the symbiotic bonds they first enjoyed with their own mothers. In Storm Jameson's autobiography, *Journey from the North* (volume number 1 1969; volume 2 1970), we see a mother turning to her daughter to fulfil emotional needs left unmet by her husband. Jameson describes herself as aware from an early age that life had disappointed her mother and that as a daughter, she must try to make up for the deficiencies of her mother's relationship with her father. So anxious and guilty did she feel whenever her literary ambitions led her away from Whitby that at one point she gave up the offer of a promising job on *The Egoist* in order to remain with her mother.

In Jameson's autobiographical trilogy *The Mirror in Darkness*, Hervey Russell's relationship with her mother is one of the central themes. The second volume *Love in Winter* (1935), describes the fourteen-year-old Hervey's anguish over her mother's unhappy marriage. Her mother's remark that her husband is cruel to her prompts Hervey to spend hours crouched outside her mother's bedroom door at night ready to rush in if her mother cries for help. The same incident is mentioned in slightly different terms in the autobiography: here the explanation is that Jameson's mother is pregnant again and distraught. The father's 'cruelty' becomes connected with sex. Unlike the classic Freudian paradigm where the daughter wants to seduce the father from the mother, here Hervey/Jameson identifies with her mother against her father.

The excerpt from *Journey from the North* shows the intensity of the bond between mother and daughter and the fluidity of identity between them. 'It seemed that a nerve led direct from my young mind to hers' wrote Jameson. 'I knew instantly what she wanted me to say, what it would please her to hear' (1969/1984: 32). This fluid identity between mother and daughter is emphasised in another strand of writing on motherhood, namely the work of the French feminists, Luce Irigaray, Hélène Cixous and Julia Kristeva. The work of these writers arises out of Jacques Lacan's combination of Freudian psychoanalysis with theories of structural linguistics. According to Lacan's theory the child only becomes a human subject when it moves out of the imaginary (a stage of imaginary wholeness and unity) into the symbolic order, the system of language and culture which he calls the law of the father. The bond with the mother must be suppressed in order that speech, writing and culture can be acquired. Language arises as a compensation for the loss of the mother.

In Lacan's theory girls make the entry into the symbolic less perfectly than boys. Because she cannot identify sexually with the father, the girl's primal repression of the mother is incomplete. She retains some hidden access to the realm of the mother. As a result her position in culture is less secure than that of a boy. Lacan's theory has been held to account for the sense of marginality women often feel to the language and culture with which they are surrounded. It can account, for example, for Woolf's feeling that language is a masculine construct which has to be reshaped for women's use.

Although Lacan's theory would seem to relegate women to their usual marginal position, some feminist writers have chosen to cele-brate girls' hidden access to the pre-oedipal mother and her language (according to others, like Jacqueline Rose, they are misreading Lacan since there can never be a language outside language, see Mitchell and Rose 1982: 49). In 'The Laugh of the Medusa' Hélène Cixous argues that women have a privileged relationship to the mother's pre-symbolic world of songs and rhythms which for men has been lost upon entry into the symbolic order. Women's imperfect repression of the mother means they can still hear the mother's language: 'a woman is never far from "mother" (I mean outside her role functions: the "mother" as nonname and source of goods). There is always within her at least a little of that good mother's milk. She writes in white ink' (Marks and de Courtivron 1981: 251). The mother is not, as in Freud and Lacan, a forbidden place that prevents speech or against which the daughter has to struggle to emerge as subject; for Cixous, the mother is the daughter's source of speaking, she liberates the daughter into her language – open-ended, anti-rational, fluid, as befits the fluidity of the body's sexual energies. 'Woman must write herself,' she urges, 'must write about women and bring women to writing, from which they have been driven away as violently as from their bodies' (Marks and de Courtivron 1981: 245).

Luce Irigaray also calls upon women to bring the body of the mother into language. In 'The Bodily Encounter with the Mother' (1981) she writes: 'we must also find, find anew, invent the words, the sentences that speak the most archaic and most contemporary relationship with the body of the mother' (Whitford 1991a: 43). She emphasises the lack of linguistic, social, iconic and religious representations of the mother-daughter relation in our culture. She reinterprets classical myths to reveal that in them daughters (Antigone, for example) have a choice between identifying with the patriarchy's laws and obliterating the mother, or identifying with the mother at the cost of social exclusion and self-destruction (which is in effect what happens to Antoinette in *Wide Sargasso Sea*). Like Adrienne Rich, Irigaray concludes that the patriarchy 'forbids the daughter to respect the blood ties with her mother' (Whitford 1991b: 119). Like Woolf in *A Room of One's Own*, she insists that women must honour their maternal inheritance: 'we must not once more kill the mother who was sacrificed to the origins of our culture. We must give her new life . . . We must refuse to let her desire be annhilated by the law of the father' (Whitford 1991a: 43; ellipsis mine).

In the lyrical monologue 'And the One Doesn't Stir Without the Other' (1981), Irigaray describes a negative mother-daughter relationship. The daughter is over-mothered. Her mother's nurturing leaves her with a feeling of paralysis. Stifled, she turns to her father but he knows only how to socialise his daughter, transforming her into 'a nearly perfect girl' (Irigaray 1981: 60) waiting for a man to come along. Robbed of her daughter's presence the mother, who has poured her entire identity into the mothering role, finds she has lost that identity: 'You look at yourself in the mirror. And already you see your own mother there. And soon your daughter, a mother. Between the two, what are you? What space is yours alone?' (Ibid 1981: 63). If she is to give her daughter an identity she must first find her own outside the patriarchal function of motherhood. The daughter pleads with her mother not to be swamped by the maternal role: 'What I wanted for you, Mother, was this: that in giving me life, you still remain alive' (Ibid 1981: 67). The only hope for a healthy mother-daughter relationship, Irigaray suggests in 'Women-Mothers, the Silent Substratum of the Social Order' (1981), is that they each detach themselves from their respective roles and see themselves as individual women, as subjects rather than objects:

> In a sense we need to say goodbye to maternal omnipotence (the last refuge) and establish a woman-to-woman relationship of reciprocity with our mothers, in which they might possibly also feel themselves to be our daughters. In a word, liberate ourselves along with our mothers. That is an indispensable precondition for our emancipation from the authority of fathers. (Whitford, 1991a: 50)

Irigarary's celebration of the mother, her emphasis on recognising the mother as subject and her call for daughters to stand with not against the mother are all very positive and counteract earlier feminists' neglect or downgrading of the mother.

Like Irigaray, Julia Kristeva points to the inadequate representation of motherhood in western culture. In 'Stabat Mater' (1977: see Moi 1986), an essay that is much indebted to Marina Warner's analysis of the cult of the Virgin Mary in *Alone of All Her Sex* (1976), Kristeva describes society's efforts to suppress the mother and the mother's body in the West but also attacks some feminists' view of motherhood as oppressive since this, she argues, leaves out of account women's continued desire to have children. Prompted by her own experience of motherhood, Kristeva insists on the need for a new understanding of the mother's body and a new discourse on maternity. She links maternity with female creativity and in 'A New Type of Intellectual: the Dissident' (1977) she argues that: 'Real female innovation (in whatever social field) will only come about when maternity, female creation and the link between them are better understood' (Moi 1986: 298). Pregnancy in Kristeva's view can provide the basis for a new ethics based on community rather than the individual: 'The child's arrival . . . extracts woman out of her oneness and gives her the possibility . . . of reaching out to the other, the ethical' (Moi 1986: 182; ellipses mine). Kristeva elaborates on this new ethic in a moving passage in 'Women's Time' (1979):

> The arrival of the child . . . leads the mother into the labyrinths of an experience that, without the child, she would only rarely encounter: love for another. Not for herself, nor for an identical being, and still less for another person with whom 'I' fuse (love or sexual passion). But the slow, difficult and delightful apprenticeship in attentiveness, gentleness, forgetting oneself. (Moi 1986: 206; ellipsis mine)

Kristeva's idea that motherhood can lead to a new ethic of attentiveness to the needs of others brings her close to the work done by Sara Ruddick in *Maternal Thinking. Towards a Politics of Peace* (1989). Ruddick argues that out of women's experience of mothering there has arisen a distinctive female approach to ethical problems with an emphasis on responsibility, openness to the needs of others, resilience and flexibility, all qualities which, she suggests, are undervalued or ignored in capitalist consumerist societies where the emphasis is on individualism and competition. Ruddick's argument is valuable for the emphasis it places on mothers' potential to contribute to society. It perhaps does not go far enough, however, in addressing the mother's own needs: an appeal to caring can be used oppressively if the mother's attentive love is not balanced by her need for self-preservation (that is, the need to limit the child's demands). Jessica Benjamin is perhaps right when in *The Bonds of Love* (1988) she claims: 'No psychological theory has adequately articulated the mother's independent existence' (Benjamin 1989/1990: 23).

In *The Bonds of Love* Benjamin investigates the notion of 'intersubjectivity' and posits the mother-child relationship as one between two mutually loving but autonomous beings, both of whom grow and change during the course of the relationship. 'The idea of mutual recognition is crucial to the intersubjective view,' she writes, 'it implies that we actually have a need to recognise the other as a separate person who is like us yet distinct. This means that the child has a need to see the mother, too, as an independent subject, not simply as the "external world" or an object of his ego' (Benjamin 1988/1990: 23). Benjamin draws on the clinical observations of developmental psychologists like Jean Piaget and Daniel Stern. In *The Interpersonal World of the Infant* (1985) Stern argues for the baby's capacity for intersubjective emotional relating from nine months. His study stresses mothering as a partnership between mother and child, unique to the individuals concerned and shaped by their interactions. Mothering becomes not a fixed, essentialised description, but a task: a mother is only a mother when interacting with her child. Moreover if, as Stern suggests, the infant is born already programmed for individuation, this frees us from the classic Freudian paradigm whereby the child is initially fused with the mother and only achieves selfhood by overthrowing her with the help of the father. Adrienne Rich, writing from personal experience, would seem to back up Stern's observation when she says: 'Nor, in pregnancy, did I experience the embryo as decisively internal in Freud's terms, but rather, as something inside and of me, yet becoming hourly and daily more separate, on its way to becoming separate from me and of itself,' Rich 1976/1977: 63).

Similarly Benjamin insists that the disposition to separation and individuation is present in the mother-child dyad and that mutual recognition is as significant a developmental goal as separation:

> Self psychology is misleading when it understands the mother's recognition of the child's feelings and accomplishments as maternal mirroring. The mother cannot (and should not) be a mirror; . . . she must be an independent other who responds in her different way. Indeed, as the child increasingly establishes his own independent centre of existence, her recognition will be meaningful only to the extent that it reflects her own equally separate subjectivity. (Benjamin 1988/1990: 24; ellipsis mine)

The observations of Benjamin, Stern and Rich have profound implications for the classical psychoanalytic theory of the mother as simply an object for her baby's needs and indeed more generally for society's approval of the self-sacrificing mother who obliterates herself for the sake of her child. Such a mother, they suggest, cannot give her infant the sense of identity a child needs. Speaking of her own experience in trying to hold onto her sense of identity while her sons were small, Rich writes:

> I don't know how we made it from their embattled childhood and my embattled motherhood into a mutual recognition of ourselves and each other.
> Probably that mutual recognition, overlaid by social and traditional circumstance, was always there, from the first gaze between mother and infant at the breast. (Rich 1976/1977: 32)

During the last three decades of the twentieth century women fiction writers have begun to pick up on similar themes to those of the theorists and acknowledge their debt to the mother. Instead of writing being something to be done in spite of and against the mother, the mother becomes, as in the work of Irigaray and Cixous, implicated in the creative act. This is foreshadowed in the extract from Virginia Woolf's 'A Sketch of the Past' where she recognises that her memories of her mother are responsible for the genesis of *To the Lighthouse*. This is not simply nostalgia for childhood memories. Resurrecting her mother and giving her a voice was for Woolf a way of laying claim to a maternal inheritance that would empower her as a writer. In *A Room of One's Own* (1929) she shows how important it is for a woman writer to find inspiring female models from the past, 'for we think back through our mothers if we are women. It is useless to go to the great men writers for help' (Woolf 1929/1992: 99).

Kathleen Raine's three volumes of autobiography celebrate her maternal inheritance as the inspiration behind her vocation as a poet. She tells us that it was from her Scottish mother that she gained a love of Scottish songs and ballads, a sense of the mystery and beauty of nature and a love of poetry as something not inaccessible but woven into one's daily life. In becoming a poet, Raine felt she was living out her mother's dreams. 'It was she who had made me a poet,' she writes in *The Lion's Mouth*, 'I was the custodian of all her unenacted possibilities' (Raine 1977: 31). She describes how, as a child before she had learned to write, she made up poems and her mother wrote them down.

Raine's moving poem, 'Heirloom', describing an epiphany her mother experienced, shows that Raine inherited not only her poetic gift from her mother but also her visionary insight. The second volume of Raine's autobiography, *The Land Unknown*, gives the background to the poem:

My mother when she was over eighty confided to me an experience she had had as a girl. 'I have never told anyone before,' she said, 'but I think you will understand.' It was simply that, one day, sitting among the heather near Kielder 'I saw that the moor was alive.' That was all. But I understood that she had seen what I had seen.' (Raine 1975: 120)

This sense of the daughter acting out unrealised maternal dreams is a strong feature of African-American women's writing. In her essay 'In Search of Our Mothers' Gardens' (1983) Alice Walker traces the roots of her own creativity not only in the literature of black foremothers (Phillis Wheatley, Zora Hurston and Nella Larsen) but in the everyday creativity of ordinary black women of the South – women like her mother who kept the creative impulse alive in circumstances which did everything to suppress it, through domestic arts like quilting, gardening, cooking and storytelling. In her review of *Second Class Citizen* by the Nigerian writer, Buchi Emecheta, 'A Writer Because Of, Not in Spite Of, Her Children' (1976: Walker 1983a), Walker points out that in some cultures motherhood is not seen as incompatible with art. Emecheta's heroine, Adah, 'integrates the profession of writer into the cultural concept of mother/worker that she retains from Ibo society. Just as the African mother has traditionally planted crops, pounded maize, and done her washing with her baby strapped to her back, so Adah can write a novel with her children playing in the same room' (Walker 1983a: 69). Motherhood becomes a symbol of creativity in all areas of life.

In her essay 'In Search of Our Mothers' Gardens' Alice Walker draws on the African-American tradition of praise for the mother that goes back to the time of slavery, linking it with Woolf's model in *A Room of One's Own* of thinking back through our mothers in order to find a tradition of black women's art in which she can place her own writing. Walker has written that 'to know ourselves as we are, we must know our mothers' names' ('A Letter to the Editor of *MS*' in Walker 1983a: 276). In her short story, 'Everyday Use', a mother, choosing between two daughters, favours the one who preserves her loyalty to her female heritage.

Maya Angelou has also spoken movingly of the heritage of

African-American women and of the importance of remembering black women writers of the past: 'We need to see our mothers, aunts, our sisters, and grandmothers. We need to see Frances Harper, Sojourner Truth, Fannie Lou Hamer, women of our heritage' (Elliot 1989: 147). For a black daughter, reclaiming her maternal heritage is part of the battle to reclaim her own life; unlike white women writers of the late 1960s and 1970s, she doesn't see the need to cut herself off from her mother in order to achieve selfhood. Part of the reason for this is that in a racist society black mothers and daughters may feel like sisters in the struggle to affirm the value of their lives: race, class and gender oppression intensify their need to uncover a strong matrilineal heritage. In a racist society a black child must look to her family for affirmation of her identity. 'Mothers and daughters in black families remain quite close,' Angelou explained in an interview she gave in 1983, 'and we do not, as a rule, blame our mothers for society' (Elliot 1989: 116).

These writers see the history of their people through the history of their mothers. In *Specifying. Black Women Writing the American Experience* (1987) Susan Willis says: 'For black women, history is a bridge defined along motherlines. It begins with a woman's particular genealogy and fans out to include all the female culture heroes' (Willis 1987: 6). One of these heroes is the black slave mother who kept alive not only her own family but the white babies she was forced to nurse: 'The black American female has nursed a nation of strangers – literally,' said Angelou. 'And has remained compassionate' (Elliot 1989: 17). In her great novel *Beloved* (1987), Toni Morrison celebrates the radicalness of the black slave woman, Sethe, who affirms her identity as a mother in the face of a system designed to break every bond between a mother and her children. Sethe's mother-in-law, Baby Suggs, has had all of her eight children but one sold away from her. Sethe's own mother, brought over on a slave ship from Africa, aborts her children by white men. The story of Sethe's mother (and of Ella in the extract) reminds us that rejection of mothering was also part of the black woman's protest against slavery.

Sethe's protest, however, is to become a mother in a situation which denied black women motherhood. *Beloved* developed from the historical case of Margaret Garner, a runaway slave who killed her children rather than let them be taken back into slavery. In the novel Morrison explores the psychic effect of slavery on the black slave mother, bringing to the surface what is left unsaid in classic slave narratives. In doing so she describes the mother-daughter relationship at its most extreme. As a baby Sethe spends only a few weeks with her mother before being handed over to a wet nurse so that her enslaved mother can return to work in the fields. Sethe loses her mother's milk and her mother's language. Later on she has to have her mother pointed out to her. As a grown woman white boys rape her and drink the milk from her breasts intended for her daughter. In the slave system the mother is made unavailable to her daughter. Rather than let her return to slavery, Sethe kills her baby daughter by cutting her throat with a handsaw.

Sethe believes she killed Beloved out of love but twenty years later, after Sethe has done time in jail and is free, a strange-looking girl appears. She says her name is Beloved. She may or may not be a ghost. She may or may not be Sethe's daughter, but she has all the neediness and rage of a small baby who demands recognition from her mother. Her incessant demands on Sethe's love devour Sethe and lead her to neglect her other daughter, Denver.

But Beloved is more than Sethe's daughter: she is a symbol of black America's relationship with its enslaved past. A survivor of the Middle Passage, she represents the suffering of all those who died in slavery and she demands to be remembered. 'They are those that died en route,' Morrison said in an interview in 1988. 'Nobody knows their names, and nobody thinks about them . . . There is a necessity for remembering the horror' (Plasa 1998: 33). Beloved forces Sethe to remember by demanding stories from her enslaved past.

There is a danger of being engulfed by the past: if Beloved is a daughter who pulls her mother into the past, her other daughter, Denver, pulls Sethe forward into the future by going out into the black community to seek help. In the excerpt Beloved is exorcised from the community in an echo of the scene of her death twenty years ago. She disappears, but she will return if communal memory dares to forget her.

Beloved is an extraordinarily powerful mother-daughter story which uses the theme of motherhood to explore the black community's relationship to its enslaved past. It also tells us something about motherhood. In the same way as the black community must remember, but not be engulfed by, its painful heritage of slavery, so Sethe as a mother must learn not to merge herself with her daughters. As Paul D tells her at the end, she must learn that she is her own best thing.

If the black woman writer looks back to her strong maternal heritage for affirmation of her identity, there is nevertheless a price to pay. The stereotype of the black woman as a strong, nurturing mother whose sacrifices have ensured the survival of the race at times weighs heavily on her daughters. In their novels, *Sula* (1973) and *Meridian* (1976), Toni Morrison and Alice Walker endeavour to counteract this stereotype by creating heroines who reject the maternal role for themselves. 'I don't want to make somebody else' Sula declares. 'I want to make myself' (Morrison 1973/1982: 92) and she looks for alternative plots for her life. In Walker's novel *Meridian*, both Meridian and her mother are trapped by the myth of black motherhood. The mother's life has been ruined by endless child-bearing, her thwarted creativity expressing itself in artificial flowers and prayer pillows. When Meridian gives away her child so as to be able to go to college she feels guilty that she has not been able to live up to the standard of mothering of black slave women whose radicalness was expressed in keeping their children in the most difficult of circumstances. Later she learns to express her maternal feelings in a wider sphere: she first appears in the novel surrounded by children whose lives she is trying to save. No longer tied to the biological, Meridian's mothering role expands into a nurturing of all life. The way Meridian puts her maternal feelings to work in the political sphere prompts obvious comparisons with the writings of Sara Ruddick on maternal thinking, discussed above.

In *Black Feminist Criticism* (1985), Barbara Christian traces the importance of motherhood in Afro-American culture to its roots in Africa, its ways of life and the many religions where motherhood was central as a symbol of creativity and continuity (Christian 1985: 213–19). In *The Temple of My Familiar* (1989) Alice Walker laments the destruction of these ancient matriarchal religions. 'We know that matriarchal societies existed before,' she told an interviewer in 1998. 'It's important that we start thinking about ancient future ways' (White 1998: 46). Yet African women writers, like black American writers, highlight the negative as well as the positive aspects of the ideology of strong motherhood in their culture. In her depiction of African village communities, the Ghanaian writer, Ama Ata Aidoo, clearly presents the difficulties of living in a society that measures the value of a woman by her ability to bear children, and she challenges the sentimental image of the African mother (1987). Her work may be compared with that of the Nigerian writer, Buchi Emecheta. In her ironically titled novel *The Joys of Motherhood* (1979) Emecheta shows, like Aidoo, the devaluation of the childless woman and questions the traditional favouring of sons over daughters. Nnu Ego, slave to the traditions of motherhood in her Ibo culture, sacrifices herself to her children and realises too late that she has lost all sense of identity. 'I don't know how to be anything else but a mother' she laments (Emecheta 1979/1994: 222). Both Aidoo and Emecheta resist the idealisation of motherhood in their cultures. They also question the traditional favouring of sons over daughters. In Aidoo's play, *The Dilemma of a Ghost* (first performed in 1964), Monka has been deprived in order to pay for her brother's education. In *The Joys of Motherhood* Nnu Ego makes her daughters hawk goods in order to finance their brothers' education. Only at the end does she begin to see a flaw in the tradition: 'Who made the law that we should not find hope in our daughters? We women subscribe to that law more than anyone. Until we change all this, it is still a man's world, which women will always help to build' (Emecheta 1979/1994: 187).

The myth of Mother Africa has weighed heavily on African women, obscuring their actual subordinate role in the culture. African women writers have had the task of opposing both African and colonial traditions which mythologised Africa as female. Writers like Aidoo and Emecheta challenge the myth of Mother Africa by portraying the realities of mothering in their fiction and by attempting to define motherhood for themselves. In a similar way the Irish poet, Eavan Boland, has struggled in a post-colonial situation to demystify the traditional romanticisation of motherhood in her culture. Boland has written of the burden the myth of Mother Ireland, so prevalent in Irish poetry written by men, has placed on women writers: 'The woman poet today is caught in a field of force. Powerful, persuasive voices are in her ear as she writes. Distorting and simplifying ideas of womanhood and poetry fall as shadows between her and the courage of her own experiences' (Boland 1987:17).

Resisting the temptation to separatism, Boland has endeavoured to rewrite the poetic tradition and reconstruct the idea of nationhood in order to give women a part in it. Her own very precise descriptions in her poems of mothering her two daughters may be seen as an attempt to counteract the idealisations of motherhood in male writers and to present real, complex mothers in place of simplified myths. Indeed, in her poem 'Tirade for a Mimic Muse', Boland suggests that it was her experience of mothering which marked a turning point in her attitude to poetic tradition: 'In a nappy stink, by a soaking wash/Among stacked dishes/Your glass cracked' (Boland 1995: 56). As she explained in an interview, after living and studying in Dublin: 'I married, moved out of the city and into the suburbs . . . and had a baby daughter. In so doing I had, without realising it, altered my whole situation' (Boland 1987: 19; ellipsis mine). There was no precedent in

Irish poetry for descriptions of the ordinary, day to day, domestic lives of women. Boland had to work hard to convince herself and her readers that the details of women's lives could be the stuff of poetry. 'Night Feed', part of a sequence titled 'Domestic Interior' and published in *Night Feed* (1982) is a good example of her art and may be compared with several other touching poems she has written to her daughters, including 'Legends' and 'The Pomegranate'.

As these African, African-American and Irish writers demonstrate, motherhood is a subject rich in social and political implications. In Caribbean women's writing, too, the mother-daughter bond is implicated in the daughter's relation to the motherland. In *Wide Sargasso Sea*, as we have seen, Antoinette is rejected both by her mother and her mother country and has difficulty holding on to a sense of identity. In Jamaica Kincaid's *The Autobiography of My Mother* (1996), Xuela's loss of her mother at birth and the colonial education designed to humiliate her leave her, like Rhys's heroine, without a mother or a mother country. Unlike Antoinette Cosway, Xuela hardens into autonomy and self-sufficiency; she will stand apart from all nations and races. In Kincaid's first novel, *Annie John* (1983), Annie's intense relationship with her mother almost overpowers her sense of self; and the colonial education she receives, and which her mother endorses, threatens to alienate Annie from herself. She has a breakdown. In order to forge her own identity she must leave behind both her mother and her mother country.

Yet Caribbean women writers, like Walker's African-American writers, look back to their mother as the source of their creativity: 'The fertile soil of my creative life is my mother' Jamaica Kincaid said in an interview (Cudjoe 1990: 222). In *Beka Lamb* (1982), Zee Edgell's coming-of-age novel set in Belize, Beka's mother gives her daughter the pen and the exercise book that will start her off on her career as a writer. It is a gesture that would have seemed inconceivable at the beginning of the century – in the extract from May Sinclair's novel. *Mary Olivier*, Mary's mother attempts to take books *away* from her daughter, fearing Mary's growing independence. By contrast, Beka's mother wishes to aid her daughter's struggle towards selfhood.

Growing up in Belize, a country inhabited by many different cultures – Creole, Carib, Spanish, Mestizo, Indian, British – Beka has to learn to negotiate a space for herself amidst the competing discourses of her society where to be a woman and black is to be doubly devalued. Her convent school reinforces this colonialism and colludes in the patriarchy's repression of the female body. Beka sees her friend, Toycie, pregnant and unmarried, destroyed by the cross-currents of racism and sexism in their society. Toycie's descent into madness recalls the fate of those other victims of colonialism and sexism, Antoinette and Annette Cosway in Jean Rhys's *Wide Sargasso Sea*.

As so often in Caribbean women's writing, reflecting the nature of a society where women frequently raise their children without male support, Beka's bonds with other women are crucial to her survival. If her creativity is fostered by her mother, she receives her political education from her Granny Ivy, a committed nationalist. By the end of the novel, Beka has accepted her Creole heritage, she ceases straightening her hair, chooses local folksongs to celebrate the Mother Provincial's visit, and excavates a bit of local history for her prize-winning essay. But it is not only Beka who grows up during the course of the novel. *Beka Lamb* is set in 1950, at the beginning of Belize's struggle for independence, and the novel intertwines the heroine's growing sense of identity with her country's struggle for self-government.

The link between the mother and the mother country is also apparent in the work of the Chinese-American writer, Amy Tan. Her novel *The Joy Luck Club* (1989) shows how the mother-daughter bond and the tie to the mother country, China, can be disrupted by patriarchal authority, economics, war and exile. Using traditional Chinese storytelling techniques, Tan's immigrant mothers struggle to retain the link with their own mothers and their mother country and pass on their stories to their American-born daughters. In a patois which emphasises their tie to the mother country, the mothers tell their daughters of their fight to hold on to a sense of themselves and their own self-worth in a country (China) that would deny value to females: 'Girls were a cheap commodity in China' (Mah 1997: 100), 'a good woman was not supposed to have a point of view at all,' (Chang 1991/1993: 45). Tan's Chinese mothers hope their daughters will grow up knowing their own worth in more favourable circumstances, but without forgetting their mothers' stories and their mother country.

The Joy Luck Club may be compared with the work of another Asian-American, Maxine Hong Kingston. In *The Woman Warrior: Memoirs of a Girlhood Among Ghosts* (1976), Kingston shows the effect of Chinese ancestry on an American-born daughter. As a child, hearing her mother's stories of China, she becomes confused over what is false, what is real, but when she grows up, she becomes a storyteller like her mother.

In *The Joy Luck Club*, the recurring motifs, the correspondences between the stories, the resemblance between the characters, put the focus on the community rather than the individual. By going back into the past to describe the Chinese mothers' relationships with their own mothers in China, Tan blurs the boundaries between the roles of mothers and daughters, reminding us that these dogmatic, fussy, perceptive mothers were once daughters themselves. Tan's novel echoes Jung's description of the continuity of identity between mother and daughter: 'Every mother contains her daughter within herself, and every daughter her mother . . . This participation and intermingling gives rise to that peculiar uncertainty as regards *time*: a woman lives earlier as a mother, later as a daughter. The conscious experience of these ties produces the feeling that her life is spread out over generations' (Jung and Kerenyi 1963: 162; ellipsis mine). Meeting her long-lost half-sisters in China after her mother's death, Jing-Mei re-establishes the mother-daughter bond disrupted by war and exile.

The Joy Luck Club may be compared with Tan's later novel, *The*

Kitchen God's Wife (1991), where silences and secrets distort the mother-daughter bond until, breaking the silence between herself and her daughter, Winnie reclaims her lost past in China, a past which has consequences for her daughter's present. In the course of the novel, like the mothers in *The Joy Luck Club*, Winnie moves from object to being subject of her own story and finds her voice. Indeed these mothers' very act of speaking out is subversive in a society where their American sons-in-law are so often shown sidelining and underestimating their foreign mothers-in-law. The fact that the mothers persist, in America, in speaking a mixture of Chinese and English highlights their subversion (see Heung 1993: 604–5).

Mothers as subversive, mothers as inspiring their daughter's creativity – we are a long way from the hostile or powerless mothers of the first half of the century. Yet two writers warn us against idealising motherhood or saying that women are superior because of their ability to mother. In her rewriting of 'Cinderella' in her short story 'Ashputtle *or* The Mother's Ghost' (1987: see Carter 1996), Angela Carter, typically, teases by giving three versions of the mother-daughter bond. The first prevents any sentimentality we may be harbouring about motherhood as we see a mother cruelly socialising her daughter to fit in with patriarchal society. We remember that Carter disliked any idealisation of motherhood and particularly any notion of mother goddesses, 'just as silly a notion as father gods' she wrote in *The Sadeian Woman* (Carter 1979: 5), a book where the daughter goes to the extreme in her sadistic savagery against her mother. In the sanctification of motherhood Carter detected attempts to keep women in their place as victims or to justify their status as outsiders. At the end of *The Passion of New Eve* (1977), Mother, as Elaine Jordan puts it, 'withers away . . . a necessary phase but one that has to be superseded. Mother ends up as the cheery but decrepit old woman on the beach: this is the end of myths of the Mother' (Jordan 1992: 37).

Then we read the second version of 'Ashputtle' and think, well maybe mothers don't have it all their own way, maybe mothers can also be devoured by their daughters. Then comes version number three, the politically correct one we have been waiting for – the mother who, like the mother in 'The Bloody Chamber', empowers her daughter and gives her, echoing the mother in Grace Nichols's poem, 'Praise Song', a future. But the other two versions still stand. Angela Carter is a writer who escapes categories. She was, as she herself said, 'in the demythologising business' (Wandor 1983: 71) and one of the myths she set out to destroy was sacred motherhood.

'Ashputtle *or* The Mother's Ghost' belongs to Carter's rewriting of fairytales. She has been criticised for this, notably by Patricia Duncker (Duncker 1984) and the question much debated by critics is whether she is contesting or colluding with the patriarchal values of the originals. For Carter the advantage of fairytales was that they were 'transformed accounts of everyday lives' (Watts 1987: 170). They removed writing from the realms of an omniscient, godlike, usually male elite and made it part of everyday life. Her tribute to everyday domestic creativity in 'The Kitchen Child' may be compared with that of Alice Walker in 'In Search of Our Mothers' Gardens'. Fairytales, Carter said, are 'anonymous and genderless' (Carter 1990: x). They allowed her to explore female sexuality and explode fictions of femininity, thus beginning what she called 'the slow process of decolonialising our language and our basic habits of thought' (Wandor 1983: 75).

In similar vein to Carter's 'Ashputtle', Margaret Atwood's short story, 'Giving Birth', though about a happy enough mother-daughter relationship, warns us against idealising motherhood. The story is an attempt to recapture in words the rapidly vanishing experience of childbirth and as such can be read in the light of French feminist theories about the difficulty of 'writing the body'. Three women feature in the story – the narrator, Jeanie (the narrator as she was before giving birth) and a shadowy woman, Jeanie's alter ego, who functions in the text in a similar way to Freud's notion of the uncanny, expressing the anxieties about giving birth that Jeanie has suppressed.

Through the use of Jeanie's shadowy double, Atwood suggests that childbirth is not a matter of rejoicing for all women – or even for any woman? Some women are forced into it through circumstances not of their choosing. The narrator reminds us that there is not even a word in the language for forced childbirth – on this theme of unwanted motherhood see also Atwood's poem 'Christmas Carols' (Atwood 1987).

As so often in Atwood, the Gothic is used to express rebellion and ambivalence towards conventional female roles. Jeanie's split self represents a fear and anxiety she cannot express in ordinary conversation. Despite A.'s supportiveness he is wrong about there being nothing to fear in childbirth; for a brief moment after giving birth, Jeanie teeters on the edge of madness. Like Kristeva's 'abject' the shadowy alter ego is expelled at the end, but not entirely – she goes off to find 'her next case'. Atwood's story follows in a long line of female Gothic writing linking childbirth with madness, an early and famous example being Charlotte Perkins Gilman's short story 'The Yellow Wallpaper' (1892).

Finally, there is the theme of giving birth: 'Who gives it? And to whom is it given?' asks the narrator, for if she has given birth to a daughter, her daughter has given birth to a mother. The woman she was, Jeanie, is no longer. In this way, Atwood expresses something of the cataclysmic change that childbirth can bring in women's lives.

In comparison with black women's praise of the mother, white women writers sometimes show a fear of the mother and an unwillingness to acknowledge their maternal inheritance. However there are signs that the black tradition is beginning to influence white women writers. Michèle Roberts's short story 'Anger' acknowledges a debt to Toni Morrison and reveals the influence of Alice Walker in showing female creativity handed on in a domestic setting from mother to daughter. As Buchi Emecheta has observed: 'The white female intellectual may still have to come to the womb of Mother Africa to re-learn how to be a woman' (McLuskie and Innes 1988: 4).

Michèle Roberts has stated that she writes out of a Kleinian desire to repair loss, beginning with the loss of her mother who, she says, didn't want daughters but a son (Wandor 1983: 64). She sees her writing as arising from a need to be reconciled with her mother and the mother inside herself: 'We recreate the mother inside ourselves, over and over again,' (Roberts 1998: 21). There has been a steady widening of theme in Roberts's work from writing about individual mothers and daughters in novels such as *A Piece of the Night* (1978) and *The Visitation* (1983) to writing about the mother principle in general which she feels has been suppressed in our patriarchal culture (Wandor 1983: 65). Her third novel, *The Wild Girl* (1984), tells the story of Mary Magdalene and reflects recent developments in feminist theology in making a plea for a Christianity that would include the mother as well as the father: 'We have lost the knowledge of the Mother' Mary Magdalene tells the disciples. 'We do not fully know God if we drive out this name of God' (Roberts 1984: 111).

Speaking of her own personal myth about art, Roberts has said that everything she used to write 'went back to maternal loss, maternal absence, and now dares to re-image maternal presence, fullness,' (Roberts 1998: 21). In her short story 'God's House' from her collection *During Mother's Absence* (1994), there is both maternal absence and maternal presence. A young girl spends time in France recovering from the death of her mother and experiences a moment of insight similar to Woolf's 'moment of being' described in 'A Sketch of the Past' (Woolf 1990: 81). The daughter sees a pattern in life and herself and her mother as part of it. The mother is not lost to her daughter. Roberts picks up another common theme in women's writing, namely nature as a nurturing mother. The story may be compared with the other stories in *During Mother's Absence*, all of which are connected in some way with the loss of a mother figure, including '*Une Glossaire*/Glossaire' where the loss is that of the mother country, France.

The work of Michèle Roberts repeats many of the themes we have noticed in other writers of the latter part of the twentieth century –

the need for reconciliation with the mother, the need to retrieve the mother's voice silenced by the patriarchy, the link between the mother and the mother country, the mother as source and inspiration for her daughter's creativity. Having no female model for becoming a poet Roberts had to make one up: 'I had to discover and invent a tradition that allowed me to become a poet. I had to imagine a maternal body made of words and milk and music and permissiveness and fierceness and sweetness and power and and and. This invisible woman became my muse' (Roberts 1998: 121).

The mother as muse: the mother-daughter story has come a long way from its muted beginnings in the early part of the century. Women of the 1980s and 1990s live out in their lives dreams that their mothers did not even dare entertain and in starting to write of their experiences as daughters and as mothers of daughters they are at last breaking the silence that has surrounded the relationship. Mothers are starting to speak openly of the difficulties of mothering, daughters are starting to see mothers as women in their own right, indeed wanting to see their mothers as separate from themselves with their own personal history. Too much self-sacrifice on the part of mothers isn't necessarily what daughters want after all. The heroine of Jamaica Kincaid's novel *Lucy* writes to her mother: 'I said that she had acted like a saint, but that since I was living in this real world I had really wanted just a mother' (Kincaid 1991: 127).

These extracts demonstrate there are more ways than one of being a mother. The excerpt from the first volume of Maya Angelou's auto-biography, *I Know Why the Caged Bird Sings* (1969), shows a mother who was not able to be there for her daughter when she was growing up suddenly knowing the right way to ease her daughter's transition into becoming a mother herself. Angelou has often stated in interviews that her mother was a poor mother for young children but that their relationship became close as she grew to adulthood (Elliot 1989: 87). What this particular extract illustrates is that mothering is not a task that can be confined to one period of life. In later life, as Angelou's autobiography shows, her mother provided important moments of mothering for her adult daughter (Angelou 1989: 119, 137).

There are many other stories that could have been included here: Dorothy Richardson's relationship with her mother, for instance, which provided the creative inspiration for *Pilgrimage*, her *roman fleuve*, or Martha Quest's troubled relationship with her mother in Doris Lessing's *Children of Violence* series. Paule Marshall's novel, *Brown Girl Brownstones* (1959), about a Barbadian family in New York, is an extraordinarily powerful depiction of a mother-daughter relationship circumscribed by the racism of white society. Selina looks at her mother and longs to understand her 'for she knew, obscurely, that she would never really understand anything until she did' (Marshall 1959/1982: 145). Only when she experiences white racism does Selina finally come to understand her mother and her people.

In many of her books Margaret Forster explores the mother-daughter relationship in the context of changing economic and social circumstances in Britain. Her memoir *Hidden Lives* (1995), for instance, portrays the clash between a working-class mother and a daughter who has educated herself into the middle class and has very different expectations of life. But mothers are changing too. They are beginning to have adventures and are capable of shocking their daughters in ways that would have been unthinkable to Mary Olivier's mother at the beginning of the century. In Esther Freud's funny and charming novel *Hideous Kinky* (1992), it is the hippie mother who is out for adventure, her small daughters who want to go home.

There is no end to stories of mothers and daughters. Antonia White's daughters both wrote memoirs of their mother, wanting to give their side of the story. So did Louise Henriksen, daughter of Anzia Yezierska. And in 1999 Sylvia Plath's daughter, Frieda Hughes, published her first volume of poetry in which she spoke of her feelings about her mother.

It is important that the exploration continues for it is from the mother-daughter bond that women gain a sense of the possibilities of their lives. As Adrienne Rich has written: 'Until a strong line of love, confirmation and example stretches from mother to daughter, from woman to woman across the generations, women will still be wandering in the wilderness' (Rich 1976/1977: 246). By passing on their stories these writers have bequeathed us a rich maternal inheritance.

Charlotte Mew (1869–1928)

Charlotte Mew was born in London, the third of seven children. It was a middle-class family – her father was an architect from the Isle of Wight, her mother an architect's daughter – but Mew's life was to be overshadowed by illness, bereavement and poverty. Her mother was an invalid and three of Mew's four brothers died in childhood. In the late 1880s, her remaining brother and her youngest sister both displayed symptoms of mental illness and had to be confined to asylums. Mew changed from being a high-spirited, passionate child into a reserved, somewhat unpredictable woman.

Charlotte Mew was educated at Gower Street School for Girls, which was run by Lucy Harrison, an educationalist and suffragist committed to furthering women's poetry. From the early 1890s onwards Mew began contributing stories and poems to journals such as *The Egoist, The English Woman* and *The Yellow Book*. She smoked, roamed the streets in tailored suits with fashionably cropped hair and generally behaved like a New Woman.

Then in 1898 her father died and Mew and her younger sister, Anne – an artist – were left in poverty to look after their invalid mother. Their reduced circumstances obliged them to take in lodgers in their house in Gordon Square, a situation of which Mew apparently felt acutely ashamed (Mew 1953: ix). She also worried that Anne was sacrificing her art by turning to furniture restoration in order to earn money (Fitzgerald 1984: 11).

All was not bleak, however. Mew made several trips to France, a country she loved and which features in many of her poems. And in 1916 her first volume of poems, *The Farmer's Bride*, was published by Harold Monro. This brought her into contact with writers such as Thomas Hardy and Walter de la Mare. Their recognition helped her gain a Civil List pension in 1923, the year her mother died. She and Anne were now left alone but the publication of a new edition of *The Farmer's Bride* in 1921 again widened Mew's circle of friends and she got to know people like Siegfried Sassoon, Robert Bridges and Ottoline Morrell. Then in January 1927 Anne, who had been ill for some time, was diagnosed as having cancer of the liver. She died in June. Lonely and depressed, Mew moved into a nursing home and in March of the following year committed suicide by drinking disinfectant.

Charlotte Mew fell in love twice in her life – with Ella D'Arcy whom she visited in Paris in 1902 (Fitzgerald 1984: 71) and with the novelist May Sinclair (Ibid. 128). Both of these loves remained unrequited. Mew developed the dramatic monologue to explore themes of frustrated sexuality, loss and isolation. In a perceptive analysis of Mew's poetry, Angela Leighton sees the motif of 'a missing life' as characteristic of Mew's writing (Leighton 1992: 283) and this is certainly present in 'The Quiet House' where the speaker is trapped in her father's house after the death of her mother. The theme of thwarted motherhood runs through several of Mew's poems. 'If there were fifty heavens, God could not give us back the child that went or never came' she wrote in 'Madeleine in Church'.

The image that remains of Mew is one of self-suppression and isolation. After 1921 she apparently wrote very little verse, attributing her small output to domestic chores and the burden of looking after her mother. Alida Monro has left us a vivid picture of Mew: 'She usually carried a horn-handled umbrella, unrolled, under her arm, as if it were psychologically necessary to her, a weapon against the world' (Mew 1953: viii).

Primary reading

Mew, C. 1953 *Collected Poems of Charlotte Mew*, with a memoir by Alida Monro, London: Duckworth.
Mew, C. 1981 *Collected Poems and Prose* V. Warner (ed.), Manchester: Carcanet.

Further reading

Fitzgerald, P. 1984 *Charlotte Mew and Her Friends*, London: Collins.
Leighton, A. 1992 *Victorian Women Poets. Writing Against the Heart*, Hemel Hempstead: Harvester Wheatsheaf.

The Quiet House

From Charlotte Mew, *Collected Poems and Prose*, V. Warner (ed.),
Manchester: Carcanet, 1981, pp. 17–19.

When we were children old Nurse used to say,
    The house was like an auction or a fair
Until the lot of us were safe in bed.
It has been quiet as the country-side
Since Ted and Janey and then Mother died
And Tom crossed Father and was sent away.
After the lawsuit he could not hold up his head,
    Poor Father, and he does not care
    For people here, or to go anywhere.

To get away to Aunt's for that week-end
    Was hard enough; (since then, a year ago,
    He scarcely lets me slip out of his sight –)
At first I did not like my cousin's friend,
    I did not think I should remember him:
    His voice has gone, his face is growing dim
And if I like him now I do not know.
    He frightened me before he smiled –
    He did not ask me if he might –
    He said that he would come one Sunday night,
    He spoke to me as if I were a child.

No year has been like this that has just gone by;
    It may be that what Father says is true,
If things are so it does not matter why:
    But everything has burned, and not quite through.
    The colours of the world have turned
    To flame, the blue, the gold has burned
In what used to be such a leaden sky.
    When you are burned quite through you die.

Red is the strangest pain to bear;
In Spring the leaves on the budding trees;
In Summer the roses are worse than these,
　More terrible than they are sweet:
　A rose can stab you across the street
　　Deeper than any knife:
　And the crimson haunts you everywhere –
Thin shafts of sunlight, like the ghosts of reddened swords
　　　have struck our stair
As if, coming down, you had spilt your life.
　I think that my soul is red
Like the soul of a sword or a scarlet flower:
　But when these are dead
　They have had their hour.

　I shall have had mine, too,
　　For from head to feet
　I am burned and stabbed half through,
　　And the pain is deadly sweet.

　The things that kill us seem
　　Blind to the death they give:
　It is only in our dream
　　The things that kill us live.

The room is shut where Mother died,
　The other rooms are as they were,
The world goes on the same outside,
　The sparrows fly across the Square,
　The children play as we four did there,
　The trees grow green and brown and bare,
The sun shines on the dead Church spire,
　And nothing lives here but the fire.

While Father watches from his chair
    Day follows day
The same, or now and then a different grey,
    Till, like his hair,
Which Mother said was wavy once and bright,
    They will all turn white.

  To-night I heard a bell again –
Outside it was the same mist of fine rain,
The lamps just lighted down the long, dim street,
    No one for me –
  I think it is myself I go to meet:
I do not care; some day I *shall* not think; I shall not *be*

May Sinclair (1863–1946)

$\mathbf{M}$ay Sinclair was born in Liverpool, the only daughter in a family with five elder sons. Around 1870 her father's shipowning business went bankrupt and the family became dispersed. Sinclair lived with her mother in Ilford, Essex (where the first part of *Mary Olivier* is set) and then in Gloucestershire. Her father declined into alcoholism and died in 1881. Her brothers suffered from hereditary heart disease. Some of them were nursed by their sister, but by 1905 all of them were dead.

Like the eponymous heroine of her novel, May Sinclair was largely self-taught. Making use of the books in her father's library, she taught herself to read Greek, German and French. When she was eighteen she spent one year at Cheltenham Ladies' College. Inspired by the pioneering educator Dorothea Beale, Sinclair began to read philosophy and psychology (Boll 1973: 34–5).

A prolific novelist, Sinclair also wrote poetry, philosophy, essays and short stories. She published her first book of poems in 1886 under a male pseudonym and in 1897 her first novel *Audrey Craven* appeared. She moved to London with her ailing mother and supported them both by reviews and German translations. She nursed her mother until the latter's death in 1901.

After her mother's death, May Sinclair's life opened out. In 1905 she went to America to promote her novel *The Divine Fire* (1904) and was hailed as the modern Charlotte Brontë (Boll 1973: 76). She began to move in literary circles, making the acquaintance of Thomas Hardy, Henry James and Charlotte Mew. Later she became friendly with the Modernists – Pound, Ford, Dorothy Richardson, H.D. and Richard Aldington. Around 1908 she was active in the suffragist cause, though she opposed militant action.

In 1914 Sinclair's interest in the work of Freud and Jung led her to become a founding member of the Medico-Psychological Clinic, the first in Britain to employ the techniques of psychoanalysis in its therapy. Sinclair was one of the first fiction writers to use psychoanalytical material and, in a review of Dorothy Richardson's *Pilgrimage*, she was the first to apply William James's term 'stream-of-consciousness' to a literary work.

May Sinclair's study of philosophy led her to publish *The Defence of Idealism* in 1917. In this work Sinclair reveals her profound dislike of what she terms the 'naif and obstinate dualism' (Sinclair 1917: 306) pervading Western Christianity and argues that the highest forms of mysticism are to be found in Eastern religions with their stress on personal insight. In *Mary Olivier* (1920) Mrs Olivier's narrow fundamentalism and her use of religion as a weapon in her fight against her daughter determines Mary's search for a different form of spirituality. By the end of the novel Mary achieves a sort of happiness and freedom based on moments of insight similar to those described in *The Defence of Idealism* and foreshadowed in this extract in the description of the young Mary's 'hidden happiness'.

In the latter part of her life May Sinclair's health declined and she spent her last fourteen years living quietly just outside Aylesbury, incapacitated by Parkinson's disease and cared for by her companion and her chauffeur.

Primary reading
Sinclair, M. 1917 *A Defence of Idealism. Some Questions and Conclusions*, London: Macmillan and Co.
Sinclair, M. 1919/1980 *Mary Olivier: A Life*, London: Virago.
Sinclair, M. 1922/1980 *The Life and Death of Harriett Frean*, London: Virago.

Further reading
Boll, T. E. M. 1973 *Miss May Sinclair: Novelist. A Biographical and Critical Introduction*, Rutherford: Fairleigh Dickinson University Press.

Mary Olivier: A Life

From May Sinclair, *Mary Olivier: A Life*, London: Virago, 1980, pp. 124–29.

Mamma whispered to Mrs Draper, and Aunt Bella whispered to Mamma: 'Fourteen.' They always made a mystery about being fourteen. They ought to have told her.

Her thoughts about her mother went up and down. Mamma was not helpless. She was not gentle. She was not really like a wounded bird. She was powerful and rather cruel. You could only appease her with piles of hemmed sheets and darned stockings. If you didn't take care she would get hold of you and never rest till she had broken you, or turned and twisted you to her own will. She would say it was God's will. She would think it was God's will.

They might at least have told you about the pain. The knives of pain. You had to clench your fists till the finger nails bit into the palms. Over the ear of the sofa cushions she could feel her hot eyes looking at her mother with resentment.

She thought: 'You had no business to have me. You had no business to have me.'

Somebody else's eyes. Somebody else's thoughts. Not yours. Not yours.

Mamma got up and leaned over you and covered you with the rug. Her white face quivered above you in the dusk. Her mouth pushed out to yours, making a small sound like a moan. You heard yourself cry: 'Mamma, Mamma, you are adorable!'

That was you.

And as if Mark had never gone, as if that awful thing had never happened to Dan, as if she had never had those thoughts about her mother, her hidden happiness came back to her. Unhappiness only pushed it to a longer rhythm. Nothing could take it away. Anything might bring it: the smell of the white dust on the road; the wind when it came up out of nowhere and brushed the young wheat blades, beat the green flats into slopes where the white light rippled and ran like water, set the green field shaking and tossing like a green sea; the five elm trees, stiff, ecstatic dancers, holding out the broken-ladder pattern of their skirts; haunting rhymes, sudden cadences; the grave *Ubique* sounding through the Beethoven Sonata.

Its thrill of reminiscence passed into the thrill of premonition, of something about to happen to her.

Poems made of the white dust, of the wind in the green corn, of the five trees – they would be the most beautiful poems in the world.

Sometimes the images of these things would begin to move before her with persistence, as if they were going to make a pattern; she could hear a thin cling-clang, a moving white pattern of sound that, when she tried to catch it, broke up and flowed away. The image pattern and the sound pattern belonged to each other, but when she tried to bring them together they fell apart.

That came of reading too much Byron.

How was it that patterns of sound had power to haunt and excite you? Like the 'potnia, potnia nux' that she found in the discarded Longfellow, stuck before his 'Voices of the Night.'

πότνια, πότνια νὺξ,υπ ὑπνοδότειρα τῶν πολυπόνων βροτῶν,
ἐρεβόθεν ἴθι, μόλε, μόλε κατάπτερος
τὸν' Ἀγαμεμνόνιον ἐπὶ δόμον.

She wished she knew Greek; the patterns the sounds made were so hard and still.

And there were bits of patterns, snapt off, throbbing wounds of sound that couldn't heal. Lines out of Mark's Homer.

Mark's Greek books had been taken from her five years ago, when Rodney went to Chelmsted. And they had come back with Rodney this Easter. They stood on the shelf in Mark's bedroom, above his writing-table.

One day she found her mother there, dusting and arranging the books. Besides the little shabby Oxford Homers there were an Aeschylus, a Sophocles, two volumes of Aristophanes, clean and new, three volumes of Euripides and a Greek Testament. On the table a well-preserved Greek Anthology, bound in green, with the owner's name, J. C. Ponsonby, stamped on it in gilt letters. She remembered Jimmy giving it to Mark.

She took the *Iliad* from its place and turned over the torn, discoloured pages.

Her mother looked up, annoyed and uneasy, like a child disturbed in the possession of its toys.

'Mark's books are to be kept where Mark put them,' she said.

'But, Mamma, I want them.'

Never in her life had she wanted anything so much as those books.

'When will you learn not to want what isn't yours?'

'Mark doesn't want them, or he'd have taken them. He'd give them me if he was here.'

'He isn't here. I won't have them touched till he comes back.'

'But, Mamma darling, I may be dead. I've had to wait five years as it is.'

'Wait? What for, I should like to know?'

'To learn Greek, of course.'

Her mother's face shivered with repugnance. It was incredible that anybody should hate a poor dead language so.

'Just because Mark learnt Greek, you think *you* must try. I thought you'd grown out of all that tiresome affectation. It was funny when you were a little thing, but it isn't funny now.'

Her mother sat down to show how tired she was of it.

'It's just silly vanity.'

Mary's heart made a queer and startling movement, as if it turned over and dashed itself against her ribs. There was a sudden swelling and aching in her throat. Her head swam slightly. The room, Mark's room, with Mark's white bed in one corner and Dan's white bed in the other, had changed; it looked like a room she had never been in before. She had never seen that mahogany washstand and the greyish blue flowers on the jug and basin. The person sitting on the yellow-painted bedroom chair was a stranger who wore, unaccountably, a brown dress and a gold watchchain with a gold tassel that she remembered. She had an odd feeling that this person had no right to wear her mother's dress and her chain.

The flash of queerness was accompanied by a sense of irreparable disaster. Everything had changed; she heard herself speaking, speaking steadily, with the voice of a changed and unfamiliar person.

'Mark doesn't think it's vanity. You only think it is because you want to.'

The mind of this unfamiliar self had a remorseless lucidity that seemed to her more shocking than anything she could imagine. It went on as if urged by some supreme necessity. 'You're afraid. Afraid.'

It seemed to her that her mother really was afraid.

'Afraid? And what of?' her mother said.

The flash went out, leaving her mind dark suddenly and defeated.

'I don't know what *of*. I only know you're afraid.'

'That's an awful thing for any child to say to any mother. Just because I won't let you have your own way in everything. Until your will is resigned to God's will I may well be afraid.'

'How do you know God doesn't want me to know Greek? He may want it as much as I do.'

'And if you did know it, what good would it do you?'

She stood staring at her mother, not answering. She knew the sound patterns were beautiful, and that was all she knew. Beauty. Beauty could be hurt and frightened away from you. If she talked about it now she would expose it to outrage. Though she knew that she must appear to her mother to be stubborn and stupid, even sinful, she put her stubbornness, her stupidity, her sinfulness, between it and her mother to defend it.

'I can't tell you,' she said.

'No. I don't suppose you can.'

Her mother followed up the advantage given her. 'You just go about dreaming and mooning as if there was nothing else in the wide world for you to do. I can't think what's come over you. You used to be content to sit still and sew by the hour together. You were more help to me when you were ten than you are now. The other day when I asked you to darn a hole in your own stocking you looked as if I'd told you to go to your funeral.

'It's time you began to take an interest in looking after the house. There's enough to keep you busy most of your time if you only did the half of it.'

'Is that what you want me to be, Mamma? A servant, like Catty?'

'Poor Catty. If you were more like Catty,' her mother said, 'you'd be happier than you are now, I can tell you. Catty is never disagreeable or disobedient or discontented.'

'No. But perhaps Catty's mother thinks she is.'

She thought: She *is* afraid.

'Do you suppose,' her mother said, 'it's any pleasure to me to find fault with my only daughter? If you weren't my only daughter, perhaps, I shouldn't find fault.'

Her new self answered again, implacable in its lucidity. 'You mean, if you'd had a girl you could do what you liked with you'd have let me alone? You'd have let me alone if you could have done what you liked with Mark?'

She noticed, as if it had a separate and significant existence, her mother's hand lying on the green cover of the Greek Anthology.

'If you were like Mark – if you were only like him!'

'If I only were!'

'Mark never hurt me. Mark never gave me a minute's trouble in his life.'

'He went into the Army.'

'He had a perfect right to go into the Army.'

Silence. 'Minky – you'll be kind to little Mamma.' A hard, light sound; the vexed fingers tap-tapping on the book. Her mother rose suddenly, pushing the book from her.

'There – take Mark's books. Take everything. Go your own way. You always have done; you always will. Some day you'll be sorry for it.'

She was sorry for it now, miserable, utterly beaten. Her new self seemed to her a devil that possessed her. She hated it. She hated the books. She hated everything that separated her and made her different from her mother and from Mark.

Her mother went past her to the door.

'Mamma – I didn't mean it – Mamma—'

Before she could reach the door it shut between them.

Anna Wickham (1884–1947)

Anna Wickham was born Edith Harper in Wimbledon. Her 'Fragment of an Autobiography' written in 1935 tells us that on her mother's side she came from a line of strong women. Her maternal grandmother, widowed early, brought up her three children single-handedly, working as an artist's model and cleaner to support them. Wickham's mother Alice, a manic, melodramatic woman, trained as a board-school teacher but she was also a gifted actress who might have turned professional had she not married.

Wickham's father, a piano salesman and witty conversationalist, wished his daughter to fulfil his failed ambition to be a writer.

According to the 'Fragment' Alice Harper resented her husband's interest in their daughter and sometimes beat her. Wickham's parents often quarrelled and as a child she yearned to reconcile them. Her childhood was punctuated by her mother's periodic suicide attempts. In 1900, the piano business failing, the family emigrated to Australia where Wickham's father continued selling pianos while her mother earned the larger part of the family income by teaching elocution and character reading. Prompted by Alice's restlessness, the family moved frequently and Wickham attended a number of different schools, including a convent which she disliked intensely.

Wickham left school at sixteen and for a while helped her mother in giving elocution lessons. Then, in 1904, she sailed to England to fulfil her father's dreams of artistic success. She obtained a scholarship to Tree's Academy of Acting and studied singing in London and Paris. She was on her way to developing a career as a singer at the Paris Conservatoire when she met and married Patrick Hepburn, a solicitor with a passion for Romanesque churches and astronomy (he later became President of the British Astronomical Association). Patrick came from a more educated family than the Harpers and Wickham felt that by marrying him she was meeting her father's standards. The marriage was, however, a turbulent one. Patrick had strong views about women as homemakers and resented his wife's commitment to her poetry, going so far as to have her certified and put in an asylum for six weeks after a volume of her poems was privately printed in 1911 under a male pseudonym.

Wickham longed for children. After a miscarriage and a daughter who died within moments of birth, her eldest son was born in 1907. In her autobiography she wrote: 'The day of this son's birth was the happiest of my life. This was the self expression which I believed in and which gave me delight' (Wickham 1984: 146–7). She became involved in social work with working-class mothers, a subject on which she lectured. Against the prevailing ethos she believed that working-class mothers had something to teach middle-class mothers and she fought for better economic conditions for impoverished mothers and their children. Her views on the social responsibility of middle-class mothers may be compared with Winifred Holtby's stress on the woman citizen.

Anna Wickham had four sons but in 1921 her third son died of scarlet fever. Devastated by this, she spent a period of time in Paris where she frequented literary circles and began a passionate correspondence with Natalie Barney. As her international reputation as a poet grew, Wickham's personal magnetism ensured that her home in Hampstead became a centre for literary gatherings – D. H. Lawrence, Katherine Mansfield, David Garnett, Dylan Thomas and Malcolm Lowry were among the writers who visited. Her disagreements with Patrick grew and in 1926 he engineered a judicial separation; the two eldest boys went to live with him but two years later the family was reunited. In 1929 Patrick died in a walking accident. Wickham continued to write poetry and to live in Hampstead. In 1947, having seen her sons safely through the war, she hanged herself.

It was an end Wickham practically predicted for herself. In many of her poems ('A Woman in Bed', 'New Eve') and in her autobiography she writes about the conflict between being a woman and a poet: 'Women of my kind are a profound mistake. There have been few women poets of distinction and . . . their despair rate has been very high' (Wickham 1984: 53; ellipsis mine). Wickham's feminist stance caused her to be linked in her lifetime with such writers as Virginia Woolf, Rebecca West, Dorothy Richardson and May Sinclair but she has been rather neglected since. She wrote several tender, wry poems to her sons but her mother is a significant absence in her poetry. Letters from her mother in later life invariably caused the adult Anna to retreat to bed.

Primary reading
Wickham, A. 1971 *Selected Poems* D. Garnett (ed.), London: Chatto & Windus.

Wickham, A. 1984 *The Writings of Anna Wickham, Free Woman and Poet*, edited and introduced by R. D. Smith, London: Virago.

The Angry Woman

From Anna Wickham, *The Writings of Anna Wickham, Free Woman and Poet*, R. D. Smith (ed.), London: Virago, 1984, pp. 202–4.

I am a woman, with a woman's parts,
And of love I bear children.
In the days of bearing is my body weak,
But why because I do you service, should you call
    me slave?

I am a woman in my speech and gait,
I have no beard, (I'll take no blame for that!)
In many things are you and I apart,
But there are regions where we coincide,
Where law for one is law for both.

There is the sexless part of me that is my mind.

You calculate the distance of a star,
I, thanks to this free age can count as well,
And by the very processes you use.
When we think differently of two times two,
I'll own a universal mastery in you!

Now of marriage,
In marriage there are many mansions,
(This has been said of Heaven).
Shall you rule all the houses of your choice
Because of manhood or because of strength?

If I must own your manhood synonym for every
   strength,
Then must I lie.
If sex is a criterion for power, and never strength,
What do we gain by union?
I lose all, while nothing worthy is so gained by
   you,
O most blessed bond!

Because of marriage, I have motherhood.
That is much, and yet not all!

By the same miracle that makes me mother
Are you a father.

It is a double honour!
Are you content to be from henceforth only
   father,
And in no other way a man?
A fantastic creature like a thing of dreams
That has so great an eye it has no head.
I am not mother to abstract Childhood, but to my
   son,
And how can I serve my son, but to be much
   myself.

My motherhood must boast some qualities,
For as motherhood is diverse
So shall men be many charactered
And show variety, as this world needs.

Shall I for ever brush my infant's hair?
Cumber his body in conceited needle-work?

Or shall I save some pains till he is grown?
Show him the consolation of mathematics
And let him laugh with me when I am old?

If he is my true son,
He will find more joy in number and in laughter
Than in all these other things.

Why should dull custom make my son my enemy
So that the privilege of his manhood is to leave
 my house?
You would hold knowledge from me because I
 am a mother,
Rather for this reason let me be wise, and very
 strong,
Power should be added to power.

And now of love!
There are many loves.
There is love, which is physiology,
And love, which has no more matter in it than is
 in the mind.
There is spiritual love, and there is good
 affection.
All these loves women need and most of all the
 last.

Kiss me sometimes in the light,
Women have body's pain of body's love.
Let me have flowers sometimes, and always joy.
And sometimes let me take your hand and kiss
 you honestly
Losing nothing in dignity by frank love.

If I must fly in love and follow in life,
Doing both things falsely,
Then am I a *mime*,
I have no free soul.

Man! For your sake and for mine, and for the
    sake of future men,
Let me speak my mind in life and love.
Be strong for love of a strong mate,
Do not ask my weakness as a sacrifice to power.
When you deny me justice
I feel as if my body were in grip of a cold octopus,
While my heart is crushed to stone.

This rapture have I of pretence!

Anzia Yezierska (?1880–1970)

Anzia Yezierska was born in a Russian-Polish village near Warsaw around 1880. She was one of nine children. Her father, Reb Yezierska, was a Talmudic scholar who believed his wife and children should support him so that he could devote himself to a life of study and prayer. 'My mother . . . dried out her days fighting at the pushcarts for another potato, another onion in the bag,' Yezierska wrote. 'My father [was] a Hebrew scholar and dreamer . . . always too much up in the air to come down to such sordid thoughts as bread and rent' (Henriksen 1988: 14). Around 1890, suffering persecution, the family emigrated to the US. Many of Yezierska's short stories describe the lives of Jewish immigrants struggling to realise the American dream in the tenements and sweatshops of Manhattan's Lower East Side.

Anzia Yezierska rejected the tradition of her Orthodox Jewish family that daughters should stay at home serving the men of the family and marry young. Instead, to her father's disapproval, she attended night school and then Columbia University for four years where she studied cooking, working in a laundry before and after classes in order to support herself. After graduation she taught cooking for several years. In 1910 she married Jacob Gordon, a lawyer. She left him almost immediately and their marriage was later annulled, though not before – in a religious ceremony – she had married Arnold Levitas, a teacher and textbook writer. She and Levitas had one daughter, Louise, born in 1912.

At home with her baby Yezierska felt increasingly trapped by the life of housewife and mother. When Louise was two, Yezierska went back to teaching but quarrels with Levitas continued and in 1916 she left him, taking Louise with her. Finding herself unable to support her daughter, she sent Louise back to live with her father.

Encouraged by the philosopher John Dewey of Columbia University (their relationship is described in *Red Ribbon on a White Horse*), Yezierska decided to live in poverty and devote herself to her short story writing. In 1920 her first collection, *Hungry Hearts*, was published. The film rights were bought by Sam Goldwyn and Yezierska went to Hollywood to work on the script. The 1920s was Yezierska's decade of success when it seemed as though she had achieved the American dream. But during the Depression she lost most of her money on the stock market, and she was obliged to take part in the WPA Writers' Project. Her reputation as a writer declined as her tales of impoverished immigrants struggling to rise above their circumstances went out of fashion. After the publication of *All I Could Never Be* in 1932, she published nothing more until her fictional autobiography *Red Ribbon on a White Horse* appeared in 1950 with an introduction by W. H. Auden. Thereafter she published short stories and reviews. She died in a nursing home in California where she had moved to be near her daughter.

In her book about Anzia's often-turbulent life Louise Levitas Henriksen gives a fascinating insight into her own difficult relationship with her mother. For a long period of her life Louise only saw her mother once a week – on a Saturday. She saw how her mother had stripped her life bare of everything to devote herself to her writing. Despite the fact that she had been excluded from her mother's life, Louise sided with her mother against her father but when she grew up she found living with her mother for any length of time exasperating: Yezierska demanded too much of her. Louise particularly resented being asked to advise and help her mother with her writing. She ends her biography of her mother:

> Out of loneliness and despair she made art. When I was a small child, I chose her against my father and never changed my allegiance. But whenever I was with her, close up, and fighting, she was always infuriating, demanding too much. Only now, in her absence, can I come this close to her again. (Henriksen 1988: 301)

Primary reading

Yezierska, A. 1925/1975 *Bread Givers*, New York: Persea Books.

Yezierska, A. 1950/1987 *Red Ribbon on a White Horse. My Story*, London: Virago.

Yezierska, A. 1987 *Hungry Hearts and Other Stories*, London: Virago.

Further reading

Henriksen, L. L. 1988 *Anzia Yezierska. A Writer's Life*, New Brunswick and London: Rutgers University Press.

Bread Givers

From Anzia Yezierska, *Bread Givers*, New York: Persea Books, 1975, pp. 165–72.

By the whole force of my will I could reason myself out of the dirt and noise around me. But how could I reason with my hungry stomach? How could I stretch my five dollars a week to meet all my needs?

I took a piece of paper and wrote it all down. A dollar and a half for rent. Sixty cents for carfare. I couldn't walk that long distance to work and back and have time for night school. No saving there. And I must put aside at least fifty cents a week to pay back Mother's rent money. What is there left for food? Two dollars and forty cents. That means thirty-four and two-sevenths cents a day. How could I have enough to eat from that? But that's all I can have now. Somehow, it's got to do.

But whenever I passed a restaurant or a delicatessen store, I couldn't tear my eyes away from the food in the window. Something wild in me wanted to break through the glass, snatch some of that sausage and corned-beef, and gorge myself just once.

One day in the laundry, while busy ironing a shirt, the thought of Mother's cooking came over me. Why was it that Mother's simplest dishes, her plain potato soup, her *gefülte* fish, were so filling? And what was the matter with the cafeteria food that it left me hungrier after eating than before?

For a moment I imagined myself eating Mother's *gefülte* fish. A happy memory floated over me. A feast I was having. What a melting taste in the mouth!

'Hey – there!' cried the boss, rushing madly at me.

Oi web! Smoke was rising from under my iron.

'Oh, I'll wash it out,' I gasped in fright, as I lifted the iron and saw the scorched triangle.

But the boss snatched the shirt away from me. 'Three dollars out of your wages for this,' he raged.

Not a word could I say. Either it was to lose my job or pay. And I could not lose my job.

Three dollars out from my wages, when every fraction of a penny was counted out where it had to go. Maybe for weeks I'd have to live on dry bread to make up the loss. I got so frightened, from weakness I longed to throw myself in some dark corner, only to weep away my bitter luck. But I dared not let go. The boss was around. I picked up the iron again, though I could hardly shift the weight back and forth.

A terrible hunger rose up in me – a hunger I had been trying to forget since my lunch of two stale slices of bread and a scrap of cheese. Just when I had to begin saving more from eating, the starvation of days and weeks began tearing and dragging down my last strength. Let me at least have one dinner with meat before I begin to starve. For that last hour of work, I saw before my eyes meat, only meat, great, big chunks of it. And I biting into the meat.

Like a wolf with hunger, I ran to the cafeteria. From the end of the line, I saw the big, printed bill of fare:

> Roast beef, 25c.
> Roast lamb, 30c.
> Beef stew, 20c.

My eyes stopped. Over the word stew, I saw big chunks of meat, carrots, and peas, with thick brown gravy. I reached for the tray, and took my place on the line. I was like a mad thing straining toward the pots of food, and the line seemed to stand for ever in one place. A big, husky, fat man stood behind me. He held his tray so that the end poked into my ribs every time he shuffled on his feet. But, thank God, the line began to move up, slowly nearer the serving table.

My anxious eyes leaped to the faces of the servers. I tried to see which one of them served the stew. My portion depended on her mood of the minute. If I'm lucky to strike her when she feels good, then the spoon will go deep down into the pot and come up heaping full. If she feels mean, then I get only from the tip of the spoon, a stingy portion. God! She holds in her hands my life, my strength, new blood for my veins, new clearness in my brain to go on with the fight. Oh! If she would only give me enough to fill myself, this one time! . . .

At last I reached the serving table.

'Stew with a lot of meat in it.'

Breathlessly, I watched how far the spoon would go into the pot. A hot sweat broke over my face as I saw the mean hunks of potato and the skinny strings of meat floating in the starched gravy which she handed me.

'Please, won't you put in one real piece of meat?' And I pushed back the plate for more.

I might as well have talked to the wall. She did not see me or hear me. Her eyes were smiling back to the fat man behind me who grinned knowingly at her.

'Stew,' was all he said.

She picked up my plate, pushed the spoon deep down into the pot and brought it up heaping with thick chunks of meat.

'Oh, thank you! Thank you! I'll take it now,' I cried, reaching for it with both hands.

'No, you don't.' And the man took the plate from the server and set it on his tray.

Speechless, bewildered, I stood there, unable to move.

'I asked for stew – *stew!*'

'I gave you some and you didn't take it.' She sniffed.

'But you didn't give me as much as you gave him. Isn't my money as good as his?'

'Don't you know they always give men more?' called a voice from the line.

'It takes a woman to be mean to a woman,' piped up another.

'You're holding up the line,' said the head lady, coming over, with quiet politeness.

'I want stew,' came again from my tight throat.

'She gave you a fair portion.'

'But why did she give more to the man just because he was a man? I'm hungry.'

All the reply I got was a cold glance. 'Please move on or step out of the line.'

People began to titter and stare at me. Even the girl at the serving table laughed as she put on a man's plate a big slice of fried liver, twice as big as she would have given me.

'Cheaters! Robbers!' I longed to cry out to them. 'Why do you have flowers on the table and cheat a starving girl from her bite of food?' But I was too trampled to speak. With tight lips, I walked out.

In the street, there was no cheap restaurant in sight. I had a dreary feeling that it was the same in every other place. Since I must starve next week, I might as well begin now. I went home boiling with hate for the whole world.

In my room, I found the tail end of a loaf of bread. Each bite I swallowed was wet with my tears.

It was so cold that night that in every tenement people huddled into their beds early and put all their clothes over themselves to keep warm. So cold it was, even the gas froze.

I stuck a candle into a bottle, took up my grammar, struggling to forget my bitterness, studying. Everything I had I wrapped around myself and, buried in my thin bedclothes, I held on to my book.

My feet were lumps of ice. How could I study? But I would. I must. I forced myself to keep to my lessons like one forcing himself awake when he's falling asleep.

A rap came to the door. It was repeated over and over again before I could drag myself out of my coverings to see who it was.

'Mother!' I cried. Yes, there stood my mother, a shawl over her head and a big bundle on her back. She threw her arms around me and kissed me hungrily.

'In a night like this, I thought you'd need a feather bed,' she said, throwing her bundle on my cot. Her face was stiff with cold, and she blew on her half-frozen fingers.

'All the way from Elizabeth for you to carry it,' I cried. In the sputtering light of the candle, her sunken eyes gleamed out of their black sockets with a dumb, pleading love that made me hate myself for my selfishness. It seemed to me I never knew till now how close to my heart my mother was.

'Here's a jar of herring that I pickled for you,' she said, unwrapping it from an old newspaper. 'A piece of herring on bread, and you have already a good meal.'

Her goodness hurt so that I began talking fast to keep back the tears in my throat.

'How is Father? How is business? How could you get away from the store?'

'It's lodge night, and your father will be away till late. With all my hurrying it took so long to get here, that I'll have to go back in a few minutes to be home before he comes.'

Hours she travelled, only to see me for a few minutes. God! How much bigger was Mother's goodness than my burning ambition to rise in the world!

'Mother! You're so good to me. What can I do back for you?' I said, feeling small under her feet with unworthiness.

'Only come to see me soon.'

'I'd do anything for you. I'd give you away my life. But I can't take time to go 'way out to Elizabeth. Every little minute must go to my studies.'

'I tore myself away from all my work to come to see you.'

'But you're not studying for college.'

'Is college more important than to see your old mother?'

'I could see you later. But I can't go to college later. Think only of the years I wasted in the shop instead of school, and I must catch up all that lost time.'

'You're young yet. You have plenty of time.'

'It's because I'm young that my minutes are like diamonds to me. I have so much to learn before I can enter college. But won't you be proud of me when I work myself up for a school teacher, in America?'

'I'd be happier to see you get married. What's a school teacher? Old maids – all of them. It's good enough for *Goyim*, but not for you.'

'Don't worry. I'll even get married some day. But to marry myself to a man that's a person, I must first make myself for a person.'

Mother shook her head. '*Ach!* Already I must go.' But her feet stuck to the floor and her hands clung to me for many minutes before she could tear herself away. Long after she had gone, I felt her still in the room.

As I tucked my shivering bones under the featherbed, I felt that nothing on earth was as warm as Mother's love. Gone was the rankling hurt I had suffered at the cafeteria. I forgot to hate even the fat man and the head lady with her cold, low-voiced politeness. All the bitterness of my heart was forgotten.

I laughed when I thought of poor dear old Mother – coming so far with that big feather bed on her back. . . . How warm I am. . . . If only I had time to go to see her. . . . To-morrow, I'll sit up in bed, warm, for once, and study my grammar.

Winifred Holtby (1898–1935)

W inifred Holtby was born at Rudston, East Yorkshire, the second of two daughters. Her father was a prosperous
farmer and her mother, Alice Holtby a formidable personality known
locally as 'deputy God' – was the first woman to be elected alderman
on the East Riding Council. She encouraged her younger daughter's
writing by having a selection of her poems privately printed in 1911.

Educated at home and then at Queen Margaret's School, Scarbor-
ough, Winifred Holtby entered Somerville College, Oxford to read
Modern History. In 1918 she interrupted her studies to join the
Women's Auxiliary Corps and went to France. In 1919, returning to

Somerville, she became friends with Vera Brittain. After Oxford, Holtby and Brittain lived together in London and embarked on their careers as writers, journalists and lecturers.

Winifred Holtby was a prolific and brilliant journalist, writing for the *Manchester Guardian*, the *News Chronicle* and *Time and Tide* (of which she became a director in 1926) amongst others. In her journalism, as in her fiction, Holtby reveals her commitment to feminism, pacifism and racial equality. A member of Lady Rhondda's Six Point Group, Holtby was an Old (equal rights) Feminist, arguing indefatigably for women's right to equal citizenship. Her second novel, *The Crowded Street* (1924), is a searing indictment of those middle-class mothers who kept their daughters at home in idleness waiting for the right man to come along. Holtby was a passionate believer that 'each of us has to find his or her work in life, and that thing greater than ourselves which gives life its meaning' (Berry and Bishop 1985: 78). She was also deeply committed to the cause of racial equality in South Africa, visiting that country in 1926 and campaigning for the unionisation of black workers. A selection of her journalism can be found in *Testament of a Generation* (1985).

Winifred Holtby continued living with Vera Brittain after the latter's marriage and she helped care for Vera's two children. In *Testament of Friendship* (1940), Brittain gives a moving portrait of her friend. Holtby's first novel, *Anderby Wold*, was published in 1923. Like *South Riding*, it depicts the East Riding farming community Holtby knew so well and from which she was to some extent exiled when an agricultural strike forced her father to give up his farm in 1919 and move to Cottingham, a suburb of Hull.

South Riding was Holtby's sixth novel. She spent much of 1934 and the early part of 1935 staying in Yorkshire researching and writing it. It was completed a month before she died of kidney failure in a London nursing home at the tragically early age of thirty-seven. *South Riding* was published posthumously in 1936 and won the James Tait Black Memorial Prize. The novel is, in part, a tribute to Holtby's mother whose life was spent caring for the local community. In her prefatory letter addressed to Alderman Mrs Holtby, Winifred Holtby writes: 'I dedicate this story, such as it is, to you, who have fought so valiant a fight for human happiness . . . At least let me record one perfect thing: the proud delight which it has meant to me to be the daughter of Alice Holtby' (Holtby 1936/1988: xii; ellipsis mine).

Primary reading

Holtby, W. 1924/1981 *The Crowded Street*, London: Virago.
Holtby, W. 1936/1988 *South Riding*, London: Virago.
Berry, P. and Bishop, A. (eds.) 1985 *Testament of a Generation. The Journalism of Vera Brittain and Winifred Holtby*, London: Virago.
Brittain, V. 1940/1989 *Testament of Friendship*, London: Virago.

South Riding

From Winifred Holtby, *South Riding*, London: Virago, 1988, pp. 173–81.

From the hour when Lydia, cycling home joyfully through the frost, found her mother in tears on the tumbled bed, life changed for her. An evil spell might have been cast upon her. She was no longer good-humoured and self-confident, assured that, in spite of present difficulty and discomfort, the future was hers and the future was good. She was afraid, and fear tormented her.

At school she was arrogant and wilful. She scribbled obscenities in her nature-book, driving Miss Sigglesthwaite to unguessed despair. She was impertinent to Miss Parsons, noisy and undisciplined on the playing-field, rough and unkind to smaller children, taking a special pleasure in tormenting Midge Carne. During the Easter term her work steadily deteriorated. She no longer wrestled with her natural faults of carelessness and disorder. Though her quick wits and retentive memory prevented her from falling to the bottom of her class, her answers lost all interest and distinction.

'You see,' smiled Miss Jameson, 'the girl's reverting to type. You can't make a silk purse out of a sow's ear. These slum children, they're quick enough till adolescence, but then the trouble begins. They can't keep it up.'

Miss Jameson spoke bitterly. The bank management still delayed Pip's promotion. She did not know how long she would be tied to a routine which bored her and to an authority which she found irksome. She might as well have applied for the headmistress-ship. It would have meant harder work, but Miss Burton was a slave-driver anyway. She had no sense of proportion.

Sarah was deeply concerned about Lydia. It's not natural, it's not right, she told herself. I don't believe the girl is either spoiled or satiated. There's something definitely wrong. A boy? She remembered the precocity of Lydia's performance at Madame Hubbard's concert. The girl undoubtedly knew everything that was to be known about certain adult experiences. 'But she's not the boy-crazy type,' thought Sarah, 'and she's not more homosexual than any other romantic adolescent.' Lydia's sturdiness, her clumsy hoydenish strength, her humour, her intelligence, prevented her from seeming a neurotic child. Sarah pondered and watched, disturbed yet patient, with the patience that was hers only when she dealt with young, confused, imperfect creatures.

The Easter holidays approached, and on Easter morning Sarah's consciousness of Lydia Holly was obliterated by her encounter with the Carnes of Maythorpe. It was not of Lydia but of Midge and her father that she talked to her sister Pattie, to whose house she had gone immediately after Easter for a week's change of air. Her brother-in-law went out one evening to a Masonic dinner, the children were in bed, and Sarah and Pattie sat, as they had often done, over the fire, exchanging their diverse experiences. As usual, Sarah monopolised most of the conversation.

She described Carne – a sporting farmer, pseudo-county, with a big pale face rather like Mussolini's – only his nose hooks a bit.

'Handsome?'

'Yes. Certainly. And knows it. Lord, how he knows it!'

Sarah lay on the fur hearthrug, plaiting its soft strands idly. Pattie, as usual, was mending socks for her family. She listened quietly to Sarah's narrative of the adventure on Easter eve.

'. . . So he sent a groom to fetch petrol from an inn down the village, and when we'd finished breakfast, there was my car ready, my clothes dried, everything splendid. Only – not a word of apology or thanks, Pattie. Well, he *did* send a stiff little note hoping I was no worse, but . . . taking everything for granted like that . . . The arrogance of it! And I shall have to spend fortunes at the cleaners, and even so that new two-piece will never be the same again. What do you think, Pattie?'

'That you're inclined to be more than half in love with him, my dear.'

'In – *love?*' gasped Sarah.

She stared at her sister, then remarked mildly, 'Marriage has had its usual deplorable effect on your intelligence, my poor one. Only one single idea nowadays.'

She went on to describe Mrs. Beddows, Alderman Astell, whom she liked increasingly, and her far-off plans for a rebuilt school.

I shall have to give up discussing personalities with Pattie, she told herself. Really she is too absurd. Yet all that night when she slept she dreamed of the governor's dark figure towering above her in the snow, and somehow incongruously intermingled with the music of Terry Bryan's solo from the *Messiah*, 'I will shake the heavens and the earth, the sea and the dry land'; and when she woke she could see Carne's profile outlined against the lantern light as he bent over the struggling terrified cow.

I dislike, I oppose everything he stands for, she told herself – feudalism, patronage, chivalry, exploitation . . . We are natural and inevitable enemies.

She returned to Kiplington before term started. She had to deal with correspondence, time-tables, workmen, repairs and contracts. Colonel Collier, Mr Tadman, and a clerk closeted themselves with Miss Parsons, going over the food contracts for the year, ordering meat for the boarders from two local butchers, lump sugar from one grocer, soft sugar from another, soap straight from the Kingsport manufacturers at a rebate, jam from a London factory, 'and I know what Tadman gets out of that,' Joe Astell said darkly. Miss Parsons was helpless before governors and contractors. Sarah ached to take her place and send the squabbling incompetents about their proper business. 'The local people pay the rates; they should get our contracts,' she protested. 'And as for ordering raisins from one shop and ground rice from another – it's ridiculous. Nothing but little finicking accounts with every tradesman. Why not get them all from one grocer and then take them in rotation?' But Miss Parsons was no fighter, and Sarah believed in delegation. She had to possess her soul in patience, with occasional explosions to Joe Astell.

But she had her own troubles. The grant for her boarding-house was hideously inadequate. The place looked desolate, and she had no money to spend on decorations. She pillaged her cottage for vases, books and woodcuts. She designed cupboards, bullied local carpenters, hung pictures and curtains, pestered governors. Far into the night she sat writing letters, drafting memoranda. She dragged any member of the Higher Education Committee whom she could lure into her buildings from cellar to garret, exposing their enormities. Her energy was unremitting. If the South Riding was not prepared to build a new school for her, she would make this old one a perpetual torment. And always as she planned and wrote and argued, she saw Councillor Carne in her mind's eye as the apostle and ringleader of reaction, the author of false economies, the culprit really responsible for leaking taps in the science room and blackbeetles in the basement. Because of this, it was a little difficult to banish the thought of him completely from her consciousness; but at least she never forgot to remember him with resentment.

In spite of her preoccupations she found time to visit Lydia Holly. One day she drove along the Maythorpe road, stopped at the Shacks, and found Lydia, in a torn overall, feeding hens with some dank-smelling mash. She called, and the girl came towards her, slouching and reluctant. Sarah spoke crisply, asked how she was getting on, praised the plump hens, mentioned Lydia's school work, asked how her mother was, and observed the girl's awkward diffident answers.

She felt snubbed by the lack of response, but would not force a confidence. She ended by asking Lydia to tea on Sunday, and determined to collect a group of girls to serve as an excuse for the party. She drove away, depressed and quite uncomforted; but as she turned her car she thought she saw in the doorway of the coach a woman's drooping figure, heavily pregnant.

Is that it? she wondered. Is that what's worrying Lydia? Still – Sarah could not see it as a tragedy.

She could not know that the moment she had driven away, Lydia rushed to the unoccupied railway coach used by her as a study. There, wrapped in old coats and sacking, she had found privacy throughout the winter. There she could read and write and copy out her home-work. Candles had spilled grease from the bottles in which she stuck them on to the table-flap of pot-ringed deal. Scraps of torn paper, dog-eared books and well-chewed pencils bore witness to her efforts. This was her own place.

But there was no longer joy in its seclusion. Its promise was betrayed, its treasure rifled. Her mother was going to die. Lydia must leave school. She must come home and look after her small brother and sisters and the new baby too. There was no choice. Her mother's sisters were both busy harassed married women with families of their own. Her father, characteristically feckless, had no kin. She would have to do it.

She was not a religious child, and did not pray about it; she was not a self-deceiving child, and did not try to tell herself that it would be all right, that her mother would get better, and she would return to school; she was not an irresponsible child, and did not dream of escaping from her obligations.

But she saw all too clearly what must happen. 'These slum children know too much,' Miss Jameson said. Lydia knew too much. Her lively imagination ran ahead and lived through the days which very soon would face her.

Quarter to five, wake Father. Put on the kettle, get his breakfast, the cocoa, the margarine, the bread. Tidy the living-room; go and wake the children; get their breakfast. (Why isn't there no bacon? Lydie, can't we have treacle?) See them off to school; look after Lennie and baby; tidy the bedroom, peel the potatoes, get the dinner ready, feed the hens, the pig – if they could keep one; give the children their dinner when they came home from school, noisy and ravenous. Lennie still needed his food shovelling in with a spoon; he was a slow eater; the baby would want a bottle. Wash up the dinner things; then do the shopping, pushing the pram along the dull road into Maythorpe; get the tea ready, the children are coming shouting across the fields; Daisy has fallen and cut her knee; Gertie is sick again. Bert back. Lyd, what's for tea, old girl? Bacon cake? I'm sick of bacon cake. Can't we have sausages? Washing the children. The heavy shallow tubs, the tepid water. Where's the flannel gone? Don't let Lennie eat the soap now! The tap stood up two feet from the ground on a twisted pipe twenty yards from the door. The slops were thrown out on to the ground behind the caravans and railway coaches. Rough weeds grew there; damel and dock and nettle soaked up the dingy water, drinking grossly. Broken pots splashed in it. Rimlets of mud seeped down from it. The rusting tubs were heavy. Lydia's strong arms ached from lifting, carrying, coping with the clamorous, wriggling children.

And throughout this day of servitude there would be no mother to applaud or scold, no draggled lumpish woman whose sharp tongue cut across tedium, whose rare rough caress lit sudden radiance. Only her father's maudlin misery or facile optimism would punctuate the days.

And all the time the High School would be there, the morning prayers in the hall, the girls in rows, white blouses and brown tunics, neat heads bowed and lifted together; there would be the hymns, the lesson, the word of command, the note struck on the piano, then the march out to a brave tune, 'Pomp and Circumstance,' or 'The Entry of the Gladiators.' There would be the classes, scripture, history. This term they were going to 'do' Nehemiah, the book about the gallant young prophet, the King's Cup Bearer, who roved by night among the ruins of Jerusalem. They were to 'do' the Civil Wars. Miss Burton had told them to read Browning's *Strafford*, 'Night hath its first supreme forsaken star.' There would be botany, physics, glorious smells and explosions in the stink-room. Teasing Siggles. Good old Siggles with her fading wisps of hair. There would be tennis. Cricket. Prize-giving. Essay prize, Lydia Holly. Maths. prize, Lydia Holly. Form prize. High average for the year, Lydia Holly. Sports junior championship, Lydia Holly. Oh, no, no, no, no, no! Other girls. Other girls, others who cared nothing for all these things, could have them. Jill Jackson, who only thought of hockey, Gladys Hubbard, who was going to be a singer, Doris Peckover, who has as much imagination as a clothes-horse – these would gain the marks, win the prizes, take the scholar-ships, be clapped at prize-giving, go on to college.

It isn't fair. None of them care like I do. None of them could do what I could do. I hate them.

I hate Sarah Burton. What did she want to come here for? 'Are these your hens? Is this your little brother?' As if that was all I should ever be good for again – the hens, the little brother!

Why did they ever let me go to school? What's never seen is never missed. 'Your work is really interesting. You have imagination.' For what? For what? 'It takes an intelligent person to be kind,' Red Sally told her. And Lydia had been kind. She had sat up for her mother when Gert was taken bad; she had got her dad his tea.

And that did for her. Kindness had done for her. Using her imagination had done for her.

'Oh God, oh God, how am I to *live?*' cried Lydia.

But she saw no respite in rebellion. With slow unchildish delib-
eration she dried her swollen tear-stained face on her torn overall,
and made her way to the railway coach across the littered turf.

It was the dead end of the afternoon – three o'clock – and the
Mitchells were both out. Mr Mitchell on his bicycle, Mrs Mitchell
shopping with her baby.

Lennie, crouched in his pen, chewed a dirty rag-book. The older
children had gone off bird's-nesting.

Unwillingly Lydia opened the door and entered. Her mother had
not finished the ironing. She had left the irons on the oil-stove, the
shirts and drawers rolled in the broken basket. She was not standing
at the table. She was not in the bedroom.

Lydia, surprised but not perturbed, went across to the Mitchells.
Mrs Holly was not there. She was not speaking to a tradesman at his
van on the road.

'Mother! Mother!' called Lydia.

No one answered.

'Mother! Mother!'

Then Lennie, in his pen, affected by the inevitable melancholy of
the human voice calling unresponsive emptiness, began to whimper:
'Mum! Mum! Mummie! Mummie!' beating with his pebble on the bar
of the pen.

'Mother! Mother!' called Lydia.

There was no one. She turned from the grey unwelcoming camp to
the grey unwelcoming field.

'Mother! Mother!'

In a sudden panic she ran to the edge of the cliff.

'Mother! Mother!'

An ashen sea swung silently against the crumbling clay.

'Mother, where are you?'

Round the field ran Lydia, terrified of horrors beyond her imagination.

'Mum! Mum! Mum!' cried Lennie, shuffling round and round his pen.

Near the hedge, behind the caravan, Lydia found her. She lay in the tangled clump of docks and nettles. In falling she had cut her head against a broken jam-jar. The cut bled. She moaned a little, her distorted body shaken by intermittent paroxysms of pain.

'Mother!' cried Lydia.

She knelt beside her, not even feeling the nettles that stung her arms and legs. With a child's panicking fear she shook her mother. 'Mother!' But it was with an adult's acceptance of inexorable anguish that she saw the woman's eyes open slowly, fix themselves on her face, and reveal the effort towards consciousness.

Mrs Holly fought for self-mastery and won.

'It's all right. I only tumbled. It's come. Get some one,' she gasped.

Strong as she might be, Lydia could not lift her mother. She left her and ran through the empty camp to the Maythorpe Road and stood there looking up and down it for help.

The dead chill windless afternoon received her cries and muffled them in distance. Sea-birds flew squawking and wheeling above her head; they mocked her impotence, then swung with effortless grace towards the town.

Should she run up the road for help? Back to her mother? Or should she wait there, risking the chance of a stray motor-car?

'Oh, come! Come! Some one. Some one must come and help me!' she sobbed, beating her hands on the gate. 'Oh, help me!'

And then she heard far away the sound of a motor approaching from the south.

It was Mr Huggins, driving one of his own lorries, who nearly ran down her gesticulating body.

'Hi, now. What's this? What's this, my girl?'

'My mother. She's fallen. You must come.'

There was no mistaking this genuine distress for mischief. Huggins followed Lydia across the field and saw enough. He was a family man.

'Pity you can't drive a car. No. We can't move her. You run in and put on kettles to boil, and get some clean sheets on the bed. Had your mother made any preparations, think you? I'll send a woman. Yes, an' I'll get doctor.'

He was gone again, but Lydia felt no longer isolated. She flew between the coach and the moaning woman; she filled kettles, she sought sheets. She hardly noticed when a neighbour sent by Huggins sprang from her cycle, when cars arrived, the lorryman, the doctor. The camp, which a few seconds ago contained only her fear, her anguish and her mother, seemed now overfull of hurrying people.

They kept her out of the coach, minding Lennie, getting tea for the children in Bella Vista; she became conscious of other things, of her father's worried face, rather cold and injured because it wasn't his fault that he was at work when Annie was taken bad; of the Mitchells' chickens, scratching in disappointment at an empty enamel basin, fouling its side with scrabbled claw-marks; of the kindly Mitchells, trying to keep the younger children quiet, of Bert, rushing off on his cycle to the chemist.

They called her at last.

'You'd better come. She wants you.'

'Is there a baby?'

'Yes. A little boy.'

She did not ask of her mother, 'Will she get better?'

She knew already. She had always known.

The interior of the coach was very hot. It smelled odd. Mrs Holly's grey drained face lay on the pillow case that Mrs Mitchell had provided.

She turned with fretful effort.

'A boy.'

'I know. Don't worry, Mum.'

'You'll have to look after him.'

'Yes, yes – don't you talk now.'

'You'll have to let the parish bury me.'

There was no hope and no reprieve. Lydia and her mother waited for the death that delayed nearly another hour, held off by the woman's stubborn spirit.

Before she died, Mrs Holly spoke once again, now fully conscious and recognising the full measure of her defeat, aware of the wreckage her death must cause, accepting it as something beyond remedy.

She opened her heavy eyes and looked straight at Lydia, and said quite clearly: 'I'm sorry, Lyd,' and died.

It was the first and only apology that she had ever made.

Virginia Woolf (1882–1941)

Virginia Woolf was born Virginia Stephen in London, daughter of Leslie Stephen, the literary critic and biographer, and Julia Duckworth. Her parents had both been married before and as well as her sister, Vanessa ('Nessa'), and brothers, Thoby and Adrian, Woolf had two half-brothers, George and Gerald and a half-sister, Stella. On her father's side, there was his daughter, Laura, referred to by Woolf in this extract from 'A Sketch of the Past' as 'an idiot' (she was possibly autistic, see Lee 1996: 103).

It was a large household to run and Leslie Stephen was a difficult and demanding man to live with. Added to this, Julia Stephen was frequently called upon to the bedsides of sick relatives and when not occupied with this she went out nursing the dying among the slums of London and of St Ives where the family spent their summer holidays. Nursing was Julia Stephen's vocation, though she was not a professional nurse and indeed she disagreed with professions for women. In 1883 she published *Notes for Sick Rooms*. She also wrote children's stories for her family and taught her children their lessons. The demands on her time were thus endless. In 'A Sketch of the Past', begun in 1939, Woolf recalls her first memory as a pattern of red and purple flowers on her mother's dress but in later life Woolf had the feeling that she had hardly spent a moment with her mother alone. In *To the Lighthouse* (1927), she recreates Julia Stephen in the portrait of Mrs Ramsay, a Victorian Angel in the House who nevertheless has private moments of dissatisfaction.

Julia Stephen died from rheumatic fever and exhaustion in 1895 when her daughter was thirteen. Woolf never got to know her mother as an adult with the result that she remained fixed in her thoughts as the idealised mother of early childhood. As Woolf herself explained in a letter to Vanessa: 'Dying at that moment, I suppose she cut a great figure in one's mind when it was just awake' (Roe 1990: 64) In all her relationships – with Vanessa, with Vita Sackville-West, with Leonard – she sought maternal nurturance. The early loss of her mother was perhaps one of the factors in Woolf's difficulty in establishing a sense of self (Lidoff 1986: 43–59). In *The Waves* (1931) all the characters are aware of the mother's language pressing against the symbolic but Rhoda lives so closely attuned to maternal rhythms that she struggles to establish an identity at all. As a writer Woolf is always attempting to recapture that sense of wholeness and safety she had experienced, all too briefly, in her mother's presence.

Woolf had a series of mental breakdowns during her life beginning with the period after the deaths of her mother and of her half-sister, Stella, in 1897. Biographers are divided about the cause of these breakdowns – perhaps they were hereditary, perhaps they were caused by events in her life, perhaps they were a response to her society's expectations of women, perhaps they were the result of abuse she suffered at hands of her half-brothers. Or perhaps they were connected, as Leonard Woolf thought, with her intense periods of creativity.

After the deaths of Julia and Stella came a period of 'Oriental gloom' (Woolf 1990: 47) when the Stephen household was dominated by Leslie Stephen's self-centred and melodramatic mourning. In between performing all the duties required of a daughter at home, Woolf continued studying and discussing her reading with her father. Intermittently she attended Greek, Latin and history classes at King's College, London and was tutored in Greek at home by Janet Case. She also reluctantly accompanied George Duckworth into the drawing rooms and ballrooms of London society.

In 1904 Leslie Stephen's death released Virginia and her sister from 'the Greek slave years' (Woolf 1990: 117). They moved to the house in Gordon Square which became central to the activities of the Bloomsbury group most of whom had been friends of their brother Thoby at Cambridge. In 1906 Thoby died after contracting typhoid, completing the decade of deaths that marked Woolf's early life.

In Gordon Square, the Stephen sisters were able to organise their lives as they pleased, Vanessa concentrating on her painting, Virginia on her writing. It was at this date that she began her career as a literary reviewer. In 1907 Vanessa married Clive Bell and Virginia moved with her brother Adrian to another part of Bloomsbury. In 1911 Leonard Woolf, back from Ceylon, rented a room in their house in Brunswick Square in which Duncan Grant and Maynard Keynes were also living. In 1912 Virginia and Leonard married. Her first novel, *The Voyage Out*, begun in 1908, was published in 1915 and in 1917 Leonard and Virginia Woolf established the Hogarth Press. During the First World War she also began writing her diary which continued until a few days before her death.

Her marriage to Leonard was one of the deepest sources of satisfaction in Woolf's life but they had no children; this was possibly

Leonard's decision, in consultation with doctors, in order to protect his wife's health. Woolf never came to terms with her childlessness and all through her diaries there runs a wistful strain of wondering about motherhood, watching Vanessa's motherhood with envy and competitiveness: if Vanessa could produce babies, she would produce novels, but she knew it wasn't the same thing and in periods of depression she felt her childlessness acutely as a failure.

In the last decade of her life, Woolf sought to bring into the public domain her opposition to the patriarchy in which she lived. In this the mother plays an important part. In *A Room of One's Own* (1929) she insists on the importance of establishing a maternal genealogy and in *Three Guineas* (1938) she argues that motherhood has a right to be recognised by society as a profession entitled to payment. But in *The Years* (1937) and *Between the Acts* (1941) her characters fail in their attempts to envisage a different type of society, a more communal one in keeping with a matriarchy. Under pressure from the war and the rise of fascism, and increasingly overwhelmed by memories of the past, particularly her father's tyranny and her half-brothers' abusive behaviour, Woolf seems to have despaired of ever creating a society which would reflect women's values. In March 1941, feeling the onset of her madness, she took her own life.

Primary reading

Woolf, V. 1915/1981 *The Voyage Out*, London: Granada.

Woolf, V. 1925/1981 *Mrs Dalloway*, London: Granada.

Woolf, V. 1927/1988 *To the Lighthouse*, London: Granada.

Woolf, V. 1931/1980 *The Waves*, London: Granada.

Woolf, V. 1937/1985 *The Years*, London: Granada.

Woolf, V. 1953/1981 *A Writer's Diary* L. Woolf (ed.), London: Granada.

Woolf, V. 1990 *Moments of Being* J. Schulkind (ed.), London: Grafton.

Woolf, V. 1992 *A Room of One's Own* [1929] *Three Guineas* [1938] M. Shiach (ed.), Oxford: Oxford University Press.

Further reading

Cramer, P. 1993 'Virginia Woolf's Matriarchal Family of Origins in *Between the Acts*', *Twentieth Century Literature* 39 (20): 166–84.

Gordon, L. 1984 *Virginia Woolf. A Writer's Life*, Oxford: Oxford University Press.

Heilbrun, C. 1991 'To the Lighthouse: The New Story of Mother and Daughter' in *Hamlet's Mother*, London: The Women's Press.

Lee, H. 1996 *Virginia Woolf*, London: Chatto & Windus.

Lidoff, J. 1986 'Virginia Woolf's Feminine Sentence', *Literature and Psychology* 32 (3): 43–59.

Lilienfield, J. 1977 ' "The Deceptiveness of Beauty": Mother Love and Mother Hate in *To the Lighthouse*', *Twentieth Century Literature* 23: 345–76.

Minow-Pinkney, M. 1987 *Virginia Woolf and the Problem of the Subject*, Brighton: Harvester Press.

Roe, S. 1990 *Writing and Gender. Virginia Woolf's Writing Practice*, Hemel Hempstead: Harvester Wheatsheaf.

Rosenman, E. 1986 *The Invisible Presence. Virginia Woolf and the Mother-Daughter Relationship*, Baton Rouge and London: Louisiana State University Press.

A Sketch of the Past

From Virginia Woolf, *Moments of Being*, J. Schulkind (ed.), London: Grafton, 1989, pp. 89–94.

Until I was in the forties – I could settle the date by seeing when I wrote *To the Lighthouse*, but am too casual here to bother to do it – the presence of my mother obsessed me. I could hear her voice, see her, imagine what she would do or say as I went about my day's doings. She was one of the invisible presences who after all play so important a part in every life. This influence, by which I mean the consciousness of other groups impinging upon ourselves; public opinion; what other people say and think; all those magnets which attract us this way to be like that, or repel us the other and make us different from that; has never been analysed in any of those Lives which I so much enjoy reading, or very superficially.

Yet it is by such invisible presences that the 'subject of this memoir' is tugged this way and that every day of his life; it is they that keep him in position. Consider what immense forces society brings to play upon each of us, how that society changes from decade to decade; and also from class to class; well, if we cannot analyse these invisible presences, we know very little of the subject of the memoir; and again how futile life-writing becomes. I see myself as a fish in a stream; deflected; held in place; but cannot describe the stream.

To return to the particular instance which should be more definite and more capable of description than for example the influence on me of the Cambridge Apostles, or the influence of the Galsworthy, Bennett, Wells school of fiction, or the influence of the Vote, or of the War – that is, the influence of my mother. It is perfectly true that she obsessed me, in spite of the fact that she died when I was thirteen, until I was forty-four. Then one day walking round Tavistock Square I made up, as I sometimes make up my books, To the Lighthouse; in a great, apparently involuntary, rush. One thing burst into another. Blowing bubbles out of a pipe gives the feeling of the rapid crowd of ideas and scenes which blew out of my mind, so that my lips seemed syllabling of their own accord as I walked. What blew the bubbles? Why then? I have no notion. But I wrote the book very quickly; and when it was written, I ceased to be obsessed by my mother. I no longer hear her voice; I do not see her.

I suppose that I did for myself what psycho-analysts do for their patients. I expressed some very long felt and deeply felt emotion. And in expressing it I explained it and then laid it to rest. But what is the meaning of 'explained' it? Why, because I described her and my feeling for her in that book, should my vision of her and my feeling for her become so much dimmer and weaker? Perhaps one of these days I shall hit on the reason; and if so, I will give it, but at the moment I will go on, describing what I can remember, for it may be true that what I remember of her now will weaken still further. (This note is made provisionally, in order to explain in part why it is now so difficult to give any clear description of her.)

Certainly there she was, in the very centre of that great Cathedral space which was childhood; there she was from the very first. My first memory is of her lap; the scratch of some beads on her dress comes back to me as I pressed my cheek against it. Then I see her in her white dressing gown on the balcony; and the passion flower with the purple star on its petals. Her voice is still faintly in my ears – decided, quick; and in particular the little drops with which her laugh ended – three diminishing ahs . . . 'Ah – ah – ah . . .' I sometimes end a laugh that way myself. And I see her hands, like Adrian's, with the very individual square-tipped fingers, each finger with a waist to it, and the nail broadening out. (My own are the same size all the way, so that I can slip a ring over my thumb.) She had three rings; a diamond ring, an emerald ring, and an opal ring. My eyes used to fix themselves upon the lights in the opal as it moved across the page of the lesson book when she taught us, and I was glad that she left it to me (I gave it to Leonard). Also I hear the tinkle of her bracelets, made of twisted silver, given her by Mr Lowell, as she went about the house; especially as she came up at night to see if we were asleep, holding a candle shaded; this is a distinct memory, for, like all children, I lay awake sometimes and longed for her to come. Then she told me to think of all the lovely things I could imagine. Rainbows and bells . . . But besides these minute separate details, how did I first become conscious of what was always there – her astonishing beauty? Perhaps I never became conscious of it; I think I accepted her beauty as the natural quality that a mother – she seemed typical, universal, yet our own in particular – had by virtue of being our mother. It was part of her calling. I do not think that I separated her face from that general being; or from her whole body. Certainly I have a vision of her now, as she came up the path by the lawn at St Ives; slight, shapely – she held herself very straight. I was playing. I stopped, about to speak to her. But she half turned from us, and lowered her eyes. From that indescribably sad gesture I knew that Philips, the man who had been crushed on the line and whom she had been visiting, was dead. It's over, she seemed to say. I knew, and was awed by the thought of death. At the same time I felt that her gesture as a whole was lovely. Very early, through nurses or casual visitors, I must have known that she was thought very beautiful. But that pride was snobbish, not a pure and private feeling: it was mixed with pride in other people's admiration. It was related to the more definitely snobbish pride caused in me by the nurses who said one night talking together while we ate our supper: 'They're very well connected . . .'

But apart from her beauty, if the two can be separated, what was she herself like? Very quick; very direct; practical; and amusing, I say at once offhand. She could be sharp, she disliked affectation. 'If you put your head on one side like that, you shan't come to the party,' I remember she said to me as we drew up in a carriage in front of some house. Severe; with a background of knowledge that made her sad. She had her own sorrow waiting behind her to dip into privately. Once when she had set us to write exercises I looked up from mine and watched her reading – the Bible perhaps; and, struck by the gravity of her face, told myself that her first husband had been a clergyman and that she was thinking, as she read what he had read, of him. This was a fable on my part; but it shows that she looked very sad when she was not talking.

But can I get any closer to her without drawing upon all those descriptions and anecdotes which after she was dead imposed themselves upon my view of her? Very quick; very definite; very upright; and behind the active, the sad, the silent. And of course she was central. I suspect the word 'central' gets closest to the general feeling I had of living so completely in her atmosphere that one never got far enough away from her to see her as a person. (That is one reason why I see the Gibbses and the Beadles and the Clarkes so much more distinctly.) She was the whole thing; Talland House was full of her; Hyde Park Gate was full of her. I see now, though the sentence is hasty, feeble and inexpressive, why it was that it was impossible for her to leave a very private and particular impression upon a child. She was keeping what I call in my shorthand the panoply of life – that which we all lived in common – in being. I see now that she was living on such an extended surface that she had not time, nor strength, to concentrate, except for a moment if one were ill or in some child's crisis, upon me, or upon anyone – unless it were Adrian. Him she cherished separately; she called him 'My Joy'. The later view, the understanding that I now have of her position must have its say; and it shows me that a woman of forty with seven children, some of them needing grown-up attention, and four still in the nursery; and an eighth, Laura, an idiot, yet living with us; and a husband fifteen years her elder, difficult, exacting, dependent on her; I see now that a woman who had to keep all this in being and under control must have been a general presence rather than a particular person to a child of seven or eight. Can I remember ever being alone with her for more than a few minutes? Someone was always interrupting. When I think of her spontaneously she is always in a room full of people; Stella, George and Gerald are there; my father, sitting reading with one leg curled round the other, twisting his lock of hair; 'Go and take the crumb out of his beard,' she whispers to me; and off I trot. There are visitors, young men like Jack Hills who is in love with Stella; many young men, Cambridge friends of George's and Gerald's; old men, sitting round the tea table talking – father's friends, Henry James, Symonds, (I see him peering up at me on the broad staircase at St Ives with his drawn yellow face and a tie made of a yellow cord with two plush balls on it); Stella's friends – the Lushingtons, the Stillmans; I see her at the head of the table underneath the engraving of Beatrice given her by an old governess and painted blue; I hear jokes; laughter; the clatter of voices; I am teased; I say something funny; she laughs; I am pleased; I blush furiously; she observes; someone laughs at Nessa for saying that Ida Milman is her B.F.; Mother says soothingly, tenderly, 'Best friend, that means.' I see her going to the town with her basket; and Arthur Davies goes with her; I see her knitting on the hall step while we play cricket; I see her stretching her arms out to Mrs Williams when the bailiffs took possession of their house and the Captain stood at the window bawling and shying jugs, basins, chamber pots onto the gravel – 'Come to us, Mrs Williams'; 'No, Mrs Stephen,' sobbed Mrs Williams, 'I will not leave my husband.' – I see her writing at her table in London and the silver candlesticks, and the high carved chair with the claws and the pink seat; and the three-cornered brass ink pot; I wait in agony peeping surreptitiously behind the blind for her to come down the street, when she has been out late the lamps are lit and I am sure that she has been run over. (Once my father found me peeping; questioned me; and said rather anxiously but reprovingly, 'You shouldn't be so nervous, Jinny.') And there is my last sight of her; she was dying; I came to kiss her and as I crept out of the room she said: 'Hold yourself straight, my little Goat.' . . . What a jumble of things I can remember, if I let my mind run, about my mother; but they are all of her in company; of her surrounded; of her generalised; dispersed, omnipresent, of her as the creator of that crowded merry world which spun so gaily in the centre of my childhood. It is true that I enclosed that world in another made by my own temperament; it is true that from the beginning I had many adventures outside that world; and often went far from it; and kept much back from it; but there it always was, the common life of the family, very merry, very stirring, crowded with people; and she was the centre; it was herself. This was proved on May 5th 1895. For after that day there was nothing left of it. I leant out of the nursery window the morning she died. It was about six, I suppose. I saw Dr Seton walk away up the street with his head bent and his hands clasped behind his back. I saw the pigeons floating and settling. I got a feeling of calm, sadness, and finality. It was a beautiful blue spring morning, and very still. That brings back the feeling that everything had come to an end.

Jean Rhys (1890–1979)

J ean Rhys was born on the island of Dominica. Her birth was intended to compensate her mother for the death of a baby girl nine months previously. Rhys's biographer, Carole Angier, traces to this circumstance Rhys's 'lifelong sense of loss and emptiness, of being wanted by no one and belonging nowhere' (Angier 1990: 11). This feeling of emptiness increased with the birth of a younger sister when Rhys was five. As she recounts in her autobiographical fragment, *Smile Please* (1979), she was now expected to look after herself. Her mother found her a nuisance, Rhys began to be afraid of her and then gradually her mother's interest in her daughter lapsed entirely (Rhys 1979/1981:

43). The relationship between Antoinette Cosway and her mother in this extract from *Wide Sargasso Sea* follows a similar pattern.

Like Antoinette, Rhys was educated at a convent school. When she was sixteen she left Dominica to attend the Perse School in Cambridge and then the Academy of Dramatic Art in London. In 1909 she got a job as a chorus girl with a touring company. She fell in love with an upper-class Englishman, Lancelot Smith, and their affair is the basis of Rhys's novel, *Voyage in the Dark* (1934). When the relationship ended in 1912, Rhys was devastated; it was to overcome her feeling of abandonment that she began to write. She frequented the Crabtree Club and earned money as an artist's model, and in 1919 she married a Dutchman, Jean Lenglet, a journalist and adventurer. For the next ten years she led a wandering life on the Continent, and this rootless life of cafés, clubs and cheap hotels is evoked in her novels.

In 1920 a son was born to Rhys and Lenglet but he died three weeks later. 1922 saw the birth of their daughter, Maryvonne. Rhys made efforts to find the money to keep her but Maryvonne spent most of her early life in a clinic paid for by friends (Angier 1990: 166). Later she went to boarding school and visited her mother only in the summer holidays. There is no mention of her in Rhys's fiction.

In Paris Rhys met Ford Madox Ford who encouraged her in her writing and with whom she had an affair, recounted in *Quartet* (1928). Ford helped her publish her first book *The Left Bank* (1927). At the end of 1927 Rhys came to England for her mother's funeral, seeing her family for the first time in years and quarrelling with them (see *After Leaving Mr Mackenzie*, 1930). The following year she moved to England and began living with her literary agent, Leslie Tilden, whom she married in 1934. Rhys disliked England, believing it a country hostile to women. She experienced all the dislocation of a white Creole at home neither in Dominica nor in England. Throughout the 1930s she spent periods alone writing in cheap hotels in Paris. Tilden encouraged her writing but his literary agency failed and he and Rhys became desperately poor, constantly on the move to cheaper lodgings. As the marriage deteriorated, Rhys began drinking heavily. In 1935 she was fined for being drunk and disorderly (Angier 1990: 348).

After the disappointing reception of *Good Morning, Midnight* in 1939, Rhys disappeared from view, her books went out of print and she was largely forgotten. It was only in 1957, as a result of a BBC broadcast, that she was traced to Cornwall where she was living with her third husband, Max Hamer (Tilden had died in 1945). Her reputation began to grow, her books were reissued and the publication of *Wide Sargasso Sea* in 1966 brought her international recognition. She is now regarded as a major figure in Caribbean literature.

Wide Sargasso Sea is a daughter's protest against a mother-text, Charlotte Brontë's *Jane Eyre* with its portrayal of the mad Creole, Bertha Rochester. Rhys was descended on her mother's side from eighteenth-century plantation owners and her novel is a West Indian daughter's attempt to affirm her identity against a white 'mother', Brontë, who denied West Indians a point of view. With her exploration of the mother-daughter relationship in this novel Rhys became foremother to a younger generation of Caribbean women writing in the 1980s and 1990s (see the extract from Zee Edgell).

Primary reading

Rhys, J. 1928/1973 *Quartet*, Harmondsworth: Penguin.

Rhys, J. 1930/1971 *After Leaving Mr Mackenzie*, Harmondsworth: Penguin.

Rhys, J. 1934/1969 *Voyage in the Dark*, Harmondsworth: Penguin.

Rhys, J. 1939/1969 *Good Morning, Midnight*, Harmondsworth: Penguin.

Rhys, J. 1966/1981 *Wide Sargasso Sea*, Harmondsworth: Penguin.

Rhys, J. 1979/1981 *Smile Please*, Harmondsworth: Penguin.

Rhys, J. 1984 *Letters 1931–1966*, F. Wyndham and D. Melly (eds), London: André Deutsch.

Further reading

Abruna, L. Niesen de 1991 'Family Connections: Mother and Mother Country in the Fiction of Jean Rhys and Jamaica Kincaid' in

Motherlands: Black Women's Writing From Africa, the Caribbean and S. Asia S. Nasta (ed.), London: The Women's Press.

Angier, C. 1990 *Jean Rhys: Life and Work*, Harmondsworth: Penguin.

Humm, H. 1994 'Jean Rhys: Race, Gender and History' in *It's My Party: Reading Twentieth-Century Women's Writing*, G. Wisker (ed.), London: Pluto.

Kloepfer, D.K. 1989 *The Unspeakable Mother: Forbidden Discourse in Jean Rhys and H.D.*, Ithaca and London: Cornell University Press.

Leigh, N.J. 1985 'Mirror, Mirror: the Development of Female Identity in Jean Rhys's Fiction', *World Literature Written in English* 25 (2): 270–85.

Scharfman, R. 1982 'Mirroring and Mothering in Simone Schwarz-Bart's *Pluie et vent sur Télumée Miracle* and Jean Rhys's *Wide Sargasso Sea*', *Yale French Studies* 62: 88–106.

Wide Sargasso Sea

From Jean Rhys, *Wide Sargasso Sea*, London: Penguin, 1968, pp. 15–26.

They say when trouble comes close ranks, and so the white people did. But we were not in their ranks. The Jamaican ladies had never approved of my mother, 'because she pretty like pretty self' Christophine said.

She was my father's second wife, far too young for him they thought, and, worse still, a Martinique girl. When I asked her why so few people came to see us, she told me that the road from Spanish Town to Coulibri Estate where we lived was very bad and that road repairing was now a thing of the past. (My father, visitors, horses, feeling safe in bed – all belonged to the past.)

Another day I heard her talking to Mr Luttrell, our neighbour and her only friend. 'Of course they have their own misfortunes. Still waiting for this compensation the English promised when the Emancipation Act was passed. Some will wait for a long time.'

How could she know that Mr Luttrell would be the first who grew tired of waiting? One calm evening he shot his dog, swam out to sea and was gone for always. No agent came from England to look after his property – Nelson's Rest it was called – and strangers from Spanish Town rode up to gossip and discuss the tragedy.

'Live at Nelson's Rest? Not for love or money. An unlucky place.'

Mr Luttrell's house was left empty, shutters banging in the wind. Soon the black people said it was haunted, they wouldn't go near it. And no one came near us.

I got used to a solitary life, but my mother still planned and hoped – perhaps she had to hope every time she passed a looking glass.

She still rode about every morning not caring that the black people stood about in groups to jeer at her, especially after her riding clothes grew shabby (they notice clothes, they know about money).

Then one day, very early, I saw her horse lying down under the frangipani tree. I went up to him but he was not sick, he was dead and his eyes were black with flies. I ran away and did not speak of it for I thought if I told no one it might not be true. But later that day, Godfrey found him, he had been poisoned. 'Now we are marooned,' my mother said, 'now what will become of us?'

Godfrey said, 'I can't watch the horse night and day. I too old now. When the old time go, let it go. No use to grab at it. The Lord make no distinction between black and white, black and white the same for Him. Rest yourself in peace for the righteous are not forsaken.' But she couldn't. She was young. How could she not try for all the things that had gone so suddenly, so without warning. 'You're blind when you want to be blind,' she said ferociously, 'and you're deaf when you want to be deaf. The old hypocrite,' she kept saying. 'He knew what they were going to do.' 'The devil prince of this world,' Godfrey said, 'but this world don't last so long for mortal man.'

She persuaded a Spanish Town doctor to visit my younger brother Pierre who staggered when he walked and couldn't speak distinctly. I don't know what the doctor told her or what she said to him but he never came again and after that she changed. Suddenly, not gradually. She grew thin and silent, and at last she refused to leave the house at all.

Our garden was large and beautiful as that garden in the Bible – the tree of life grew there. But it had gone wild. The paths were overgrown and a smell of dead flowers mixed with the fresh living smell. Underneath the tree ferns, tall as forest tree ferns, the light was green. Orchids flourished out of reach or for some reason not to be touched. One was snaky looking, another like an octopus with long thin brown tentacles bare of leaves hanging from a twisted root. Twice a year the octopus orchid flowered – then not an inch of tentacle showed. It was a bell-shaped mass of white, mauve, deep purples, wonderful to see. The scent was very sweet and strong. I never went near it.

All Coulibri Estate had gone wild like the garden, gone to bush. No more slavery – why should *anybody* work? This never saddened me. I did not remember the place when it was prosperous.

My mother usually walked up and down the *glacis*, a paved roofed-in terrace which ran the length of the house and sloped upwards to a clump of bamboos. Standing by the bamboos she had a clear view to the sea, but anyone passing could stare at her. They stared, sometimes they laughed. Long after the sound was far away and faint she kept her eyes shut and her hands clenched. A frown came between her black eyebrows, deep – it might have been cut with a knife. I hated this frown and once I touched her forehead trying to smooth it. But she pushed me away, not roughly but calmly, coldly, without a word, as if she had decided once and for all that I was useless to her. She wanted to sit with Pierre or walk where she pleased without being pestered, she wanted peace and quiet. I was old enough to look after myself. 'Oh, let me alone,' she would say, 'let me alone,' and after I knew that she talked aloud to herself I was a little afraid of her.

So I spent most of my time in the kitchen which was in an outbuilding some way off. Christophine slept in the little room next to it.

When evening came she sang to me if she was in the mood. I couldn't always understand her patois songs – she also came from Martinique – but she taught me the one that meant 'The little ones grow old, the children leave us, will they come back?' and the one about the cedar tree flowers which only last for a day.

The music was gay but the words were sad and her voice often quavered and broke on the high note. 'Adieu.' Not adieu as we said it, but *à dieu*, which made more sense after all. The loving man was lonely, the girl was deserted, the children never came back. Adieu.

Her songs were not like Jamaican songs, and she was not like the other women.

She was much blacker – blue-black with a thin face and straight features. She wore a black dress, heavy gold earrings and a yellow handkerchief – carefully tied with the two high points in front. No other negro woman wore black, or tied her handkerchief Martinique fashion. She had a quiet voice and a quiet laugh (when she did laugh), and though she could speak good English if she wanted to, and French as well as patois, she took care to talk as they talked. But they would have nothing to do with her and she never saw her son who worked in Spanish Town. She had only one friend – a woman called Maillotte, and Maillotte was not a Jamaican.

The girls from the bayside who sometimes helped with the washing and cleaning were terrified of her. That, I soon discovered, was why they came at all – for she never paid them. Yet they brought presents of fruit and vegetables and after dark I often heard low voices from the kitchen.

So I asked about Christophine. Was she very old? Had she always been with us?

'She was your father's wedding present to me – one of his presents. He thought I would be pleased with a Martinique girl. I don't know how old she was when they brought her to Jamaica, quite young. I don't know how old she is now. Does it matter? Why do you pester and bother me about all these things that happened long ago?

Christophine stayed with me because she wanted to stay. She had her own very good reasons you may be sure. I dare say we would have died if she'd turned against us and that would have been a better fate. To die and be forgotten and at peace. Not to know that one is abandoned, lied about, helpless. All the ones who died – who says a good word for them now?'

'Godfrey stayed too,' I said. 'And Sass.'

'They stayed,' she said angrily, 'because they wanted somewhere to sleep and something to eat. That boy Sass! When his mother pranced off and left him here – a great deal *she* cared – why he was a little skeleton. Now he's growing into a big strong boy and away he goes. We shan't see him again. Godfrey is a rascal. These new ones aren't too kind to old people and he knows it. That's why he stays. Doesn't do a thing but eats enough for a couple of horses. Pretends he's deaf. He isn't deaf – he doesn't want to hear. What a devil he is!'

'Why don't you tell him to find somewhere else to live?' I said and she laughed.

'He wouldn't go. He'd probably try to force us out. I've learned to let sleeping curs lie,' she said.

'Would Christophine go if you told her to?' I thought. But I didn't say it. I was afraid to say it.

It was too hot that afternoon. I could see the beads of perspiration on her upper lip and the dark circles under her eyes. I started to fan her, but she turned her head away. She might rest if I left her alone, she said.

Once I would have gone back quietly to watch her asleep on the blue sofa – once I made excuses to be near her when she brushed her hair, a soft black cloak to cover me, hide me, keep me safe.

But not any longer. Not any more.

These were all the people in my life – my mother and Pierre, Christophine, Godfrey, and Sass who had left us.

I never looked at any strange negro. They hated us. They called us white cockroaches. Let sleeping dogs lie. One day a little girl followed me singing, 'Go away white cockroach, go away, go away.' I walked fast, but she walked faster. 'White cockroach, go away, go away. Nobody want you. Go away.'

When I was safely home I sat close to the old wall at the end of the garden. It was covered with green moss soft as velvet and I never wanted to move again. Everything would be worse if I moved. Christophine found me there when it was nearly dark, and I was so stiff she had to help me to get up. She said nothing, but next morning Tia was in the kitchen with her mother Maillotte, Christophine's friend. Soon Tia was my friend and I met her nearly every morning at the turn of the road to the river.

Sometimes we left the bathing pool at midday, sometimes we stayed till late afternoon. Then Tia would light a fire (fires always lit for her, sharp stones did not hurt her bare feet, I never saw her cry). We boiled green bananas in an old iron pot and ate them with our fingers out of a calabash and after we had eaten she slept at once. I could not sleep, but I wasn't quite awake as I lay in the shade looking at the pool – deep and dark green under the trees, brown-green if it had rained, but a bright sparkling green in the sun. The water was so clear that you could see the pebbles at the bottom of the shallow part. Blue and white and striped red. Very pretty. Late or early we parted at the turn of the road. My mother never asked me where I had been or what I had done.

Christophine had given me some new pennies which I kept in the pocket of my dress. They dropped out one morning so I put them on a stone. They shone like gold in the sun and Tia stared. She had small eyes, very black, set deep in her head.

Then she bet me three of the pennies that I couldn't turn a somersault under water 'like you say you can'.

'Of course I can.'

'I never see you do it,' she said. 'Only talk.'

'Bet you all the money I can,' I said.

But after one somersault I still turned and came up choking. Tia laughed and told me that it certainly look like I drown dead that time. Then she picked up the money.

'I did do it,' I said when I could speak but she shook her head. I hadn't done it good and besides pennies didn't buy much. Why did I look at her like that?

'Keep them then, you cheating nigger,' I said, for I was tired, and the water I had swallowed made me feel sick. 'I can get more if I want to.'

That's not what she hear, she said. She hear all we poor like beggar. We ate salt fish – no money for fresh fish. That old house so leaky, you run with calabash to catch water when it rain. Plenty white people in Jamaica. Real white people, they got gold money. They didn't look at us, nobody see them come near us. Old time white people nothing but white nigger now, and black nigger better than white nigger.

I wrapped myself in my torn towel and sat on a stone with my back to her, shivering cold. But the sun couldn't warm me. I wanted to go home. I looked round and Tia had gone. I searched for a long time before I could believe that she had taken my dress – not my underclothes, she never wore any – but my dress, starched, ironed, clean that morning. She had left me hers and I put it on at last and walked home in the blazing sun feeling sick, hating her. I planned to get round the back of the house to the kitchen, but passing the stables I stopped to stare at three strange horses and my mother saw me and called. She was on the *glacis* with two young ladies and a gentleman. Visitors! I dragged up the steps unwillingly – I had longed for visitors once, but that was years ago.

They were very beautiful I thought and they wore such beautiful clothes that I looked away down at the flagstones and when they laughed – the gentleman laughed the loudest – I ran into the house, into my bedroom. There I stood with my back against the door and I could feel my heart all through me. I heard them talking and I heard them leave. I came out of my room and my mother was sitting on the blue sofa. She looked at me for some time before she said that I had behaved very oddly. My dress was even dirtier than usual.

'It's Tia's dress.'

'But why are you wearing Tia's dress? Tia? Which one of them is Tia?'

Christophine, who had been in the pantry listening, came at once and was told to find a clean dress for me. 'Throw away that thing. Burn it.'

Then they quarrelled.

Christophine said I had no clean dress. 'She got two dresses, wash and wear. You want clean dress to drop from heaven? Some people crazy in truth.'

'She must have another dress,' said my mother. 'Somewhere.' But Christophine told her loudly that it shameful. She run wild, she grow up worthless. And nobody care.

My mother walked over to the window. ('Marooned,' said her straight narrow back, her carefully coiled hair. 'Marooned.')

'She has an old muslin dress. Find that.'

While Christophine scrubbed my face and tied my plaits with a fresh piece of string, she told me that those were the new people at Nelson's Rest. They called themselves Luttrell, but English or not English they were not like old Mr Luttrell. 'Old Mr Luttrell spit in their face if he see how they look at you. Trouble walk into the house this day. Trouble walk in.'

The old muslin dress was found and it tore as I forced it on. She didn't notice.

No more slavery! She had to laugh! 'These new ones have Letter of the Law. Same thing. They got magistrate. They got fine. They got jail house and chain gang. They got tread machine to mash up people's feet. New ones worse than old ones – more cunning, that's all.'

All that evening my mother didn't speak to me or look at me and I thought, 'She is ashamed of me, what Tia said is true.'

I went to bed early and slept at once. I dreamed that I was walking in the forest. Not alone. Someone who hated me was with me, out of sight. I could hear heavy footsteps coming closer and though I struggled and screamed I could not move. I woke crying. The covering sheet was on the floor and my mother was looking down at me.

'Did you have a nightmare?'

'Yes, a bad dream.'

She sighed and covered me up. 'You were making such a noise. I must go to Pierre, you've frightened him.'

I lay thinking, 'I am safe. There is the corner of the bedroom door and the friendly furniture. There is the tree of life in the garden and the wall green with moss. The barrier of the cliffs and the high mountains. And the barrier of the sea. I am safe. I am safe from strangers.'

The light of the candle in Pierre's room was still there when I slept again. I woke next morning knowing that nothing would be the same. It would change and go on changing.

I don't know how she got money to buy the white muslin and the pink. Yards of muslin. She may have sold her last ring, for there was one left. I saw it in her jewel box – that, and a locket with a shamrock inside. They were mending and sewing first thing in the morning and still sewing when I went to bed. In a week she had a new dress and so had I.

The Luttrells lent her a horse, and she would ride off very early and not come back till late next day – tired out because she had been to a dance or a moonlight picnic. She was gay and laughing – younger than I had ever seen her and the house was sad when she had gone.

So I too left it and stayed away till dark. I was never long at the bathing pool, I never met Tia.

I took another road, past the old sugar works and the water wheel that had not turned for years. I went to parts of Coulibri that I had not seen, where there was no road, no path, no track. And if the razor grass cut my legs and arms I would think 'It's better than people.' Black ants or red ones, tall nests swarming with white ants, rain that soaked me to the skin – once I saw a snake. All better than people.

Better. Better, better than people.

Watching the red and yellow flowers in the sun thinking of nothing, it was as if a door opened and I was somewhere else, something else. Not myself any longer.

I knew the time of day when though it is hot and blue and there are no clouds, the sky can have a very black look.

I was bridesmaid when my mother married Mr Mason in Spanish Town. Christophine curled my hair. I carried a bouquet and everything I wore was new – even my beautiful slippers. But their eyes slid away from my hating face. I had heard what all these smooth smiling people said about her when she was not listening and they did not guess I was. Hiding from them in the garden when they visited Coulibri, I listened.

'A fantastic marriage and he will regret it. Why should a very wealthy man who could take his pick of all the girls in the West Indies, and many in England too probably?' 'Why *probably?*' the other voice said. '*Certainly.*' 'Then why should he marry a widow without a penny to her name and Coulibri a wreck of a place? Emancipation troubles killed old Cosway? Nonsense – the estate was going downhill for years before that. He drank himself to death. Many's the time when – well! And all those women! She never did anything to stop him – she encouraged him. Presents and smiles for the bastards every Christmas. Old customs? Some old customs are better dead and buried. Her new husband will have to spend a pretty penny before the house is fit to live in – leaks like a sieve. And what about the stables and the coach house dark as pitch, and the servants' quarters and the six-foot snake I saw with my own eyes curled up on the privy seat last time I was here. Alarmed? I screamed. Then that horrible old man she harbours came along, doubled up with laughter. As for those two children – the boy an idiot kept out of sight and mind and the girl going the same way in my opinion – a *lowering* expression.'

'Oh I agree,' the other one said, 'but Annette is such a pretty woman. And what a dancer. Reminds me of that song 'light as cotton blossom on the something breeze', or is it air? I forget.'

Yes, what a dancer – that night when they came home from their honeymoon in Trinidad and they danced on the *glacis* to no music. There was no need for music when she danced. They stopped and she leaned backwards over his arm, down till her black hair touched the flagstones – still down, down. Then up again in a flash, laughing. She made it look so easy – as if anyone could do it, and he kissed her – a long kiss. I was there that time too but they had forgotten me and soon I wasn't thinking of them. I was remembering that woman saying 'Dance! He didn't come to the West Indies to dance – he came to make money as they all do. Some of the big estates are going cheap, and one unfortunate's loss is always a clever man's gain. No, the whole thing is a mystery. It's evidently useful to keep a Martinique obeah woman on the premises.' She meant Christophine. She said it mockingly, not meaning it, but soon other people were saying it – and meaning it.

While the repairs were being done and they were in Trinidad, Pierre and I stayed with Aunt Cora in Spanish Town.

Mr Mason did not approve of Aunt Cora, an ex-slave-owner who had escaped misery, a flier in the face of Providence.

'Why did she do nothing to help you?'

I told him that her husband was English and didn't like us and he said, 'Nonsense.'

'It isn't nonsense, they lived in England and he was angry if she wrote to us. He hated the West Indies. When he died not long ago she came home, before that what could she do? *She* wasn't rich.'

'That's her story. I don't believe it. A frivolous woman. In your mother's place I'd resent her behaviour.'

'None of you understand about us,' I thought.

Tillie Olsen (?1913–)

T illie Olsen was born in either 1912 or 1913 in Wahoo, Omaha or Mead, Nebraska (both the date and place of her birth are uncertain, see Pearlman and Werlock 1991: 9). She was the daughter of Russian Jewish immigrants whose move to the US was precipitated by the failure of the 1905 Russian revolution in which they were involved. Her father worked in a variety of jobs – farming, paperhanging, packing – as well as being state secretary for the Nebraska Socialist Party. The second of six children, Olsen was strongly influenced both by her parents' socialist beliefs and by her father's work as a labour organiser. She started writing in high school, composing skits and musicals for the Young People's Socialist League. She left school after eleventh grade and worked in various jobs, as a waitress, a packer and a tie presser. When she was seventeen she joined the Young Communist League and was sent by them to Kansas City. She contracted pleurisy as a result of working in a tie factory and this worsened when she was incarcerated in the Argentine Jail for organising a strike in the packing houses.

In 1932 Olsen moved to Minnesota and began writing *Yonnondio*. She gave birth to her first daughter, Karla, and moved to San Francisco where she continued her political work and was arrested for her involvement in the 1934 San Francisco Maritime strike. She began living with her comrade in the YCL, Jack Olsen, a warehouseman and printer whom she married in 1943. She had three more daughters with him.

In 1934 'The Iron Throat' (the first part of *Yonnondio*) was published in the *Partisan Review*, as were two of her poems and two essays. Eventually, however, the demands of raising and supporting her four daughters, together with her political activities, forced Olsen to give up writing fiction. During the McCarthy era, her work in connection with educational issues led to the accusation that she was 'an agent of Stalin' though, unlike her husband, she was never subpoenaed.

It was not until 1954 that Olsen was able to write again in a sustained way. 'I Stand Here Ironing', which appeared in 1956, was Olsen's first published story in over twenty years. It forms part of the collection *Tell Me a Riddle* which was published in 1962, the title story winning the O. Henry Award.

In 1962, Olsen was appointed scholar at the Radcliffe Institute and came into contact with Anne Sexton and other women artists whom she greatly influenced (Hedges and Fishkin 1994: 17–22). It was here that Olsen began her public discussion of the ideas that would later form the subject of *Silences* (1978), a founding text of feminist criticism which has had a profound influence in changing what is taught in the academy. In *Silences* Olsen examines the social forces which can lead to the silencing of an author, particularly a female author, circumstances such as domestic responsibility, poverty, race, class and, above all, motherhood. She points out that until recently almost all literary achievement came from childless women. *Silences* provided the impetus to recover forgotten women writers and to expand the canon to include diaries, journals, oral history and so on. It has been a crucial influence on the development of women's studies. In the early 1970s Olsen was also instrumental in encouraging the Feminist Press to reprint forgotten women writers.

Yonnondio was finally published in 1974, forty years after its inception.

Primary reading

Olsen, T. 1978/1980 *Silences*, London: Virago.

Olsen, T. 1990 *Tell Me A Riddle* and *Yonnondio*, London: Virago.

Further reading

Aarons, V. 1987 'The Outsider Within: Women in Contemporary Jewish-American Fiction', *Contemporary Literature* 28 (3): 378–93.

Burstein, J. H. 1996 *Writing Mothers, Writing Daughters. Tracing the Maternal in Stories by American Jewish Women*, Urbana and Chicago: University of Illinois Press.

Coiner, C. 1992 ' "No One's Private Ground': A Bakhtinian Reading of Tillie Olsen's *Tell Me A Riddle*', *Feminist Studies* 18 (2): 257–81.

Frye, J. S. 1981 ' "I Stand Here Ironing": Motherhood as Experience and Metaphor', *Studies in Short Fiction* 18 (3): 287–92.

Hedges, E. and Fishkin, S. F. 1994 *Listening to Silences. New Essays in Feminist Criticism*, Oxford: Oxford University Press.

Pearlman, M. and Werlock, A. H. P. 1991 *Tillie Olsen*, Boston: Twayne.

Rosenfelt, D. 1981 'From the Thirties: Tillie Olsen and the Radical Tradition', *Feminist Studies* 7 (3): 371–406.

I Stand Here Ironing

From Tillie Olsen, *Tell Me A Riddle* and *Yonnondio*, London: Virago, 1990, pp. 13–25.

I stand here ironing, and what you asked me moves tormented back and forth with the iron.

'I wish you would manage the time to come in and talk with me about your daughter. I'm sure you can help me understand her. She's a youngster who needs help and whom I'm deeply interested in helping.'

'Who needs help. . . .' Even if I came, what good would it do? You think because I am her mother I have a key, or that in some way you could use me as a key? She has lived for nineteen years. There is all that life that has happened outside of me, beyond me.

And when is there time to remember, to sift, to weigh, to estimate, to total? I will start and there will be an interruption and I will have to gather it all together again. Or I will become engulfed with all I did or did not do, with what should have been and what cannot be helped.

She was a beautiful baby. The first and only one of our five that was beautiful at birth. You do not guess how new and uneasy her tenancy in her now-loveliness. You did not know her all those years she was thought homely, or see her poring over her baby pictures, making me tell her over and over how beautiful she had been – and would be, I would tell her – and was now, to the seeing eye. But the seeing eyes were few or non-existent. Including mine.

I nursed her. They feel that's important nowadays. I nursed all the children, but with her, with all the fierce rigidity of first motherhood, I did like the books then said. Though her cries battered me to trembling and my breasts ached with swollenness, I waited till the clock decreed.

Why do I put that first? I do not even know if it matters, or if it explains anything.

She was a beautiful baby. She blew shining bubbles of sound. She loved motion, loved light, loved colour and music and textures. She would lie on the floor in her blue overalls patting the surface so hard in ecstasy her hands and feet would blur. She was a miracle to me, but when she was eight months old I had to leave her daytimes with the woman downstairs to whom she was no miracle at all, for I worked or looked for work and for Emily's father, who 'could no longer endure' (he wrote in his good-bye note) 'sharing want with us.'

I was nineteen. It was the pre-relief, pre-WPA world of the depression. I would start running as soon as I got off the streetcar, running up the stairs, the place smelling sour, and awake or asleep to startle awake, when she saw me she would break into a clogged weeping that could not be comforted, a weeping I can yet hear.

After a while I found a job hashing at night so I could be with her days, and it was better. But it came to where I had to bring her to his family and leave her.

It took a long time to raise the money for her fare back. Then she got chicken pox and I had to wait longer. When she finally came, I hardly knew her, walking quick and nervous like her father, looking like her father, thin, and dressed in a shoddy red that yellowed her skin and glared at the pock marks. All the baby loveliness gone.

She was two. Old enough for nursery school they said, and I did not know then what I know now – the fatigue of the long day, and the lacerations of group life in the kinds of nurseries that are only parking places for children.

Except that it would have made no difference if I had known. It was the only place there was. It was the only way we could be together, the only way I could hold a job.

And even without knowing, I knew. I knew the teacher that was evil because all these years it has curdled into my memory, the little boy hunched in the corner, her rasp, 'why aren't you outside, because Alvin hits you? that's no reason, go out, scaredy.' I knew Emily hated it even if she did not clutch and implore 'don't go Mommy' like the other children, mornings.

She always had a reason why we should stay home. Momma, you look sick. Momma, I feel sick. Momma, the teachers aren't there today, they're sick. Momma, we can't go, there was a fire there last night. Momma, it's a holiday today, no school, they told me.

But never a direct protest, never rebellion. I think of our others in their three-, four-year-oldness – the explosions, the tempers, the denunciations, the demands – and I feel suddenly ill. I put the iron down. What in me demanded that goodness in her? And what was the cost, the cost to her of such goodness?

The old man living in the back once said in his gentle way: 'You should smile at Emily more when you look at her.' What *was* in my face when I looked at her? I loved her. There were all the acts of love.

It was only with the others I remembered what he said, and it was the face of joy, and not of care or tightness or worry I turned to them – too late for Emily. She does not smile easily, let alone almost always as her brothers and sisters do. Her face is closed and sombre, but when she wants, how fluid. You must have seen it in her pantomimes, you spoke of her rare gift for comedy on the stage that rouses a laughter out of the audience so dear they applaud and applaud and do not want to let her go.

Where does it come from, that comedy? There was none of it in her when she came back to me that second time, after I had had to send her away again. She had a new daddy now to learn to love, and I think perhaps it was a better time. Except when we left her alone nights, telling ourselves she was old enough.

'Can't you go some other time, Mommy, like tomorrow?' she would ask. 'Will it be just a little while you'll be gone? Do you promise?'

The time we came back, the front door open, the clock on the floor in the hall. She rigid awake. 'It wasn't just a little while. I didn't cry. Three times I called you, just three times, and then I ran downstairs to open the door so you could come faster. The clock talked loud. I threw it away, it scared me what it talked.'

She said the clock talked loud again that night I went to the hospital to have Susan. She was delirious with the fever that comes before red measles, but she was fully conscious all the week I was gone and the week after we were home when she could not come near the new baby or me.

She did not get well. She stayed skeleton thin, not wanting to eat, and night after night she had nightmares. She would call for me, and I would rouse from exhaustion to sleepily call back: 'You're all right, darling, go to sleep, it's just a dream,' and if she still called, in a sterner voice, 'now go to sleep, Emily, there's nothing to hurt you.' Twice, only twice, when I had to get up for Susan anyhow, I went in to sit with her.

Now when it is too late (as if she would let me hold and comfort her like I do the others) I get up and go to her at once at her moan or restless stirring. 'Are you awake, Emily? Can I get you something, dear?' And the answer is always the same: 'No, I'm all right, go back to sleep, Mother.'

They persuaded me at the clinic to send her away to a convalescent home in the country where 'she can have the kind of food and care you can't manage for her, and you'll be free to concentrate on the new baby.' They still send children to that place. I see pictures on the society page of sleek young women planning affairs to raise money for it, or dancing at the affairs, or decorating Easter eggs or filling Christmas stockings for the children.

They never have a picture of the children so I do not know if the girls still wear those gigantic red bows and the ravaged looks on the every other Sunday when parents can come to visit 'unless otherwise notified' – as we were notified the first six weeks.

Oh it is a handsome place, green lawns and tall trees and fluted flower beds. High up on the balconies of each cottage the children stand, the girls in their red bows and white dresses, the boys in white suits and giant red ties. The parents stand below shrieking up to be heard and the children shriek down to be heard, and between them the invisible wall 'Not To Be Contaminated by Parental Germs or Physical Affection.'

There was a tiny girl who always stood hand in hand with Emily. Her parents never came. One visit she was gone. 'They moved her to Rose Cottage,' Emily shouted in explanation. 'They don't like you to love anybody here.'

She wrote once a week, the laboured writing of a seven-year-old. 'I am fine. How is the baby. If I write my leter nicely I will have a star. Love.' There never was a star. We wrote every other day, letters she could never hold or keep but only hear read – once. 'We simply do not have room for children to keep any personal possessions,' they patiently explained when we pieced one Sunday's shrieking together to plead how much it would mean to Emily, who loved so to keep things, to be allowed to keep her letters and cards.

Each visit she looked frailer. 'She isn't eating,' they told us.

(They had runny eggs for breakfast or mush with lumps, Emily said later, I'd hold it in my mouth and not swallow. Nothing ever tasted good, just when they had chicken.)

It took us eight months to get her released home, and only the fact that she gained back so little of her seven lost pounds convinced the social worker.

I used to try to hold and love her after she came back, but her body would stay stiff, and after a while she'd push away. She ate little. Food sickened her, and I think much of life too. Oh she had physical lightness and brightness, twinkling by on skates, bouncing like a ball up and down up and down over the jump rope, skimming over the hill; but these were momentary.

She fretted about her appearance, thin and dark and foreign-looking at a time when every little girl was supposed to look or thought she should look a chubby blonde replica of Shirley Temple. The door-bell sometimes rang for her, but no one seemed to come and play in the house or be a best friend. Maybe because we moved so much.

There was a boy she loved painfully through two school semesters. Months later she told me how she had taken pennies from my purse to buy him candy. 'Liquorice was his favourite and I brought him some every day, but he still liked Jennifer better'n me. Why, Mommy?' The kind of question for which there is no answer.

School was a worry to her. She was not glib or quick in a world where glibness and quickness were easily confused with ability to learn. To her overworked and exasperated teachers she was an overconscientious 'slow learner' who kept trying to catch up and was absent entirely too often.

I let her be absent, though sometimes the illness was imaginary. How different from my now-strictness about attendance with the others. I wasn't working. We had a new baby, I was home anyhow. Sometimes, after Susan grew old enough, I would keep her home from school, too, to have them all together.

Mostly Emily had asthma, and her breathing, harsh and laboured, would fill the house with a curiously tranquil sound. I would bring the two old dresser mirrors and her boxes of collections to her bed. She would select beads and single ear-rings, bottle tops and shells, dried flowers and pebbles, old postcards and scraps, all sorts of oddments; then she and Susan would play Kingdom, setting up landscapes and furniture, peopling them with action.

Those were the only times of peaceful companionship between her and Susan. I have edged away from it, that poisonous feeling between them, that terrible balancing of hurts and needs I had to do between the two, and did so badly, those earlier years.

Oh there are conflicts between the others too, each one human, needing, demanding, hurting, taking – but only between Emily and Susan, no, Emily toward Susan that corroding resentment. It seems so obvious on the surface, yet it is not obvious. Susan, the second child, Susan, golden- and curly-haired and chubby, quick and articulate and assured, everything in appearance and manner Emily was not; Susan, not able to resist Emily's precious things, losing or sometimes clumsily breaking them; Susan telling jokes and riddles to company for applause while Emily sat silent (to say to me later: that was *my* riddle, Mother, I told it to Susan); Susan, who for all the five years' difference in age was just a year behind Emily in developing physically.

I am glad for that slow physical development that widened the difference between her and her contemporaries, though she suffered over it. She was too vulnerable for that terrible world of youthful competition, of preening and parading, of constant measuring of yourself against every other, of envy, 'If I had that copper hair,' or 'If I had that skin. . . .' She tormented herself enough about not looking like the others, there was enough of the unsureness, the having to be conscious of words before you speak, the constant caring – what are they thinking of me? What kind of an impression am I making? – there was enough without having it all magnified by the merciless physical drives.

Ronnie is calling. He is wet and I change him. It is rare there is such a cry now. That time of motherhood is almost behind me when the ear is not one's own but must always be racked and listening for the child cry, the child call. We sit for a while and I hold him, looking out over the city spread in charcoal with its soft aisles of light. 'Shoogily,' he breathes and curls closer. I carry him back to bed, asleep. Shoogily. A funny word, a family word, inherited from Emily, invented by her to say: comfort.

In this and other ways she leaves her seal, I say aloud. And startle at my saying it. What do I mean? What did I start to gather together, to try and make coherent? I was at the terrible, growing years. War years. I do not remember them well. I was working, there were four smaller ones now, there was not time for her. She had to help be a mother, and housekeeper, and shopper. She had to set her seal. Mornings of crisis and near hysteria trying to get lunches packed, hair combed, coats and shoes found, everyone to school or Child Care on time, the baby ready for transportation. And always the paper scribbled on by a smaller one, the book looked at by Susan then mislaid, the homework not done. Running out to that huge school where she was one, she was lost, she was a drop; suffering over her unpreparedness, stammering and unsure in her classes.

There was so little time left at night after the kids were bedded down. She would struggle over books, always eating (it was in those years she developed her enormous appetite that is legendary in our family) and I would be ironing, or preparing food for the next day, or writing V-mail to Bill, or tending the baby. Sometimes to make me laugh, or out of her despair, she would imitate happenings or types at school.

I think I said once: 'Why don't you do something like this in the school amateur show?' One morning she phoned me at work, hardly understandable through the weeping: 'Mother, I did it. I won, I won; they gave me first prize; they clapped and clapped and wouldn't let me go.'

Now suddenly she was Somebody, and as imprisoned in her difference as she had been in her anonymity.

She began to be asked to perform at other high schools, even in colleges, then at city and state-wide affairs. The first one we went to, I only recognized her that first moment when thin, shy, she almost drowned herself into the curtains. Then: Was this Emily? The control, the command, the convulsing and deadly clowning, the spell, then the roaring, stamping audience, unwilling to let this rare and precious laughter out of their lives.

Afterwards: You ought to do something about her with a gift like that – but without money or knowing how, what does one do? We have left it all to her, and the gift has as often eddied inside, clogged and clotted, as been used and growing.

She is coming. She runs up the stairs two at a time with her light graceful step, and I know she is happy tonight. Whatever it was that occasioned your call did not happen today.

'Aren't you ever going to finish the ironing, Mother? Whistler painted his mother in a rocker. I'd have to paint mine standing over an ironing-board.' This is one of her communicative nights and she tells me everything and nothing as she fixes herself a plate of food out of the icebox.

She is so lovely. Why did you want me to come in at all? Why were you concerned? She will find her way.

She starts up the stairs to bed. 'Don't get me up with the rest in the morning.' 'But I thought you were having midterms.' 'Oh, those,' she comes back in, kisses me, and says quite lightly, 'in a couple of years when we'll all be atom-dead they won't matter a bit.'

She has said it before. She *believes* it. But because I have been dredging the past, and all that compounds a human being is so heavy and meaningful in me, I cannot endure it tonight.

I will never total it all. I will never come in to say: She was a child seldom smiled at. Her father left me before she was a year old. I had to work her first six years when there was work, or I sent her home and to his relatives. There were years she had care she hated. She was dark and thin and foreign-looking in a world where the prestige went to blondness and curly hair and dimples, she was slow where glibness was prized. She was a child of anxious, not proud, love. We were poor and could not afford for her the soil of easy growth. I was a young mother, I was a distracted mother. There were the other children pushing up, demanding. Her younger sister seemed all that she was not. There were years she did not let me touch her. She kept too much in herself, her life was such that she had to keep too much in herself. My wisdom came too late. She has much to her and probably little will come of it. She is a child of her age, of depression, of war, of fear.

Let her be. So all that is in her will not bloom – but in how many does it? There is still enough left to live by. Only help her to know – help make it so there is cause for her to know that she is more than this dress on the ironing-board, helpless before the iron.

Sylvia Plath (1932–1963)

S ince her suicide in 1963, the interpretation of Sylvia
Plath's life has been a major source of contention for biographers,
academics and feminists.

Plath was born in Boston, Massachusetts. Her father, Otto Plath,
was a German immigrant who had worked his way up to become
Professor of Entomology at Boston University. His death when Plath
was eight years old left her psychologically scarred for life. Dying
before she was old enough to question his authority, Otto Plath left
his daughter with a myth of her father as a god and a desire to join
him in death.

Plath's mother, Aurelia, had been a high-school teacher before her marriage but gave up her profession at her husband's request. After his death she was obliged to return to work to support her two children. The child of immigrants Aurelia, like Otto, believed in hard work and educational attainments. Plath learned early on that the way to please her mother was to achieve high marks; indeed she felt she had a responsibility to prove herself worthy of her mother's continual sacrifices to give her and her brother the best educational opportunities. From her parents, as well as from the culture of the period, Plath learned to equate hard work, high marks, money and fame with personal happiness.

A straight 'A' student, Plath entered the prestigious Smith College on a scholarship in 1950. She had already embarked on her career as a professional author, submitting stories to magazines and earning money from her writing. She put herself under enormous pressure to shine academically and at the same time conform to the image of the Smith College girl whose education was seen essentially as a preparation for marriage. The image she projected at this time masked an inner self racked by fear and self-doubt which eventually led to a suicide attempt in August 1953. She later recorded this episode in her novel *The Bell Jar* (1963). In the novel, Esther Greenwood's mother reacts in an obtuse and uncomprehending way to her daughter's breakdown, suggesting they forget all about it. For Esther, however, her breakdown and her stay in an asylum 'were part of me. They were my landscape' (Plath 1963/1966: 250).

In 1955 Plath went to Cambridge on a Fulbright scholarship. There she met and later married the poet, Ted Hughes, seeing in him a reincarnation of her hero father. Their troubled relationship inspired many of her disturbing late poems. In 1998 Hughes published his response in *Birthday Letters*.

In the early years Plath worked hard to promote Hughes's poetry and supported him financially by teaching for a year at Smith College. On 1 April 1960 their daughter, Frieda, was born in London.

In February 1961 Plath suffered a miscarriage and then in January 1962, after their move to Devon, their son, Nick, was born.

Although Plath's first volume of poems, *Colossus*, was published in 1960, her fame was gradually eclipsed by Hughes's growing reputation. It became apparent that the marriage was in difficulty and in October 1962 Hughes moved out. In December Plath returned to London with her two children. A combination of circumstances – the failure of her marriage and with it her failure to live up to conventional expectations of a woman's life, the bitterly cold winter, her isolation in an underheated flat with two young children, perhaps also the chauvinism of the London literary establishment – led her to take her own life on 11 February 1963.

Sylvia Plath's relationship with her mother has been much discussed, particularly since the publication of her *Letters Home* (1975) where Plath adopts a bright, optimistic persona and a gushing tone at odds with her poetry and her journals. Certainly for many years after Otto's death the relationship between mother and daughter was close to the point of claustrophobia, resulting in the intense hostility of poems like 'Medusa' (1962) and passages in *The Bell Jar*.

Plath's relationship with her children has been less extensively discussed. In 1999 her daughter Frieda Hughes published her first collection of poems. It includes the poem 'Readers' where she angrily attacks those biographers and critics who have plundered her mother's life for their own purposes. The mother-daughter story continues . . .

Primary reading

Plath, S. 1963/1966 *The Bell Jar*, London: Faber & Faber.

Plath, S. 1975 *Letters Home: Correspondence 1950–1963* Aurelia Schober Plath (ed.), London: Faber & Faber.

Plath, S. 1977/1979 *Johnny Panic and the Bible of Dreams and Other Prose Writings*, London: Faber & Faber.

Plath, S. 1981 *Collected Poems* edited with an introduction by Ted Hughes, London: Faber & Faber.

Further reading

Hughes, F. 1999 *Wooroloo*, Newcastle: Bloodaxe.

Rose, J. 1991 *The Haunting of Sylvia Plath*, London: Virago.

Stevenson, A. 1989 *Bitter Fame. A Life of Sylvia Plath*, Harmondsworth: Penguin.

Wagner-Martin L. 1987 *Sylvia Plath: A Biography*, New York: Simon & Schuster.

Balloons

From Sylvia Plath, *Collected Poems* Ted Hughes (ed.), London: Faber & Faber, 1981, pp. 271–2.

Since Christmas they have lived with us,
Guileless and clear,
Oval soul-animals,
Taking up half the space,
Moving and rubbing on the silk

Invisible air drifts,
Giving a shriek and pop
When attacked, then scooting to rest, barely trembling.
Yellow cathead, blue fish—
Such queer moons we live with

Instead of dead furniture!
Straw mats, white walls
And these traveling
Globes of thin air, red, green,
Delighting

The heart like wishes or free
Peacocks blessing

Old ground with a feather
Beaten in starry metals.
Your small

Brother is making
His balloon squeak like a cat.
Seeming to see
A funny pink world he might eat on the other side of it,
He bites,

Then sits
Back, fat jug
Contemplating a world clear as water.
A red
Shred in his little fist.

Margaret Drabble (1939–)

Margaret Drabble was born in Sheffield, the younger sister of the novelist and critic Antonia Byatt (Drabble writes shrewdly of the rivalries between sisters in her first novel *A Summer Bird-Cage*, 1963). Drabble attended the Mount School, York, a Quaker boarding-school where her mother taught English. Many of Drabble's early novels feature difficult mother-daughter relationships and she told an interviewer (Hardin 1973a: 278) that for several years her mother had suffered severe depression and that consequently Drabble had sought other mother figures, much as Clara Maugham does in *Jerusalem the Golden* (1967). In this novel Mrs

Maugham's stoic endurance of life in the grim Northern town which has 'crushed and deformed and dissembled' all her gifts (Drabble 1967/1969: 8) casts a blight over her daughter's life. As soon as possible Clara escapes to university in London.

Drabble herself escaped to read English at Newnham College, Cambridge where she received a double first. For a couple of years she acted with the Royal Shakespeare Company in Stratford but she turned to writing after her marriage to the actor, Clive Swift, and the birth of their first child. Drabble had three children with Swift from whom she was divorced in 1972. In 1982 she married the biographer Michael Holroyd.

Margaret Drabble has written novels, short stories and criticism. Her novels belong to the English realist tradition and document British women's lives from the 1960s onwards against the changing political, social and economic climate. Her early 1960s novels, written before the resurgence of feminism in Britain in the 1970s, portray the plight of educated, middle-class women who find themselves trapped by marriage and motherhood. She depicts something of the earth-shattering changes that motherhood can wreak in the lives of such women. In *The Garrick Year*, Emma reflects: 'Time and maternity can so force and violate a personality that it can hardly remember what it was' (Drabble 1964/1966: 171). Yet Emma knows that motherhood can bring its own sort of salvation. When her friend Julian drowns himself, she thinks: 'I used to be like Julian myself, but now I have two children, and you will not find me at the bottom of any river. I have grown into the earth, I am terrestrial' (Ibid.: 170).

Primary reading
Drabble, M. 1964/1966 *The Garrick Year*, Harmondsworth: Penguin.
Drabble, M. 1965/1968 *The Millstone*, Harmondsworth: Penguin.
Drabble, M. 1967/1969 *Jerusalem the Golden*, Harmondsworth: Penguin.
Drabble, M. 1969/1971 *The Waterfall*, Harmondsworth: Penguin.
Drabble, M. 1975/1977 *The Realms of Gold*, Harmondsworth: Penguin.

Further reading

Cunningham, G. 1982 'Women and Children First: the Novels of Margaret Drabble' in *Twentieth-Century Women Novelists* T. F. Staley (ed.), London: Macmillan, pp. 130–52.

Hannay, J. 1987 'Margaret Drabble: An Interview', *Twentieth-Century Literature* 33 (1): 129–49.

Hardin, N. S. 1973a 'An Interview with Margaret Drabble', *Contemporary Literature* 14 (3): 273–95.

Hardin, N. S. 1973b 'Drabble's *The Millstone*: A Fable for our Times', *Critique* 15 (1): 22–34.

Harper, M. F. 1982 'Margaret Drabble and the Resurrection of the English Novel', *Contemporary Literature* 23 (1): 145–68.

Myer, V. G. 1974 *Margaret Drabble: Puritanism and Permissiveness*, London: Vision Press.

Rose, E. C. 1980 *The Novels of Margaret Drabble*, London: Macmillan.

The Millstone

From Margaret Drabble, *The Millstone*, London: Penguin, 1968, pp. 126–42.

The night before Octavia's operation I lay awake, enduring what might have been my last battle with the vast shadowy monsters of doubt. Some on such occasions must doubt the existence of God; it does not seem to me natural to survive such disasters with faith unimpaired. I find it more honourable to take events into consideration, when speaking of the mercy of God. But, in fact, the subject of God did not much cross my mind, for I had never given it much thought, having been brought up a good Fabian rationalist, and notions such as the after-life and heaven seem to me crude quite literally beyond belief. Justice, however, preoccupied me. I could not rid myself of the notion that if Octavia were to die, this would be a vengeance upon my sin. The innocent shall suffer for the guilty. What my sin had been I found difficult to determine, for I could not convince myself that sleeping with George had been a sin; on the contrary, in certain moods I tended to look on it as the only virtuous action of my life. A sense of retribution nevertheless hung heavily over me, and what I tried to preserve that night was faith not in God but in the laws of chance.

Towards morning, I began to think that my sin lay in my love for her. For five minutes or so, I almost hoped that she might die, and thus relieve me of the corruption and the fatality of love. Ben Jonson said of his dead child, my sin was too much hope of thee, loved boy. We too easily take what the poets write as figures of speech, as pretty images, as strings of *bons mots*. Sometimes perhaps they speak the truth.

In the morning, when it was time to get up and get dressed and gather together her pitiably small requirements, I got out of bed and got down on my knees and said, Oh God, let her survive, let her live, let her be all right, and God was created by my need, perhaps.

We went to hospital and I handed her over, and she smiled at me, then cried when they took her away. The world had contracted to the small size of her face and her clenching, waving hands. The poignancy was intolerable: her innocence, her gaiety, her size. I went away, and I walked up and down Marylebone Road. I cannot think what I did with the hours. I did not go back till half an hour after they had told me to inquire, and when I got there I did not dare to ask. I stood there, waiting, till someone recognized me and came over smiling and told me that everything had gone extremely well, and that Mr Protheroe sent his regards and hoped to see me, and that there was every hope of complete success. As on the day when I had first guessed at her condition, I could not believe that a mere recital of facts could thus change my fate: I stood there, dumbly, wondering if it could be the truth that she had told me, or whether she had got the wrong name, the wrong data, the wrong message. But she went on smiling and reassuring me, and soon I believed her, for it became suddenly clear that it was quite out of the question that anything should have gone wrong, that of course we had been lucky, Octavia and I. When I got round to speaking, I asked if I could see her, and they said to come back in the morning, as she was still unconscious and not to be disturbed. Of course, I said humbly, and backed away, full of gratitude towards the lot of them: then I went and wept copiously in the Cloakroom, and then I went home.

It was only when I got home that I began to be preoccupied by certain details upon which I had not previously dared to exercise my mind. What would Octavia think when she woke in hospital? Would she be in terrible pain from the operation? Would they feed her properly? Would she cry? Earlier it had seemed presumptuous to have considered these things, but now their importance swelled minute by minute in my mind. The threat of fatality removed, the conditions of life at once resumed their old significance. It was the strangeness, I thought, more than the pain that would afflict her, for she liked nobody but me; even Mrs Jennings and Lydia she regarded only with tolerance, and strangers she disliked with noisy vehemence. Lord knows what incommunicable small terrors infants go through, unknown to all. We disregard them, we say they forget, because they have not the words to make us remember, because they cannot torment our consciences with a recital of their woes. By the time they learn to speak they have forgotten the details of their complaints, and so we never know. They forget so quickly, we say, because we cannot contemplate the fact that they never forget. We cannot stand the injustice of life, so we pretend that a baby can forget hours spent wrapped in newspaper on the floor of a telephone kiosk, the vicious blows of the only ones that might have loved it, the sight of its elder, unsaved brothers in a blazing mass of oil-stove flames. Like Job's comforters, we cannot believe that the innocent suffer. And yet they do. We see, but we cannot believe.

When I went round in the morning to visit her, I found myself met by a certain unhelpful stalling. The lady in charge, a lady in white whose title was not clear to me, assured me that all was well, that all was progressing most satisfactorily, that the child was as comfortable as could be expected. 'I'd like to go and see her,' I said then, summoning up a little courage.

'I'm afraid that won't be possible,' said the lady in white with calm certainty, looking down at her file of notes.

'Why not?' I said. 'I would like to see her, I know she'd like to see me.'

The lady in white embarked upon a long explanation about upsetting children, upsetting mothers, upsetting other children, upsetting other mothers, justice to all, disturbing the nurses' routine, and such topics. As she talked, in her smooth even tones, all kinds of memories filtered back into my mind, memories of correspondence in *The Times* and the *Guardian* upon this very subject, composed of letters from mothers like myself who had not been allowed in. 'What about visiting hours?' I said, and back came the civil, predictable answer,

'I'm afraid that for such small infants we don't allow any visiting time at all. We really do find that it causes more inconvenience to staff and patients than we can possibly cope with. Really, Mrs Stacey, you must understand that it is of no practical use to visit such a young child, she will settle much more happily if she doesn't see you. You'd be amazed to see how soon they settle down. Mothers never believe us, but we know from experience how right we are to make this regulation.'

I didn't like the sound of that word 'settle': it suggested a settling into lethargy and torpor, such as I remembered to have read of in *The Times*. Octavia had never been settled in her short life, and I did not want her to begin now. Already, in twenty-four hours, we had endured the longest separation of our lives, and I began to see it stretching away, indefinitely prolonged. Also, because they would not let me see the child, I suspected that they had not told me the whole truth about her recovery; was there now in her small countenance something too dreadful for me to behold? I voiced this fear, feeling that it would have effect, and be at least appreciated.

'I can't believe until I see her,' I said, 'that everything really is all right. I just can't believe it.'

She took my point. 'Mrs Stacey,' she said, looking up and meeting with straight, woman-to-woman frankness my anxious gaze, 'you must believe me when I say that I have given you all the information there is about your daughter. We are making no attempt to conceal anything from you because there is nothing to conceal. Mr Protheroe expressed personal satisfaction at the progress of the operation and is calling in this morning to check on progress. If you would like to see his report, here it is.'

And she detached a piece of paper from the file marked Not To Be Seen By Patient and pushed it over to me. I glanced at it, but could see it was nothing but a mass of technicalities, so I did not try to read it. I felt better, though, by virtue of the fact that she had let me look, for she could not reasonably have relied upon the exact extent of my ignorance. By this time it was quite easy to tell from her expression that she considered I was nothing but an ordinary and tedious time-waster, and as I dislike being any such thing, and as I could see that I was making no progress, I decided that I had no choice but to leave gracefully, so I did.

'Oh well,' I said, 'perhaps you're right. I'm sure you're looking after her properly; it was just that I wanted to see her, I thought she might be missing me. But perhaps you're right, perhaps it wouldn't do any good to see her so soon.'

And I picked up my bag and prepared to go. She got up from behind her desk and opened the door for me; I was out in the corridor before I heard her saying that perhaps in a fortnight or so I might be able to visit. I half turned to retort, but had not the energy, so I continued on down the corridor and out of the building. I knew my way round that place now as well as if it were my school or my college or the British Museum itself.

I had not expected that they would let me stay with her all day, and had arrived prepared to go on to the BM to work, intending to call back at tea-time. I went on to the BM mechanically, and spent an hour or two there trying to check up on some very insignificant footnotes, but it was not the kind of work that could occupy the mind, and by lunch time I had had enough. My thesis was so nearly finished that I anyway somewhat disliked the prospect of its final completion and all the rethinking and restarting on new projects that it would entail. I went downstairs for a sandwich and a coffee, and while there sat quietly and told myself that I should be grateful, that I should not now be worrying about not seeing my child for a fortnight, that regulations were regulations, that I should be grateful and should not obstruct. But the more I told myself all this, the less I convinced myself, for I had only to think of my baby's small lonely awakening for the whole pack of thoughts to seem so much waste irrelevant rubbish. And when I had finished my coffee, I got up and put my books back in my bag and went back to the hospital.

It was lunch time and I could not find the lady in white. There were a couple of nurses guarding her office, who said she would not be back till two.

'That doesn't matter,' I said. 'It wasn't her I wanted to see, it was my baby. Would one of you take me to see my baby? She's in ward 21G. Octavia Stacey, her name is.'

The two nurses looked at each other, nervously, as though I were a case.

'You're not allowed to visit in this ward,' one of them said, with timid politeness, propitiating, kind, as one speaks to the sick or the mad.

'I don't really care,' I said, 'whether I'm allowed to visit or not. If you'll tell me where it is, I'll get there by myself, and you needn't even say you saw me.'

'I'm afraid we can't possibly do that,' the other one said when the first speaker said nothing. Like her friend, she had a timid, undetermined note in her voice, and I felt mean to pursue my point. I did pursue it, however; I told them I had no intention of not seeing my baby, that I didn't think it would upset her at all, but that on the contrary it would cheer her up, and cheer me up, and was in every way desirable, and that if they didn't tell me how to find her I would just go and look for myself. No, no, I couldn't possibly do that, they both said at once, their voices hardening from personal timidity and embarrassment into the weight of authority. They had that whole building behind them, they knew, and I had nothing behind me at all except my intention. I have never been good at getting what I want; every impulse in me tells me to give up at the first breath of opposition. And yet this time I felt that I would not be the only one to lose; somewhere Octavia was lying around and waiting for me. It was no longer a question of what I wanted: this time there was someone else involved. Life would never be a simple question of self-denial again.

'I must see her,' I repeated. 'If you won't let me, go and get Sister, or Matron, or whatever she's called. Go and fetch her for me. Or I'll wait here till she comes.'

'She won't be here till two,' said one, and the other said, 'You can't wait here, you aren't allowed to wait.'

'What do you mean, I'm not allowed?' I said crossly, suffering greatly from this as yet mild degree of self-assertion. 'Who doesn't allow me? Who says I can't wait?'

'Sister won't see anyone anyway, at this time of day,' they said. 'And she says that no one must be allowed to wait.'

They began to look frightened; I could see that they were going to get into trouble if I were still there when Sister came back. I was sorry for them, but not as sorry as I was for Octavia. I sat down on the desk and I waited. After five minutes one of them disappeared, perhaps in an effort to find someone more persuasive to dislodge me, but before she returned Sister arrived, and the remaining girl had to bear the brunt of her wrath.

'Well, well, Mrs Stacey,' she said snappily as she bustled in. 'So you're here again, are you? Now then, Miss Richards, how many times have I told you that this isn't a convenient time for visitors? Mrs Stacey, I'm afraid that I can't possibly talk . . .'

'I'm not supposed to be on duty now,' said Miss Richards querulously, interrupting. 'I was only here because of Mavis, and then Mavis went off to look for . . .'

'I don't care who went off where,' said Sister, fiercely, 'I have said again and again that my office must not be used as a waiting-room. Mrs Stacey, I'm afraid I am far too busy to talk to you now. Miss Richards, would you show Mrs Stacey to the lift, please. If there is anything you wish to discuss, you must . . .'

'I don't want to discuss anything,' I said. 'I've come to visit my baby.'

I felt happier now; I had not enjoyed upsetting those unimpressive nurses, whose discomfort in the situation had been almost as great as mine. In Sister, however, I sensed the kind of will that can be fought: she found pleasure, not torment, in assertion, so I felt free to assert myself too.

'I told you this morning,' said Sister, 'that visiting is quite out of the question.'

'I don't care what you told me,' I said. 'I want to see my baby. If you don't take me straight there, I shall walk round until I find the way myself. She's not kept under lock and key, I assume?'

'Miss Stacey,' said Sister, 'you are behaving most foolishly, and I must ask you to leave at once.'

'I won't leave,' I said. 'You'd much better take me straight there, I don't want to be compelled to wander round upsetting the whole of your hospital until I find my baby.'

'Now then, now then,' said Sister, 'this is neither the time nor the place for hysterical talk like that. We must all be grateful that your child is . . .'

'Grateful,' I said. 'I am grateful. I admire your hospital, I admire your work, I am devoted to the National Health Service. Now I want to see my baby.'

She came over to me and took my arm and started to push me

gently towards the door; I have spent so much of my life in intelligent, superior effort to understand ignorance that I recognized her look at once. She pitied me and she was amazed. I let her get me as far as the door, being unable at first to resist the physical sense of propulsion, but when we got to the door I stopped and said, 'No, I'm not going to leave. I'm going to stay here until you change your mind.'

'I have no intention of changing my mind,' she said, and once more took hold of my elbow and started to push. I resisted. We stood there for a moment; I could not believe that physical violence could possibly take place, but on the other hand I did not see what else I could do. So when she started to push, I started to scream. I screamed very loudly, shutting my eyes to do it, and listening in amazement to the deafening shindy that filled my head. Once I had started, I could not stop; I stood there, motionless, screaming, whilst they shook me and yelled at me and told me that I was upsetting everybody in earshot. 'I don't care,' I yelled, finding words for my inarticulate passion, 'I don't care, I don't care, I don't care about anyone, I don't care, I don't care, I don't care.'

Eventually they got me to sit down, but I went on screaming and moaning and keeping my eyes shut; through the noise I could hear things happening, people coming and going, someone slapped my face, someone tried to put a wet flannel on my head, and all the time I was thinking I must go on doing this until they let me see her. Inside my head it was red and black and very hot, I remember, and I remember also the clearness of my consciousness and the ferocity of my emotion, and myself enduring them, myself neither one nor the other, but enduring them, and not breaking in two. After a while I heard someone shouting above the din, 'For God's sake tell her she can see the baby, someone try and tell her,' and I heard these words and instantly stopped and opened my eyes and beheld the stricken, confused silence around me.

'Did you say I could see the baby?' I said.

'Of course you can see the baby,' said Mr Protheroe. 'Of course you can see the baby. I cannot imagine why you should ever have been prevented from seeing the baby.'

I looked at the breathless circle surrounding me, which had changed its composition considerably since I had last seen it: Mr Protheroe himself looked agitated and white with anger, Sister was sitting in a corner and crying into a handkerchief, the nurses were looking stunned, and there were a couple more men also looking angry. It was as though I had opened my eyes on a whole narrative caught in a single picture, a narrative in which I myself had taken no part; it had been played out between the Sister and the others, quite clearly, and she had lost and was now suffering her defeat. It was nothing to do with me at all, I felt; I shut my eyes, wearily, upon them, for I did not want to know. I had no interest in their story; I wished to know only my own. I felt I could no longer bother to endure their conflicts; if I had gained my point, that was enough for me.

'Can I go now and see my baby?' I asked.

'I will take you myself,' said Mr Protheroe, and I got up, and he took my arm and conducted me down the corridor. To my surprise I found that I needed his arm, for my knees were weak and the blood was singing in my ears, sensations odd enough for one who had always looked and felt as strong as a horse, as my parents used to say. We went along various devious passages, through swing doors and up and down half-flights of stairs, while I tried in vain to memorize the route, like Theseus in the labyrinth, and finally emerged in a long, cubicle ward full of small children. The cubicles must have been sound-proofed, for when we reached Octavia I heard nothing until they opened the door, and at once her sad, piercing and recognizable wails met my ear. She was lying there in a cot much like the one in which she had spent the first days of her life, and wearing the same kind of institution nightie, but this time she was strapped in. I stood on the threshold, overcome with feeling, and she turned her eyes towards me, and I was afraid she would weep all the more bitterly, or fail to recognize me at all, but instead she stopped crying, and I went up to her, and her face became suffused with its habitual enchanted and enchanting total smile. She lay there smiling, unable to move but smiling, and I went up to her and stroked her cheek and she smiled more and more. She had forgiven me for our day of separation, I could see, and such generosity I found amazing, for I am not generous. Fair, but not generous.

I stayed with her all day, and helped to feed her, and watched her sleep and watched her wake and watched her cry, for she did cry, but through restless boredom and pain, not through desertion. Mr Protheroe, who had had to leave me after five minutes, had said that they were to find me a chair and to let me in any day I wished to come, and that I could eat in the canteen. I asked him, when no one was there, whether this was preferential treatment, and whether I was receiving it because I made a fuss, or because he had known my father: he said that it was not preferential treatment, the policy of the hospital was to admit mothers with children, the policy of the nation was to admit mothers with children, but that nevertheless the human element intervened. 'Our buildings here are old,' he said, 'and our staff are old. We have to put up with it.' 'Admit it, though,' I said. 'I only got in because I made a fuss. Other mothers don't get in, do they?'

'They don't all want to,' he said. 'They don't all have time to. Some of them have families at home to worry about. I wouldn't think about the others, if I were you. Think about yourself.'

So I did think about myself and I went on coming, regardless of all the others who couldn't come. They did not like me to be there, most of them, and they never found me a chair, but I wasn't bothered about a chair, and when I could not find one for myself I sat on the floor. It was quite peaceful, as she slept much of the time, so I was able to read and get bored in a fairly normal fashion. Sister Watkins would not speak to me, so deep was her resentment for what she had endured through my innocent agency, but the twinges of guilt that I felt whenever I encountered her were fainter than any I can recollect. Towards the end, however, try as I would, I could no longer stifle awareness of the other small ones, crying quietly and unheard behind their glass doors, or lying in a stupor of nothingness at the other end of the long ward, unprotected by partitions. There were only very small children in that part of the hospital; I did manage to see some larger ones, on one of my detours to the canteen, and some of them looked much better, and were reading and playing and shouting at each other. I saw some terrible sights, and even from time to time indulged the dreadful fancy that I was glad that Octavia's illness, however grave, had in no way marred her beauty. But this was but a fancy, for who would not rather endure a hare lip? Before Octavia was born, I used to think that love bore some relation to merit and to beauty, but now I saw that this was not so.

It must have been the saddest place in the world, that hospital. The décor made faint attempts at cheer, for there were friezes of bunny rabbits round the walls, and from time to time one particularly enthusiastic nurse would come and talk to me and dangle teddy bears at Octavia. Octavia took no interest in teddy bears, being at an age where she would play only with hard chewable objects or paper, but the nurse did not notice. I seemed to spend weeks there, for she was in for a long time, and during those weeks I saw only one other mother; we met, twice, at the entrance to the ward, and the second time accompanied each other more or less accidentally down to the canteen, where we sat, after brief and watery smiles, at the same table with our cups of tea. There seemed little small talk in which one could indulge, for any however trivial inquiry might well in those circumstances let loose unwelcome, dormant fear and tragedy, so finally all I said was, 'How did you manage to get in?' I wanted to talk to her, for she looked a nice woman: older than myself, with fair hair parted in the middle and draped looping gently backwards, and wearing a belted grey coat with a fur collar. Her face was one of those mild, round-chinned, long-cheeked faces, without angles or edges, but nevertheless shapely and memorable, with a kind of soft tranquillity. She looked, too, as if she could talk, and I had had enough of my endless battle with the official and the inarticulate.

'Oh, I got in all right,' she said. 'I made them give it me in writing before I let him in, that I could come. Then all one has to do is show them the letter.'

'That shows foresight,' I said. 'I had to have hysterics.'

'Really?' she smiled, impressed. 'And it worked, did it?'

'Evidently.'

'I was always afraid,' she said, 'that if I made a real fuss, they wouldn't let me in anyway, because they'd say I was in too bad a state to see the children. I was afraid they'd put me to bed, too.'

I thought that this might well have been more than likely in my case too, and I thought about what Lydia had said about not being allowed to have an abortion because it would upset her; degrees of madness were a tricky matter, it seemed, as were degrees of responsibility.

'Anyway,' I said, 'you didn't have to make a fuss. You did it all properly. I didn't realize what it would be like; if I'd realized I would have done something about it earlier too, perhaps.'

'One doesn't realize,' she said. 'The first time, I'd no idea. They wouldn't let me in with the first child. I had to get my husband to write a letter.'

'And that worked?'

'Oh yes. My husband has some influence here, you see. Some. I don't know what one would do without a little influence.' She smiled, wanly, and I noticed that she looked very, very tired.

'But how many children?' I asked. 'More than one child?'

'It's my second,' she said, 'that's in now. My second boy.'

There was a pause; she expected me to ask her what was wrong, perhaps, but I did not like to, and I could see that she was relieved by my abstention, for she went on, 'It's the same thing with both of them. So I knew it was coming this time, I've known for years. It makes it worse. People think it makes it better, but it makes it worse.'

'Why did you let him come here, after the other one?'

'Why? It's the best place, you know. They must have told you it's the best place.'

'Oh yes, they did. But I thought they said that everywhere.'

She smiled once more, her grave slow liquid smile, a smile not of amusement but of tired well-meaning. 'Oh no,' she said, 'it really is. You're very lucky. They really are wonderful here. It's your first, isn't it?'

'Yes, my first.'

'I wish you luck,' she said, finishing her cup of tea, 'with your second.'

'I'm not having any more,' I said.

'That's what I said,' she said. 'They said it wasn't likely to happen twice. And afterwards they told me the odds. Not that it matters. I'd have done it anyway.'

'But how,' I said, 'how do you bear it?' I did not mean to say it, but I said it in spite of myself and then wished I had not spoken, for her manner, though kind, had been impersonal, a sort of cool human sympathy rather than a personal interest. She did not mind, however; she seemed used to the question.

'I don't bear it,' she said. She picked up her spoon and started to stir the leaves in the bottom of her cup, staring at them intently as though fate were indeed lying there amongst them, sodden and dark brown, to be altered by the movement of a tin spoon. 'At first I used to pretend not to mind, I used to laugh it off to my friends and underestimate its gravity when talking to my family, you know what I mean. Extraordinary, the impulse to play things down, don't you think? But in the end I got fed up with it. I got tired of pretending it was nothing just to save other people's feelings. Now I don't care who sees I care.'

She stopped talking as though she had said all she had to say. I too said nothing, awed by this testimony of long-term sorrow. There was still something in me that protested, that told me that it was not possible that a mere accident of birth, the slight misjudgement of part of one organ should so mould and pin and clamp a nature that it could grow like this, warped and graceful, up the one sunny wall of dignity left to it. For, no doubt about it, she wore her grief well: she spared herself and her associates the additional infliction of ugliness, which so often accompanies much pain.

We sat there for a moment or two, quietly, and I meant to say no more, but after a while my nature returned, relentless, to its pre-occupations, like a dog to some old dried marrowless bone. I could not help but ask; I had no hope of an answer, having always known that there is no answer, but it seemed to me that this woman would at least understand the terms of my question.

'What,' I said to her then, 'what about all the others?'

'The others?' she said slowly.

'The others,' I said. 'Those that don't even get in. Those without money. Those without influence. Those who would not dare to have hysterics.'

'Ah, those,' she said.

'Yes, those. What about them?'

'I don't know,' she said, still speaking slowly, her eyes still down-cast. 'I don't know. I can't see that I can do anything about them.'

'But don't they worry you?' I said, reluctant to disturb her yet unable to desist.

With difficulty she began to attach herself to the question. She began to speak, and I waited with ridiculous expectation for her answer.

'They used to worry me,' she said. 'When I first started on all this, they worried me almost as much as my own. And I comforted myself by saying that nobody felt what I felt. They don't care, I said, or they would do what I do. But that's not true, of course.'

She looked at me for confirmation, and I nodded, for I agreed with what she had said.

'They do care,' she went on, 'but they don't set about it as I do. As time went on, though, and after years of this, I began to think that it was after all nothing to do with me. And it isn't, you know. My concerns are my concerns, and that's where it ends. I haven't the energy to go worrying about other people's children. They're nothing to do with me. I only have enough time to worry about myself. If I didn't put myself and mine first, they wouldn't survive. So I put them first and the others can look after themselves.'

She finished speaking; she had no more to say. I was, inevitably, touched almost to tears, for it is very rare that one meets someone who will give one such an answer to my question. She had spoken without harshness; I think it was that that had touched me most. I had so often heard these views expressed, but always before they had been accompanied by a guilty sneer at those who must be neglected, or a brisk Tory contempt for the ignorant, or a business-like blinkered air of proud realism. I had never heard them thus gently put forward as the result of sad necessity. I saw what she meant; I saw, in her, what all the others meant. I don't think I replied, and after a while she put on her gloves and stood up.

'Good-bye,' she said.

'Good-bye,' I said. And she went.

It was about a week later that I was able to take Octavia home. She was by this time quite gay and mobile once more, and seemingly unaffected, apart from loss of weight, by her ordeal. I arrived on the morning of her release with a small suitcase full of real clothes for her to wear; I had been looking forward to dressing her in something other than the white institutional nighties the hospital provided. In fact, I had whiled away some of my vigil by her cot-side by making her some new dresses; I had been taught at school to smock, an accomplishment I had never thought to use, but I do not like to let anything be wasted, and I had made her some very pretty small garments in various dark smart shades of Viyella. It had given me much satisfaction to make them; it was more profitable than jigsaws, for it actually saved money, while at the same time gratifying the need to do something mechanical with my hands, which otherwise occupied themselves by ripping holes in my cuticles or tearing strips off the wicker-seated chair I had finally acquired. I put her in my masterpiece to take her home: it was dark blue with a very small check. She looked very charming in it and jumped happily on my knee. I shook hands with all the nurses and even with Sister, who was glad to see me go. I got into the waiting taxi and off we went: I remembered the last time she and I had left the place together in this way, when she had been ten days old. I now knew better than to hope I would never have to go back again, for I knew that at the best she and I were in for a lifetime of checks and examinations, but nevertheless it seemed to me that I was more happy and more fortunate now than I had been then.

It was the middle of the afternoon: owing to the curious nature of the one-way street system, the quickest way to approach the flat was to go round Queens Crescent and then to the right off Portland Place. The air was bright and clear, and as we drove past the formal determined structure of the crescent, ever-demolished, ever-renewed, I suddenly thought that perhaps I could take it and survive. I had thought this before when drunk but never when sober; up till that moment I had been inwardly convinced that too much worry would rot my nature beyond any hope of fruit or even of flower. But then, however fleetingly, I felt that I could take what I had been given to take. I felt, for the first time since Octavia's birth, a sense of adequacy. Like Job, I had been threatened with the worst and, like Job, I had kept my shape. I knew something now of the quality of life, and anything in the way of happiness that I should hereafter receive would be based on fact and not on hope.

Adrienne Rich (1929–)

P oet, essayist, feminist theorist and activist, Adrienne
Rich was born into an intellectual, middle-class family in Baltimore.
She was the elder of two sisters. Her father, a pathology professor at
John Hopkins University, was Jewish and Rich has written movingly
of her Jewish inheritance and its effect on her life in 'Split at the Root'
(Rich 1987: 100–23). Her mother, from a Southern Protestant
background, was an accomplished musician who gave up a promising
career as a concert pianist when she married. Rich's poem, 'Solfeg-
gietto' (dated 1985–88), recalls her mother's talent as a pianist and the
tension-filled lessons with her ungifted daughter.

According to a scheme devised by their ambitious, autocratic father, Rich and her sister were taught all their lessons at home by their mother, only entering school at fourth grade. In her chapter on 'Motherhood and Daughterhood' in *Of Woman Born* (1976), Rich describes her mother's anxious, guilty mothering and her feeling of failure because she had not produced the son her husband wanted. She shows how a daughter's relationship with her mother can be wrenched apart, as hers was, by the mother's obedience to an over-controlling husband.

Rich graduated from Radcliffe College in 1951, the same year as her first book of poetry, *A Change of World*, was published. It was selected by W. H. Auden for the Yale Younger Poets Award. In 1953 Rich married Alfred Conrad, a Jewish economist: they moved to Cambridge, Massachusetts and their first son was born in 1955, followed by two more in 1957 and 1959. *Of Woman Born* describes the conflict Rich experienced at this time between mothering three small boys and writing poetry.

In 1966 Rich and her family moved to New York where she became involved in the campaign for civil rights, anti-Vietnam protests and the emergent women's movement. She taught in the SEEK programme, a remedial English programme for poor, black and Third World students entering college.

Rich's collection, *Snapshots of a Daughter-in-Law* (1963), marked a turning-point in her writing as she began to speak more directly, exploring themes of womanhood, women's relationship to language and the effects of the patriarchy on the female psyche. In 1970 she left her husband to live with a woman. In her groundbreaking and controversial essay, 'Compulsory Heterosexuality and Lesbian Existence' (1980), she writes of a 'lesbian continuum' in women's lives and defines a lesbian as 'a woman-identified woman', that is, one who forms close emotional and intellectual, but not necessarily sexual, bonds with other women. Heterosexuality she sees as a patriarchal institution imposed on women by force which wrenches them away from their bonds with other women, much as she showed in *Of Woman Born* the father diverting the mother's attention from her daughter and interrupting the bond between them.

Adrienne Rich has lectured extensively and won numerous awards, fellowships and prizes, including two Guggenheim Fellowships and the Fellowship of the Academy of American Poets. Since *Snapshots of a Daughter-in-Law* she has continued to record her personal and political journeys, widening her themes to explore the situation of women across cultures, history and ethnicity, pursuing her project of speaking for the speechless and bringing to the surface stories that, like the mother-daughter story, have remained unwritten.

Primary reading

Rich, A. 1976/1977 *Of Woman Born. Motherhood as Experience and Institution*, London: Virago.

Rich, A. 1979/1980 *On Lies, Secrets and Silence. Selected Prose 1966–1978*, London: Virago.

Rich, A. 1980 *The Dream of a Common Language*, New York and London: W.W. Norton.

Rich, A. 1981 *A Wild Patience Has Taken Me This Far. Poems 1978–1981*, New York and London: W.W. Norton.

Rich, A. 1984 *The Fact of a Doorframe. Poems Selected and New 1950–1984*, New York and London: W.W. Norton.

Rich, A. 1987 *Blood, Bread, and Poetry. Selected Prose 1979–1985*, London: Virago.

Rich, A. 1989 *Time's Power. Poems 1985–1988*, New York and London: W.W. Norton.

Further reading

Ostriker, A. 1983 'Her Cargo: Adrienne Rich and the Common Language' in *Writing Like A Woman*, Michigan: University of Michigan Press.

Ostriker, A. 1987 *Stealing the Language. The Emergence of Women's Poetry in America*, London: The Women's Press.

Mother-in-Law

From Adrienne Rich, *The Fact of a Doorframe. Poems Selected and New 1950–1984*, New York and London: W. W. Norton, 1984, pp. 290–2.

Tell me something

              you say

Not: What are you working on now, is there anyone
special,

   how is the job

   do you mind coming back to an empty house

   what do you do on Sundays

Tell me something . . .

            Some secret

   we both know and have never spoken?

   Some sentence that could flood with light

   your life, mine?

Tell me what daughters tell their mothers
everywhere in the world, and I and only I
even have to ask. . . .

Tell me something.

   Lately, I hear it: Tell me something true,

   daughter-in-law, before we part,

   tell me something true before I die

   And time was when I tried.

You married my son, and so
strange as you are, you're my daughter
Tell me. . . .

   I've been trying to tell you, mother-in-law

   that I think I'm breaking in two

   and half of me doesn't even want to love

   I can polish this table to satin because I don't care

   I am trying to tell you, I envy

the people in mental hospitals their freedom
and I can't live on placebos
or Valium, like you

A cut lemon scours the smell of fish away
You'll feel better when the children are in school
   I would try to tell you, mother-in-law
   but my anger takes fire from yours and in the oven
   the meal bursts into flames
Daughter-in-law, before we part
tell me something true
   I polished the table, mother-in-law
   and scrubbed the knives with half a lemon
   the way you showed me to do
   I wish I could tell you—
                 Tell me!
They think I'm weak and hold
things back from me. I agreed to this years ago.
Daughter-in-law, strange as you are,
tell me something true
tell me something
        Your son is dead
  ten years, I am a lesbian,
  my children are themselves.
  Mother-in-law, before we part
  shall we try again? Strange as I am,
  strange as you are? What do mothers
  ask their own daughters, everywhere in the world?
  Is there a question?
           Ask me something.

Storm Jameson (1891–1986)

M̲argaret Storm Jameson was born in Whitby, the
eldest in a family of three girls and a boy. Her mother was a
shipowner's daughter, her father a sea captain. As a very young
child Jameson travelled with her mother on her father's ship but with
the birth of her siblings this became impossible. Her father's long
absences at sea alienated him from his children, none of whom seem
to have felt much affection for him. In her autobiography *Journey from
the North* Jameson makes it clear that she believed her mother married
beneath her, emotionally and intellectually. Her mother's boredom at
being left alone with her children in Whitby and her dissatisfaction at

the limitations of her life are well caught in Jameson's autobiography.

Jameson was educated privately in Whitby and then spent one year at the co-educational Municipal School in Scarborough in order to prepare for matriculation. Her mother, who had high ambitions for all her children, helped her daughter apply for and get one of the three County Scholarships available. They were worth sixty pounds. With the aid of this money plus money found by her mother for living expenses, Jameson went to Leeds University in 1910 to study English. This is a rare example at this date of a mother actually encouraging her daughter to go on to higher education (contrast Vera Brittain's struggle to persuade her parents to allow her to follow her brother to Oxford, as recounted in *Testament of Youth*). Jameson's autobiography provides a valuable record of a girl's life in a co-ed school and at a provincial university in the early part of the century.

In 1912 Jameson graduated from Leeds and moved down to London to write an MA thesis on European drama. Her autobiography portrays the stimulating and carefree life she led as a postgraduate but in 1913 she made a disastrous marriage, fictionalised in her novel *Company Parade*. Her son, Bill, was born in 1915 in her mother's house in Whitby. In 1917 her brother was killed in the war, ending what was left of her mother's happiness. When the war was over Jameson, by now separated from her husband, had to support herself and her son. In her autobiography she describes her agonising decision to leave her three-year-old son in Whitby while she returned to London to work as a copywriter (Jameson 1969/1984: 135). She was to be separated from Bill for most of the next four years.

In 1919 her first novel, *The Pot Boils*, was published. It had been written at night while her child slept. Like many of the writers in this anthology Jameson found the conflict between mothering and writing almost unbearable (Jameson 1970/1984: 379–80). Her autobiography shows her constantly torn between her restless ambitions and her agonising, overwhelming love for her son.

Between 1923 and 1925 Jameson acted as British agent for the

American publisher Alfred Knopf. In 1925 she married the historian Guy Chapman, and for three years they co-managed Knopf's UK firm. In the 1930s the threat of fascism increasingly occupied Jameson and she became active in left wing and humanitarian causes. In 1938 she was a British delegate to the P.E.N. Congress in Prague and saw the effects of Nazism in central Europe. In 1939 she became the first woman president of the British section of International P.E.N. and during the war she helped refugee writers who had fled Nazi Germany. After the war she and Chapman travelled widely, particularly in France, a country Jameson loved. Chapman died in 1972 and Jameson lived on alone in Cambridge until her own death.

Between 1919 and 1976, Jameson published forty-five novels, works of criticism, essays and a two-volume autobiography. Her early novels deal with the gap between men who fought in the First World War and the women who stayed at home. *Company Parade* (1934), the first volume of her 1930s' trilogy *The Mirror in Darkness*, closely follows events described in her autobiography and Jameson's alter ego, Hervey Russell, has the same intense relationship with her mother. 'Her mother was at the centre of her life. She rebelled against her, at times with dislike, but she was bound to her by a love in which bitter and hurting things were drowned' (Jameson 1934/1982: 297).

Primary reading
Jameson, S. 1934/1982 *Company Parade*, London: Virago.
Jameson, S. 1969/1984 *Journey from the North*. Vol. 1, London: Virago.
Jameson, S. 1970/1984 *Journey from the North*. Vol. 2, London: Virago.

Journey from the North

From Storm Jameson, *Journey from the North*, Vol. 1, London: Virago, 1984, pp. 347–55.

In May that year my mother stayed with me in Reading. It was a superb spring, the lilacs and chestnuts so full that each tree was a single massive flower, dazzling.

She could not walk far. I drove her about the countryside to look, with that blue fixed stare, at an inordinate beauty, almost too much, too cruel and insistent an energy.

'I shan't see them again,' she said suddenly.

To hear her say it angered me sharply, and I said, 'Of course you will, you'll be here next May and I'll bring you to see them.'

She looked at me without answering; she had wanted to be reassured and was not.

In August, my middle sister wrote from Whitby that she had had 'an attack', and was very ill. All the way in the train, an eight-hour journey, I was nagged by anxiety, and then impatient when I thought of the book I had had to abandon, and must finish soon: I needed the money.

'She thinks she has had a heart attack,' my sister said, 'so be careful.'

When I went into her room and saw her lying in bed on her side, my heart shrank; her face, her soft hair screwed into a plait, her eyes, all had in some way given up, as if this time she were really defeated. She spoke in a voice I had never heard from her, slow, slurred, coming from a great distance.

'I'm glad you're feeling better,' I said.

She was a long time answering. 'Am I?' she said at last, like a child who has been told by an adult something it can't take in.

I was both anguished and numbed, I refused to believe what I could see. Deliberately and yet as if blind and deaf, refused. She must not be dying – that was not thinkable. And, if she were, I could not leave her and go back to my life and my work.

Her recovery was very slow. Time confused her terribly. The kind thing would have been to let her live in her own time, waking and sleeping as she pleased. But she had to live by others' time, and it was a torment to her. She slept, and woke bewildered; or she forgot she had just eaten, and demanded her lunch, and then begged us to give it to her, half weeping. Sometimes the railing voice of a lively self-willed child broke from her; sometimes it was the strong full voice of a young woman I could just recall.

I knew when she was living in the past, because her mouth shut in a hard stubborn line; she was thinking of her dead son, and my father's unkindness to him, or of some other bitter cause she had for not forgiving her husband. She forgave him nothing. The dry indifference she had come to feel broke, and now she could not endure him. When he came into her room – as once a day he did, and stood awkwardly, looking down at her, for a minute – she closed her eyes.

'How are you feeling?' he asked, pretending ease.

'Better,' she said icily, and waited, clenched, until he had hurried away.

I think that now she hated him simply because she had married him, not for anything he had done. He stood for the disappointment her life had been, for the absence of all an ardent quick-witted young woman had expected from it and had not had.

We talked about my young sister, and her house and her baby, endlessly, since I was the one person who would listen endlessly. Even this was not completely safe, and once, as she had said about the chestnuts, she said,

'I shan't see Do and Nicholas again. I shall never be well enough.'

'You'll be as well as ever,' I said lightly. 'You've had a bad heart attack, but if you're careful you won't have any more.'

There was a long silence. Then she said slowly,

'I don't remember the heart attack.'

It shamed me that I, her child, was deceiving her. And that perhaps she was not really deceived.

One evening when she and I were alone in her room – she was strong enough now to sit in the window, looking, looking, looking – she said in a hesitant voice,

'Sometimes, in the night, Daisy, I feel afraid.'

I shut away, at once, the agony of grief. 'Why should you be afraid?'

'I don't know. But I am afraid.'

'There is something you could say to yourself; you could say: *In quietness and in confidence shall be my strength*. It's what *I* say when I'm afraid.'

I would not let her fear reach me. Would not. I kept it away from me, I would not know or feel what was taking place in her. She was not going to die, so why think about it, why suffer? I shut both mind and heart against what, if I let it in, would destroy too many of my defences and pretences. There were moments when I thought it would be better for us all if she died. And this, too, I did not look at.

Days and weeks went by. When she was strong enough to walk the short distance to the nearest shops, though not alone, I prepared to go back to Reading, to Guy and my unfinished novel. She did not want me to go.

It was like all the other times I had left her. I had to go, I had to get away – back into my life, into the world. As I had done at these other times, I hardened my heart.

To catch the only train that would get me to Reading that evening, I had to leave the house very early, at half-past six, and when I went into her room to say goodbye, she was half asleep: she was lying in the bed as though she were sinking in it, her eyes closed. I could scarcely hear her when she spoke.

'Don't go.'

For less than a moment I knew that I should hear that remote barely audible voice in the deepest recesses of my brain, and those two words, all the rest of my life. Then I closed my ears.

'I *must* go,' I said. 'But I'll come back – I'll come as soon as I can.'

She did not answer or lift her eyelids to look at me – as though she had lost interest. Or as though she had known all along that she could not count on me, had known I would fail her, and were turning away from me.

I did not go again until, in February, my sister wired me to come. Because, in winter, there were fewer trains to Whitby, the journey was endlessly roundabout, and I was tormented by the thought that I might not get there in time. Time for what? My mind drew back sharply from that edge.

The dark, the cold North Sea wind, the empty streets – it could have been any of the evenings when I jumped out of the school train from Scarborough and hurried home.

'Do didn't think of coming with you?' my sister said.

'How could she? She can't leave the baby.'

'Well, it doesn't matter,' my sister said wearily, 'she's forgotten her.'

'What do you mean?'

'Last week, when Do's box of snowdrops came and I took them in to her and told her Do had sent them, she asked: Who is Do?'

For all these years the abiding passion of every moment, and it had dropped out of her hand. Why, then you have had nothing, I thought, oh, my poor love, nothing.

She was reared up on pillows, her face empty, a skull, not a face, the cheeks sunk, the eyes a blue absence of sight: she was the image of her father, my hard grandfather: nothing of her was left except the life of her Gallilee tribe.

I bent down, thinking I should be able to reach her.

'Here I am, Mother.'

Slowly, almost imperceptibly, her eyes turned towards my voice. For less than a second.

'She's going fast on her journey,' the nurse said loudly. She saw my frown, and said, 'Oh, she's completely unconscious, y'know.'

I no longer remember whether she was two days or three finishing that journey. I slept through the nights. During the day, whenever I could be alone with her, I bent over her and said softly, 'Don't be afraid, I'm here.' But she made no sign that she heard me. Once I said, 'Don't worry, I'll look after Do for you.' I was forced to believe that, somewhere in the silence, she must remember her youngest. My breath was cut off in my throat by the knot of pain. Tears came against the hard effort I made; I could not bear it that she did not know I was there.

'You and I have been on so many journeys,' I said, 'and now you are going alone.'

I was ashamed to be crying, afraid that I was crying over myself, and ashamed to be seen crying. When the nurse came into the room, I hurried out.

On the second or was it the third evening my sister said that we had better begin to destroy or put out of reach things she would not want my father to touch.

She lay in her bed in the lighted room, seeming asleep, breathing lightly and rapidly, while her daughters turned out drawers and looked into cupboards. I came on the box full of my brother's letters from France. I began destroying them, then stopped. They can live with me, I thought: let someone else destroy them. I took the photographs of him, the young blurred image, a boy still, in the uniform of the Flying Corps, and the parchment *au nom du Président de la République*, awarding him his *Médaille Militaire*.

Laid under gloves in a drawer there was a letter from my father, written thirty-three years ago, in 1904. 'My darling wife, this wishes you Many Happy Returns on your Birthday. I am enclosing you £5 (five pounds) cheque to buy yourself something as a present. Well my Dear your welcome letter to hand well I am sorry you have such hard work and trouble with the children. You should let them run wild like animals that is what they are. It doesn't do any good making a fuss of them spending money on their clothes all they want is enough to cover them never mind looks. I don't give myself trouble about clothes and none the worse for it. Well we have had a lovely week.

Sunshine all day and a smooth sea and this morning the sun is shining and a blue sky and 60° in the shade. I am happy and in good health and the air here is beautiful coming in the berth. Well my Dear I trust you are feeling alright and get all the sunshine you can for it will be best for you both for health and happiness. Now I will close with best love and best wishes and take care of yourself. Your loving husband Will.'

Very distinctly I saw the sea captain in his shabby uniform bent over the table in his cabin writing, in his backward-sloping hand . . . Why did she keep this single letter out of hundreds? Is it silly to think that, perhaps, under the bitterness, a single flicker, of warmth, regret, was still alive? . . . I put the letter in my pocket without showing it to my sister.

We found a large crudely coloured photograph of the three of us as very young children, my middle sister and Harold – he still in petticoats – smiling like idiots, I looking sullen and stolid. We laughed over it madly, and tore it up. I remembered suddenly that it used to stand in my father's cabin in the *Saxon Prince*. He must have brought it home, or it would have been sunk by the German cruiser in 1916, with his other possessions.

The night nurse came in as we were finishing. She looked closely at my mother and said quietly,

'She's going home.'

I would not take this in. Mechanically, without conscious effort, I refused. I went to bed and slept, in the next room, leaving her with the nurse.

Towards one o'clock the woman roused me. I went in. She died so quickly that even if I had cared to speak to her with other people in the room there would not have been time.

When I saw her again, it was daylight. Between them, the two nurses had made an image of her, lips upturned as never in life, an almost suave smile, not hers at all, her face ivory, small, ice-cold, fine soft hair drawn back from her arched forehead. Now I knew that she had really gone. It was a purely physical agony, a nerve being ripped out of me, slowly.

Downstairs in the hall I came on my father, standing at the foot of the staircase, crying. He was wearing the frightful suit, soiled and green with age, he insisted on wearing in the morning until he went out. I spoke to him awkwardly, with a false pity, and he turned his back on me, vexed. He cheered up later, and went out to be shaved in the town, first asking me if I had seen the chequebook of the joint account. I gave it to him and he took it away to his room. What a time he'll have going through the counterfoils, I thought.

When he came back, shaved, he handed me a paper bag. 'Here's something for you and the other one,' he said, smiling pleasantly. There were two grapefruit in it. He always bought these at Christmas, one for each person in the house. I suppose he had felt this was a day to be marked, and since the nurses had taken on all the business of a death, he had nothing to occupy him.

I kept going into her room to speak to her, when I could do it without anyone noticing. The cold of her cheeks shocked me, and the silence, but I could not let her lie there alone all day. (Why – since I had slept during her last night?) Each time, another piece of my life was ripped slowly out.

'I'm here,' I told her, 'I'm here, you're not alone.'

The agony came up again, tears poured down my face: I forced them back, and went away. No one must see me.

When she was alive, my father never entered her sitting-room. This evening, when the men brought the coffin, he came in. He was shivering with cold. He stood in the middle of the room, throwing quick glances round him, and said,

'I'll go out. I'll go out at the back.'

'Why?' I asked. 'Why go out? You're better here. Do sit down.'

He sat down in one of the armchairs, and began to talk about a pain in his chest. 'I shan't last long,' he said.

I despised him for trying to get attention and sympathy. Besides, he did not mean it; he had every intention now of living for ever. The men were walking about in the room overhead. I knelt and poked the fire noisily.

'Are you warmer?'

'Oh, I'm warm enough,' he said jauntily. 'I don't believe in warm rooms. Hers were always too warm for me. I've been forty-eight hours on the bridge in bad weather without so much as a hot drink. That's nothing, that's nothing.'

He laughed his short defensive laugh and went on talking about himself until the steps overhead ceased. Then he shambled away.

Later that night when I went into the kitchen, he had put aside his endless newspaper competitions – he never won anything – and was turning the pages of his scrap-book, and crying.

'Look,' he said, 'look what I've found.'

He pressed a long brown knotted finger on a yellowed cutting from some Australian paper. 'Y'see?'

I read the lines, shutting my mind against them.

'Then home, get her home, where the drunken rollers comb,
    And the shouting seas drive by,
And the engines stamp and ring, and the wet bows reel and swing,
    And the Southern Cross rides high!
Yes, the old lost stars wheel back, dear lass,
    That blaze in the velvet blue . . .'

'All them voyages,' he said.

What does he see? I wondered. A foreign quay that no longer exists as he knew it, blinding sunlight in a street in Vera Cruz, in Santos, in Montevideo, and a young woman who holds a sunshade over her as she walks with that light step towards the corner and the waiting cab, and is gone.

I left him sitting there. I had been sorry for him for a minute.

Shut in my room, I waited for him to come upstairs. When he had come and gone, padding quickly, almost silently, across the landing and up the further stairs, I went in to say goodnight to her.

'You're so cold,' I said to her.

I touched her hands, her cheek. The skin was soft.

'Goodnight, my love, goodnight, goodnight. Don't think about anything. The journey is over. Oh, my love, my love.'

Bitter grief hardened my throat and scalded my eyelids, and it was all no use.

The next day when I went in I saw that a faint colour had come into her cheeks. She seemed younger and vulnerable, and yet more nearly serene. This new image of her, this tranquil, inconceivably tranquil face, masked, at least for now, the tormented skull of the last days, and wiped out the image of the last few years, the blue fixed stare, the face which had become shapeless because her mind had given up bothering to mould it. Yet the last was what I ought not to forget.

I tried to recall other images of her. They must, each of them, have been familiar – the very young woman, tireless, the woman touched by time but still so eager to live. But nothing would come except an image drawn from a photograph, shallow and meaningless.

This smiling tranquil dead woman threatened to efface all the others. I turned away. Suddenly and piercingly, I saw her standing before the long glass in her other bedroom; she was trying on a new hat and looking at herself with such intentness that she seemed to be willing another self to step out from behind the one she saw.

My only chance of seeing her again is to catch her off guard in moments like this, I thought. And in sleep.

My father had been standing outside the room, waiting to say something. He was holding a painting on silk, made by a Japanese artist from the coloured photograph my sister and I had torn up. He gave it to me.

'It's no use keeping this,' he said hurriedly, 'since you're all going.'

I preferred not to glance at the abyss under the words – all but hidden from him, too. I am like him in the cowardice with which, when I can, I dodge an unpleasant reality.

It was her last day and night in her house. I went in and out of her room, and talked to her. The delicately flushed cheeks, the smooth rounded forehead, the smiling mouth, the rigid body, dreamed their own dream, indifferent to us, the living.

I stood there in the dark, alone as I had never been.

'This is your last night with us,' I said. 'Forgive me for all I have thought against you in vile moments, forgive me for all I did not do for you. Remember me only as the child I was, wholly in your hands.'

The searing grief ran over me. I felt drained of life, naked, and defenceless. Help me, I thought, help me.

That is a long time ago, many years. All but a few of the things she saw every day, and liked, have disappeared from my life. I keep a few. It is a long time, too, since I made the effort to see with her eyes the harbour, the old houses crouched against the side of the cliff, the abandoned shipyard, the old church, landmark for sailors, the fields and woods she knew. On the rare, very rare, occasions when I go back, no shadow comes to meet me. But – at any time since then I could have said this – the story is not at an end. Her life did not end then; it goes on echoing through mine, and will echo there until it and I are both silenced.

Kathleen Raine (1908–)

Kathleen Raine was born in Ilford. She was an only child, and in her three volumes of autobiography she describes her divided inheritance. Her English father stood for education, progress and socialist Methodism. He wished his daughter to become a school-teacher like himself, dedicated to the service of others. From her Scottish mother Raine inherited the songs, legends and language of Scotland. 'The poet in me is my mother's daughter' she wrote (Raine 1973: 20). She was not sent to school until she was six, for which she thanks her mother in her autobiography, saying that she owes her formation as a poet to those early years of solitude (Raine 1973: 82).

Raine attended local schools in Ilford but holidays were spent with her maternal grandparents in Northumberland. Early consciousness of her vocation as a poet led Raine to rebel against Ilford surburbia and her father's Methodism. She sought escape in books and in close observation of nature.

In 1926 Raine won a scholarship to Cambridge to study natural sciences. She began to mix with other writers including John Cornford, William Empson and Julian Bell, but she found the scientific materialism then prevalent at Cambridge not conducive to the kind of poetry she wished to write. In her autobiography she recalls being present when Virginia Woolf read her paper, 'A Room of One's Own', but disagreed with Woolf's premise that the problems of the woman writer differ from those of male writers.

On graduation, uncertain of what direction her life should take, she was briefly married to Hugh Sykes Davies, but left him for the poet Charles Madge whom she later married and with whom she had a son and a daughter. She left Madge too, however, and moved to Cumberland, feeling a sense of homecoming. She lived alone with her two children earning money by book reviewing.

During the war, Raine left her children in Cumberland while she returned to London to work. She later regretted this decision, believing that she had left her children at too early an age. She secured wartime work for the BBC in Bush House where she met Antonia White and Graham Greene. Under their influence she converted to Roman Catholicism but eventually found her true spiritual home in Neoplatonism, the cabbala and theosophy. She became an expert on the Neoplatonic tradition in British poetry and has published scholarly works on Blake and Yeats. Her first volume of poetry, *Stone and Flower*, appeared in 1943.

Raine's platonic relationship with the poet and naturalist Gavin Maxwell is described in the third volume of her autobiography. In loving Maxwell – who was of Scottish and Northumbrian ancestry – Raine felt she was loving as her mother would have wished. Raine's relationship with her mother runs as a leitmotif through her three volumes of autobiography. After her mother's death in 1973, she wrote some moving poems celebrating her mother's life, her independent spirit and her love of nature. They were published in 1977 in *The Oval Portrait*.

Primary reading

Raine, K. 1956 *Collected Poems*, London: Hamish Hamilton.

Raine, K. 1973 *Farewell Happy Fields. Memories of Childhood*, London: Hamish Hamilton.

Raine, K. 1975 *The Land Unknown*, London: Hamish Hamilton.

Raine, K. 1977 *The Lion's Mouth. Concluding Chapters of Autobiography*, London: Hamish Hamilton.

Raine, K. 1981 *Collected Poems 1935–1980*, London: Allen & Unwin.

Heirloom

From Kathleen Raine, *Collected Poems*, London: Allen & Unwin, 1981.

She gave me childhood's flowers,
Heather and wild thyme,
Eyebright and tormentil,
Lichen's mealy cup
Dry on wind-scored stone,
The corbies on the rock,
The rowan by the burn.

Sea-marvels a child beheld
Out in the fisherman's boat,
Fringed pulsing violet
Medusa, sea-gooseberries,
Starfish on the sea-floor,
Cowries and rainbow-shells
From pools on a rocky shore,

Gave me her memories.
But kept her last treasure:
'When I was a lass,' she said,
'Sitting among the heather,
'Suddenly I saw
'That all the moor was alive!
'I have told no one before.'

That was my mother's tale.
Seventy years had gone
Since she saw the living skein
Of which the world is woven,
And having seen, knew all:
Through long indifferent years
Treasuring the priceless pearl.

Alice Walker (1944–)

A̲lice Walker was born in Eatonton, Georgia, the young-
est of eight children in a family of sharecroppers. In her groundbreaking
essay, 'In Search of our Mothers' Gardens', Walker describes her mother
as a formidable woman who worked alongside her husband in the fields
yet still found time to make all her children's clothes, sew beautiful
quilts, can vegetables and fruit during the summer months and express
her creativity in tending to her garden. It was her mother who battled
with their landlord to keep her children out of the fields and in school.
As a result of her mother's efforts, Walker started school at four. She was
a bright pupil but when she was eight she suffered a traumatic accident.

One of her brothers shot her in the eye, blinding it and disfiguring her. The accident caused the little girl to turn in on herself. As she grew up, Walker was always painfully self-conscious about her eye until, as she describes in 'Beauty: When the Other Dancer is the Self', her small daughter helped her to come to terms with it.

In 1961, Walker left home. She took with her the gifts her mother had given her – a suitcase for independence, a typewriter for creativity and a sewing-machine for self-sufficiency. She entered Spelman College, Atlanta on a scholarship. The college, dedicated to turning out young ladies, is described in Walker's novel *Meridian* (1976). Walker began to participate in the civil rights movement and she visited Finland in the summer of 1962 as a delegate to the World Youth Peace Festival. In August 1963 she participated in the March on Washington for Jobs and Freedom where she was part of the crowd listening to Martin Luther King deliver his 'I Have a Dream' speech. In 1963 she was offered a scholarship to the prestigious Sarah Lawrence College in New York from where she graduated in 1965.

Walker moved to Mississippi to work for the civil rights movement and met and married the white civil rights lawyer Mel Leventhal. They became the first legally married interracial couple in Jackson and, as such, they suffered considerable harassment and threats. Their daughter, Rebecca, was born in 1969. Walker settled down to a life of teaching and writing. In 1968 her first poetry collection, *Once*, was published and in 1970 her first novel, *The Third Life of Grange Copeland*, appeared to favourable reviews. She taught black studies at Jackson State University and in 1972 she began teaching black women's writing at Wellesley College.

In 1973 Walker's collection of thirteen stories, *In Love and Trouble*, was published to great acclaim. In 1974 she was offered the post of editor of *Ms* magazine and she and her family moved to New York. In 1976 her civil rights novel *Meridian* was published and she was offered a prestigious Guggenheim Fellowship – that same year she was amicably divorced from Leventhal. With her companion, Robert

Allen, she moved to California where she still lives.

Motherhood and the difficulties of mothering are themes which run through much of Alice Walker's work. Her essay, 'A Child of One's Own' (1979), recounts her struggle to combine motherhood with writing. She decided early on, much to her mother's disapproval, that in order to fulfill her vocation she could only have one child. Walker's best-selling novel *The Color Purple* (1982), shows the violence inflicted on black women and children and their powerlessness to resist. Celie's children are taken away from her, as are Sophie's when she is imprisoned by whites. *The Color Purple* established Walker's international reputation and won the Pulitzer Prize. Motherhood continues to feature in her later work. *The Temple of my Familiar* (1989) laments the loss of Africa's ancient matriarchal religions and cultures. But, though she celebrates black women's strong maternal inheritance, Walker never sentimentalises motherhood nor underestimates the difficulties of the mothering task.

Primary reading

Walker, A. 1976/1982 *Meridian*, London: The Women's Press.

Walker, A. 1983 *In Search of Our Mothers' Gardens. Womanist Prose*, New York and London: Harcourt Brace.

Walker, A. 1983 *The Color Purple*, London: The Women's Press.

Walker, A. 1989/1990 *The Temple of My Familiar*, Harmondsworth: Penguin.

Walker, A. 1992 *Possessing the Secret of Joy*, New York: Simon & Schuster.

Walker, A. 1994 *The Complete Stories*, London: The Women's Press.

Further reading

Christian, B. 1985 'An Angle of Seeing: Motherhood in Buchi Emecheta's *The Joys of Motherhood* and Alice Walker's *Meridian*' in *Black Feminist Criticism: Perspectives on Black Women Writers*, New York: Pergamon Press.

In Search of Our Mothers' Gardens

From Alice Walker, *In Search of Our Mothers' Gardens. Womanist Prose*, New York and London: Harcourt Brace, 1983, pp. 238–43.

I described her own nature and temperament. Told how they needed a larger life for their expression. . . . I pointed out that in lieu of proper channels, her emotions had overflowed into paths that dissipated them. I talked, beautifully I thought, about an art that would be born, an art that would open the way for women the likes of her. I asked her to hope, and build up an inner life against the coming of that day. . . . I sang, with a strange quiver in my voice, a promise song.

— *Jean Toomer, 'Avey,'*
CANE

The poet speaking to a prostitute who falls asleep while he's talking –

When the poet Jean Toomer walked through the South in the early twenties, he discovered a curious thing: black women whose spirituality was so intense, so deep, so *unconscious*, that they were themselves unaware of the richness they held. They stumbled blindly through their lives: creatures so abused and mutilated in body, so dimmed and confused by pain, that they considered themselves unworthy even of hope. In the selfless abstractions their bodies became to the men who used them, they became more than 'sexual objects,' more even than mere women: they became 'Saints.' Instead of being perceived as whole persons, their bodies became shrines: what was thought to be their minds became temples suitable for worship. These crazy Saints stared out at the world, wildly, like lunatics – or quietly, like suicides; and the 'God' that was in their gaze was as mute as a great stone.

Who were these Saints? These crazy, loony, pitiful women?

Some of them, without a doubt, were our mothers and grand-mothers.

In the still heat of the post-Reconstruction South, this is how they seemed to Jean Toomer: exquisite butterflies trapped in an evil honey, toiling away their lives in an era, a century, that did not acknowledge them, except as 'the *mule* of the world.' They dreamed dreams that no one knew – not even themselves, in any coherent fashion – and saw visions no one could understand. They wandered or sat about the countryside crooning lullabies to ghosts, and drawing the mother of Christ in charcoal on courthouse walls.

They forced their minds to desert their bodies and their striving spirits sought to rise, like frail whirlwinds from the hard red clay. And when those frail whirlwinds fell, in scattered particles, upon the ground, no one mourned. Instead, men lit candles to celebrate the emptiness that remained, as people do who enter a beautiful but vacant space to resurrect a God.

Our mothers and grandmothers, some of them: moving to music not yet written. And they waited.

They waited for a day when the unknown thing that was in them would be made known; but guessed, somehow in their darkness, that on the day of their revelation they would be long dead. Therefore to Toomer they walked, and even ran, in slow motion. For they were going nowhere immediate, and the future was not yet within their grasp. And men took our mothers and grandmothers, 'but got no pleasure from it.' So complex was their passion and their calm.

To Toomer, they lay vacant and fallow as autumn fields, with harvest time never in sight: and he saw them enter loveless marriages, without joy; and become prostitutes, without resistance; and become mothers of children, without fulfillment.

For these grandmothers and mothers of ours were not Saints, but Artists; driven to a numb and bleeding madness by the springs of creativity in them for which there was no release. They were Creators, who lived lives of spiritual waste, because they were so rich in spirituality – which is the basis of Art – that the strain of enduring their unused and unwanted talent drove them insane. Throwing away this spirituality was their pathetic attempt to lighten the soul to a weight their work-worn, sexually abused bodies could bear.

What did it mean for a black woman to be an artist in our grandmothers' time? In our great-grandmothers' day? It is a question with an answer cruel enough to stop the blood.

Did you have a genius of a great-great-grandmother who died under some ignorant and depraved white overseer's lash? Or was she required to bake biscuits for a lazy backwater tramp, when she cried out in her soul to paint watercolors of sunsets, or the rain falling on the green and peaceful pasturelands? Or was her body broken and forced to bear children (who were more often than not sold away from her) – eight, ten, fifteen, twenty children – when her one joy was the thought of modeling heroic figures of rebellion, in stone or clay?

How was the creativity of the black woman kept alive, year after year and century after century, when for most of the years black people have been in America, it was a punishable crime for a black person to read or write? And the freedom to paint, to sculpt, to expand the mind with action did not exist. Consider, if you can bear to imagine it, what might have been the result if singing, too, had been forbidden by law. Listen to the voices of Bessie Smith, Billie Holiday, Nina Simone, Roberta Flack, and Aretha Franklin, among others, and imagine those voices muzzled for life. Then you may begin to comprehend the lives of our 'crazy,' 'Sainted' mothers and grandmothers. The agony of the lives of women who might have been Poets, Novelists, Essayists, and Short-Story Writers (over a period of centuries), who died with their real gifts stifled within them.

And, if this were the end of the story, we would have cause to cry out in my paraphrase of Okot p'Bitek's great poem:

O, my clanswomen
Let us all cry together!
Come,
Let us mourn the death of our mother,
The death of a Queen
The ash that was produced
By a great fire!
O, this homestead is utterly dead
Close the gates
With *lacari* thorns,
For our mother
The creator of the Stool is lost!
And all the young women
Have perished in the wilderness!

But this is not the end of the story, for all the young women – our mothers and grandmothers, *ourselves* – have not perished in the wilderness. And if we ask ourselves why, and search for and find the answer, we will know beyond all efforts to erase it from our minds, just exactly who, and of what, we black American women are.

One example, perhaps the most pathetic, most misunderstood one, can provide a backdrop for our mothers' work: Phillis Wheatley, a slave in the 1700s.

Virginia Woolf, in her book *A Room of One's Own*, wrote that in order for a woman to write fiction she must have two things, certainly: a room of her own (with key and lock) and enough money to support herself.

What then are we to make of Phillis Wheatley, a slave, who owned not even herself? This sickly, frail black girl who required a servant of her own at times – her health was so precarious – and who, had she been white, would have been easily considered the intellectual superior of all the women and most of the men in the society of her day.

Virginia Woolf wrote further, speaking of course not of our Phillis, that 'any woman born with a great gift in the sixteenth century [insert 'eighteenth century,' insert 'black woman,' insert 'born or made a slave'] would certainly have gone crazed, shot herself, or ended her days in some lonely cottage outside the village, half witch, half wizard [insert 'Saint'], feared and mocked at. For it needs little skill and psychology to be sure that a highly gifted girl who had tried to use her gift for poetry would have been so thwarted and hindered by contrary instincts [add 'chains, guns, the lash, the ownership of one's body by someone else, submission to an alien religion'], that she must have lost her health and sanity to a certainty.'

The key words, as they relate to Phillis, are 'contrary instincts.' For when we read the poetry of Phillis Wheatley – as when we read the novels of Nella Larsen or the oddly false-sounding autobiography of that freest of all black women writers, Zora Hurston – evidence of 'contrary instincts' is everywhere. Her loyalties were completely divided, as was, without question, her mind.

But how could this be otherwise? Captured at seven, a slave of wealthy, doting whites who instilled in her the 'savagery' of the Africa they 'rescued' her from . . . one wonders if she was even able to remember her homeland as she had known it, or as it really was.

Yet, because she did try to use her gift for poetry in a world that made her a slave, she was 'so thwarted and hindered by . . . contrary instincts, that she . . . lost her health. . . .' In the last years of her brief life, burdened not only with the need to express her gift but also with a penniless, friendless 'freedom' and several small children for whom she was forced to do strenuous work to feed, she lost her health, certainly. Suffering from malnutrition and neglect and who knows what mental agonies, Phillis Wheatley died.

So torn by 'contrary instincts' was black, kidnapped, enslaved Phillis that her description of 'the Goddess' – as she poetically called the Liberty she did not have – is ironically, cruelly humorous. And, in fact, has held Phillis up to ridicule for more than a century. It is usually read prior to hanging Phillis's memory as that of a fool. She wrote:

> The Goddess comes, she moves divinely fair,
> Olive and laurel binds her *golden* hair.
> Wherever shines this native of the skies,
> Unnumber'd charms and recent graces rise. [My italics]

It is obvious that Phillis, the slave, combed the 'Goddess's' hair every morning; prior, perhaps, to bringing in the milk, or fixing her mistress's lunch. She took her imagery from the one thing she saw elevated above all others.

With the benefit of hindsight we ask, 'How could she?'

But at last, Phillis, we understand. No more snickering when your stiff, struggling, ambivalent lines are forced on us. We know now that you were not an idiot or a traitor; only a sickly little black girl, snatched from your home and country and made a slave; a woman who still struggled to sing the song that was your gift, although in a land of barbarians who praised you for your bewildered tongue. It is not so much what you sang, as that you kept alive, in so many of our ancestors, *the notion of song*.

Black women are called, in the folklore that so aptly identifies one's status in society, 'the *mule* of the world,' because we have been handed the burdens that everyone else – *everyone* else – refused to carry. We have also been called 'Matriarchs,' 'Superwomen,' and 'Mean and Evil Bitches.' Not to mention 'Castraters' and 'Sapphire's Mama.' When we have pleaded for understanding, our character has been distorted; when we have asked for simple caring, we have been handed empty inspirational appellations, then stuck in the farthest corner. When we have asked for love, we have been given children. In short, even our plainer gifts, our labors of fidelity and love, have been knocked down our throats. To be an artist and a black woman, even today, lowers our status in many respects, rather than raises it: and yet, artists we will be.

Therefore we must fearlessly pull out of ourselves and look at and identify with our lives the living creativity some of our great-grand-mothers were not allowed to know. I stress *some* of them because it is well known that the majority of our great-grandmothers knew, even without 'knowing' it, the reality of their spirituality, even if they didn't recognize it beyond what happened in the singing at church – and they never had any intention of giving it up.

How they did it – those millions of black women who were not Phillis Wheatley, or Lucy Terry or Frances Harper or Zora Hurston or Nella Larsen or Bessie Smith; or Elizabeth Catlett, or Katherine Dunham, either – brings me to the title of this essay, 'In Search of Our Mothers' Gardens,' which is a personal account that is yet shared, in its theme and its meaning, by all of us. I found, while thinking about the far-reaching world of the creative black woman, that often the truest answer to a question that really matters can be found very close.

In the late 1920s my mother ran away from home to marry my father. Marriage, if not running away, was expected of seventeen-year-old girls. By the time she was twenty, she had two children and was pregnant with a third. Five children later, I was born. And this is how I came to know my mother: she seemed a large, soft, loving-eyed woman who was rarely impatient in our home. Her quick, violent temper was on view only a few times a year, when she battled with the white landlord who had the misfortune to suggest to her that her children did not need to go to school.

She made all the clothes we wore, even my brothers' over-alls. She made all the towels and sheets we used. She spent the summers canning vegetables and fruits. She spent the winter evenings making quilts enough to cover all our beds.

During the 'working' day, she labored beside – not behind – my father in the fields. Her day began before sunup, and did not end until late at night. There was never a moment for her to sit down, undisturbed, to unravel her own private thoughts; never a time free from interruption – by work or the noisy inquiries of her many children. And yet, it is to my mother – and all our mothers who were not famous – that I went in search of the secret of what has fed that muzzled and often mutilated, but vibrant, creative spirit that the black woman has inherited, and that pops out in wild and unlikely places to this day.

But when, you will ask, did my overworked mother have time to know or care about feeding the creative spirit?

The answer is so simple that many of us have spent years discovering it. We have constantly looked high, when we should have looked high – and low.

For example: in the Smithsonian Institution in Washington, D.C., there hangs a quilt unlike any other in the world. In fanciful, inspired, and yet simple and identifiable figures, it portrays the story of the Crucifixion. It is considered rare, beyond price. Though it follows no known pattern of quilt-making, and though it is made of bits and pieces of worthless rags, it is obviously the work of a person of powerful imagination and deep spiritual feeling. Below this quilt I saw a note that says it was made by 'an anonymous Black woman in Alabama, a hundred years ago.'

If we could locate this 'anonymous' black woman from Alabama, she would turn out to be one of our grandmothers – an artist who left her mark in the only materials she could afford, and in the only medium her position in society allowed her to use.

As Virginia Woolf wrote further, in A Room of One's Own:

Yet genius of a sort must have existed among women as it must have existed among the working class. [Change this to 'slaves' and 'the wives and daughters of sharecroppers.'] Now and again an

Emily Brontë or a Robert Burns [change this to 'a Zora Hurston or a Richard Wright'] blazes out and proves its presence. But certainly it never got itself on to paper. When, however, one reads of a witch being ducked, of a woman possessed by devils [or 'Sainthood'], of a wise woman selling herbs [our root workers], or even a very remarkable man who had a mother, then I think we are on the track of a lost novelist, a suppressed poet, of some mute and inglorious Jane Austen. . . . Indeed, I would venture to guess that Anon, who wrote so many poems without signing them, was often a woman . . .

And so our mothers and grandmothers have, more often than not anonymously, handed on the creative spark, the seed of the flower they themselves never hoped to see: or like a sealed letter they could not plainly read.

And so it is, certainly, with my own mother. Unlike 'Ma' Rainey's songs, which retained their creator's name even while blasting forth from Bessie Smith's mouth, no song or poem will bear my mother's name. Yet so many of the stories that I write, that we all write, are my mother's stories. Only recently did I fully realize this: that through years of listening to my mother's stories of her life, I have absorbed not only the stories themselves, but something of the manner in which she spoke, something of the urgency that involves the knowledge that her stories – like her life – must be recorded. It is probably for this reason that so much of what I have written is about characters whose counterparts in real life are so much older than I am.

But the telling of these stories, which came from my mother's lips as naturally as breathing, was not the only way my mother showed herself as an artist. For stories, too, were subject to being distracted, to dying without conclusion. Dinners must be started, and cotton must be gathered before the big rains. The artist that was and is my mother showed itself to me only after many years. This is what I finally noticed:

Like Mem, a character in *The Third Life of Grange Copeland*, my mother adorned with flowers whatever shabby house we were forced to live in. And not just your typical straggly country stand of zinnias, either. She planted ambitious gardens – and still does – with over fifty different varieties of plants that bloom profusely from early March until late November. Before she left home for the fields, she watered her flowers, chopped up the grass, and laid out new beds. When she returned from the fields she might divide clumps of bulbs, dig a cold pit, uproot and replant roses, or prune branches from her taller bushes or trees – until night came and it was too dark to see.

Whatever she planted grew as if by magic, and her fame as a grower of flowers spread over three counties. Because of her creativity with her flowers, even my memories of poverty are seen through a screen of blooms – sunflowers, petunias, roses, dahlias, forsythia, spirea, delphiniums, verbena . . . and on and on.

And I remember people coming to my mother's yard to be given cuttings from her flowers; I hear again the praise showered on her because whatever rocky soil she landed on, she turned into a garden. A garden so brilliant with colors, so original in its design, so magnificent with life and creativity, that to this day people drive by our house in Georgia – perfect strangers and imperfect strangers – and ask to stand or walk among my mother's art.

I notice that it is only when my mother is working in her flowers that she is radiant, almost to the point of being invisible – except as Creator: hand and eye. She is involved in work her soul must have. Ordering the universe in the image of her personal conception of Beauty.

Her face, as she prepares the Art that is her gift, is a legacy of respect she leaves to me, for all that illuminates and cherishes life. She has handed down respect for the possibilities – and the will to grasp them.

For her, so hindered and intruded upon in so many ways, being an artist has still been a daily part of her life. This ability to hold on, even in very simple ways, is work black women have done for a very long time.

This poem is not enough, but it is something, for the woman who literally covered the holes in our walls with sunflowers:

> They were women then
> My mama's generation
> Husky of voice – Stout of
> Step
> With fists as well as
> Hands
> How they battered down
> Doors
> And ironed
> Starched white
> Shirts
> How they led
> Armies
> Headragged Generals
> Across mined
> Fields
> Booby-trapped
> Kitchens
> To discover books
> Desks
> A place for us
> How they knew what we
> *Must* know
> Without knowing a page
> Of it
> Themselves.

Guided by my heritage of a love of beauty and a respect for strength – in search of my mother's garden, I found my own.

And perhaps in Africa over two hundred years ago, there was just such a mother; perhaps she painted vivid and daring decorations in oranges and yellows and greens on the walls of her hut; perhaps she sang – in a voice like Roberta Flack's – *sweetly* over the compounds of her village; perhaps she wove the most stunning mats or told the most ingenious stories of all the village storytellers. Perhaps she was herself a poet – though only her daughter's name is signed to the poems that we know.

Perhaps Phillis Wheatley's mother was also an artist. Perhaps in more than Phillis Wheatley's biological life is her mother's signature made clear.

Maya Angelou (1928–)

―――――――――――――――――――――――

Marguerite Johnson (she was given the name Maya by her brother) was born in St Louis, Missouri. Her father was a hotel doorman and later a dietician with the navy, her mother had trained as a nurse. After her parents' divorce she was sent, aged three and wearing an identification tag round her wrist, with her brother (aged four) in a train across America to her paternal grandmother in Stamps, Arkansas.

Maya Angelou has published five volumes of autobiography which have been linked to the tradition of black slave narratives. In the first volume, *I Know Why the Caged Bird Sings* (1969), Angelou describes growing up in Stamps during the Depression. Stamps was a town so segregated that many black children didn't know what white people looked like (Angelou 1969/84: 24–5). Her grandmother, a strict and devout woman, owned a general store and Angelou describes reading and serving in the store.

When she was seven her father appeared, without warning, to take her and her brother back to their mother. Angelou was terrified. She describes the meeting with her mother: 'My mother's beauty literally assailed me . . . I was struck dumb. I knew immediately why she had sent me away. She was too beautiful to have children. I had never seen a woman as pretty as she who was called "Mother" ' (Angelou 1969/1984: 58; ellipsis mine).

Her mother ran a gambling saloon in St Louis. She entranced customers with her singing and dancing. Angelou remained in awe of her feisty mother and fearful of being rejected again. Then, aged eight, she was raped by her mother's boyfriend. He was tried and then released and later found beaten to death. Racked by fear and guilt, Angelou stopped speaking. She and her brother, Bailey, were returned to their grandmother in Stamps. It was there that a Mrs Bertha Flowers helped Angelou to come out of her shell by giving her books to read aloud and by encouraging her to recite poems. About this time Angelou began to write poetry herself.

In 1940 Angelou graduated as a star pupil from Lafayette County Training School and went to live with her mother in San Francisco. She became one of the few black students at the George Washington High School and won a scholarship to study drama and dance at night school. Bored with school, however, she became the first black streetcar conductor in San Francisco, winning her mother's admiration for her courage.

In 1945 Angelou graduated from high school and her son, Guy, was born, as described in the following excerpt. Her mother offered to take care of the child but, remembering her own childhood, Angelou decided she could not trust her. She earned money for herself and her son by working variously as a cook, a dancer, a brothel owner and a prostitute (see *Gather Together in My Name*, 1974). In 1952 she was married briefly to Enistasious Angelous and after the marriage broke down, began performing at the Purple Onion nightclub in San Francisco. In 1954–55 she toured internationally as a dancer in *Porgy and Bess*. This time she did leave her son with her mother.

Angelou's singing career blossomed. At the same time she began testing out her poems and stories with the Harlem Writers' Guild. She became involved in the civil rights movement and met the South African freedom fighter, Vusumzi Make, with whom she moved to Cairo in 1961. After that relationship broke up, she moved with Guy to Ghana – the first place, she told an interviewer, where she had ever felt at home (Elliot 1989: 33). She worked as a journalist and taught at the university (see *All God's Children*, 1986).

In 1965 Angelou returned to America to devote herself to her writing and with the publication in 1969 of her first volume of autobiography her fame began to grow. In 1982 she was given the prestigious post of lifetime Reynolds Professor of American Studies at Wake Forest University. In 1993 she read her poem 'On the Pulse of Morning' at the inauguration of President Clinton.

Triumphing over a difficult and often traumatic childhood, Maya Angelou has been a pioneer in many different fields. As she grew older and began to see her mother as a person separate from herself, their relationship grew closer. In 1983 she told an interviewer that her closest relationships have been with her son and her mother (Elliot 1989: 138).

Primary reading

Angelou, M. 1969/1984 *I Know Why the Caged Bird Sings*, London: Virago.

Angelou, M. 1974/1985 *Gather Together in My Name*, London: Virago.

Angelou, M. 1976 *Singin' and Swingin' and Gettin' Merry Like Christmas*, New York: Random House.

Angelou, M. 1981 *The Heart of a Woman*, New York: Random House.
Angelou, M. 1986 *All God's Children Need Travelling Shoes*, New York: Random House.

Further reading

Elliot, J. M. (ed.) 1989 *Conversations with Maya Angelou*, Mississippi: University Press of Mississippi.

I Know Why the Caged Bird Sings

From Maya Angelou, *I Know Why the Caged Bird Sings*, London: Virago, 1984, pp. 265–81.

The Well of Loneliness was my introduction to lesbianism and what I thought of as pornography. For months the book was both a treat and a threat. It allowed me to see a little of the mysterious world of the pervert. It stimulated my libido and I told myself that it was educational because it informed me of the difficulties in the secret world of the pervert. I was certain that I didn't know any perverts. Of course I ruled out the jolly sissies who sometimes stayed at our house and cooked whopping eight-course dinners while the perspiration made paths down their made-up faces. Since everyone accepted them, and more particularly since they accepted themselves, I knew that their laughter was real and that their lives were cheerful comedies, interrupted only by costume changes and freshening of make-up.

But true freaks, the 'women lovers,' captured yet strained my imagination. They were, according to the book, disowned by their families, snubbed by their friends and ostracized from every society. This bitter punishment was inflicted upon them because of a physical condition over which they had no control.

After my third reading of *The Well of Loneliness* I became a bleeding heart for the downtrodden misunderstood lesbians. I thought 'lesbian' was synonymous with hermaphrodite, and when I wasn't actively aching over their pitiful state, I was wondering how they managed simpler body functions. Did they have a choice of organs to use, and if so, did they alternate or play favorite? Or I tried to imagine how two hermaphrodites made love, and the more I pondered the more confused I became. It seemed that having two of everything other people had, and four where ordinary people just had two, would complicate matters to the point of giving up the idea of making love at all.

It was during this reflective time that I noticed how heavy my own voice had become. It droned and drummed two or three whole tones lower than my schoolmates' voices. My hands and feet were also far from being feminine and dainty. In front of the mirror I detachedly examined my body. For a sixteen-year-old my breasts were sadly undeveloped. They could only be called skin swellings, even by the kindest critic. The line from my rib cage to my knees fell straight without even a ridge to disturb its direction. Younger girls than I boasted of having to shave under their arms, but my armpits were as smooth as my face. There was also a mysterious growth developing on my body that defied explanation. It looked totally useless.

Then the question began to live under my blankets: How did lesbianism begin? What were the symptoms? The public library gave information on the finished lesbian – and that woefully sketchy – but on the growth of a lesbian, there was nothing. I did discover that the difference between hermaphrodites and lesbians was that hermaphrodites were 'born that way.' It was impossible to determine whether lesbians budded gradually, or burst into being with a suddenness that dismayed them as much as it repelled society.

I had gnawed into the unsatisfying books and into my own unstocked mind without finding a morsel of peace or understanding. And meantime, my voice refused to stay up in the higher registers where I consciously pitched it, and I had to buy my shoes in the 'old lady's comfort' section of the shoe stores.

I asked Mother.

Daddy Clidell was at the club one evening, so I sat down on the side of Mother's bed. As usual she woke completely and at once. (There is never any yawning or stretching with Vivian Baxter. She's either awake or asleep).

'Mother, I've got to talk to you . . .' It was going to kill me to have to ask her, for in the asking wouldn't it be possible that suspicion would fall on my own normality? I knew her well enough to know that if I committed almost any crime and told her the truth about it she not only wouldn't disown me but would give me her protection. But just suppose I was developing into a lesbian, how would she react? And then there was Bailey to worry about too.

'Ask me, and pass me a cigarette.' Her calmness didn't fool me for a minute. She used to say that her secret to life was that she 'hoped for the best, was prepared for the worst, so anything in between didn't come as a surprise.' That was all well and good for most things but if her only daughter was developing into a . . .

She moved over and patted the bed, 'Come on, baby, get in the bed. You'll freeze before you get your question out.'

It was better to remain where I was for the time being.

'Mother . . . my pocketbook . . .'

'Ritie, do you mean your vagina? Don't use those Southern terms. There's nothing wrong with the word 'vagina.' It's a clinical description. Now, what's wrong with it?'

The smoke collected under the bed lamp, then floated out to be free in the room. I was deathly sorry that I had begun to ask her anything.

'Well? . . . Well? Have you got crabs?'

Since I didn't know what they were, that puzzled me. I thought I might have them and it wouldn't go well for my side if I said I didn't. On the other hand, I just might not have them, and suppose I lied and said I did?

'I don't know, Mother.'

'Do you itch? Does your vagina itch?' She leaned on one elbow and jabbed out her cigarette.

'No, Mother.'

'Then you don't have crabs. If you had them, you'd tell the world.'

I wasn't sorry or glad not to have them, but made a mental note to look up 'crabs' in the library on my next trip.

She looked at me closely, and only a person who knew her face well could have perceived the muscles relaxing and interpreted this as an indication of concern.

'You don't have a venereal disease, do you?'

The question wasn't asked seriously, but knowing Mother I was shocked at the idea. 'Why, Mother, of course not. That's a terrible question.' I was ready to go back to my room and wrestle alone with my worries.

'Sit down, Ritie. Pass me another cigarette.' For a second it looked as if she was thinking about laughing. That would really do it. If she laughed, I'd never tell her anything else. Her laughter would make it easier to accept my social isolation and human freakishness. But she wasn't even smiling. Just slowly pulling in the smoke and holding it in puffed cheeks before blowing it out.

'Mother, something is growing on my vagina.'

There, it was out. I'd soon know whether I was to be her ex-daughter or if she'd put me in hospital for an operation.

'Where on your vagina, Marguerite?'

Uh-huh. It was bad all right. Not 'Ritie' or 'Maya' or 'Baby.' 'Marguerite.'

'On both sides. Inside.' I couldn't add that they were fleshy skin flaps that had been growing for months down there. She'd have to pull that out of me.

'Ritie, go get me that big *Webster's* and then bring me a bottle of beer.'

Suddenly, it wasn't all that serious. I was 'Ritie' again, and she just asked for beer. If it had been as awful as I anticipated, she'd have ordered Scotch and water. I took her the huge dictionary that she had bought as a birthday gift for Daddy Clidell and laid it on the bed. The weight forced a side of the mattress down and Mother twisted her bed lamp to beam down on the book.

When I returned from the kitchen and poured her beer, as she had taught Bailey and me beer should be poured, she patted the bed.

'Sit down, baby. Read this.' Her fingers guided my eyes to VULVA. I began to read. She said, 'Read it out loud.'

It was all very clear and normal-sounding. She drank the beer as I read, and when I had finished she explained it in every-day terms. My relief melted the fears and they liquidly stole down my face.

Mother shot up and put her arms around me. 'There's nothing to worry about, baby. It happens to every woman. It's just human nature.'

It was all right then to unburden my heavy, heavy heart. I cried into the crook of my arm. 'I thought maybe I was turning into a lesbian.'

Her patting of my shoulder slowed to a still and she leaned away from me.

'A lesbian? Where the hell did you get that idea?'

'Those things growing on my . . . vagina, and my voice is too deep and my feet are big, and I have no hips or breasts or anything. And my legs are so skinny.'

Then she did laugh. I knew immediately that she wasn't laughing at me. Or rather that she was laughing at me, but it was something about me that pleased her. The laugh choked a little on the smoke in its way, but finally broke through cleanly. I had to give a small laugh too, although I wasn't tickled at all. But it's mean to watch someone enjoy something and not show your understanding of their enjoyment.

When she finished with the laughter, she laid it down a peal at a time and turned to me, wiping her eyes.

'I made arrangements, a long time ago, to have a boy and a girl. Bailey is my boy and you are my girl. The Man upstairs, He don't make mistakes. He gave you to me to be my girl and that's just what you are. Now, go wash your face, have a glass of milk and go back to bed.'

I did as she said but I soon discovered my new assurance wasn't large enough to fill the gap left by my old uneasiness. It rattled around in my mind like a dime in a tin cup. I hoarded it preciously, but less than two weeks later it became totally worthless.

A classmate of mine, whose mother had rooms for herself and her daughter in a ladies' residence, had stayed out beyond closing time. She telephoned me to ask if she could sleep at my house. Mother gave her permission, providing my friend telephoned her mother from our house.

When she arrived, I got out of bed and we went to the upstairs kitchen to make hot chocolate. In my room we shared mean gossip about our friends, giggled over boys and whined about school and the tedium of life. The unusualness of having someone sleep in my bed (I'd never slept with anyone except my grandmothers) and the frivolous laughter in the middle of the night made me forget simple courtesies. My friend had to remind me that she had nothing to sleep in. I gave her one of my gowns, and without curiosity or interest I watched her pull off her clothes. At none of the early stages of undressing was I in the least conscious of her body. And then suddenly, for the briefest eye span, I saw her breasts. I was stunned.

They were shaped like light-brown falsies in the five- and-ten-cent store, but they were real. They made all the nude paintings I had seen in museums come to life. In a word they were beautiful. A universe divided what she had from what I had. She was a woman.

My gown was too snug for her and much too long, and when she wanted to laugh at her ridiculous image I found that humor had left me without a promise to return.

Had I been older I might have thought that I was moved by both an esthetic sense of beauty and the pure emotion of envy. But those possibilities did not occur to me when I needed them. All I knew was that I had been moved by looking at a woman's breasts. So all the calm and casual words of Mother's explanation a few weeks earlier and the clinical terms of Noah Webster did not alter the fact that in a fundamental way there was something queer about me.

I somersaulted deeper into my snuggery of misery. After a thorough self-examination, in the light of all I had read and heard about dykes and bulldaggers, I reasoned that I had none of the obvious traits – I didn't wear trousers, or have big shoulders or go in for sports, or walk like a man or even want to touch a woman. I wanted to be a woman, but that seemed to me to be a world to which I was to be eternally refused entrance.

What I needed was a boyfriend. A boyfriend would clarify my position to the world and, even more important, to myself. A boyfriend's acceptance of me would guide me into that strange and exotic land of frills and femininity.

Among my associates, there were no takers. Understandably the boys of my age and social group were captivated by the yellow- or light-brown-skinned girls, with hairy legs and smooth little lips, and whose hair 'hung down like horses' manes.' And even those sought-after girls were asked to 'give it up or tell where it is.' They were reminded in a popular song of the times, 'If you can't smile and say yes, please don't cry and say no.' If the pretties were expected to make the supreme sacrifice in order to 'belong,' what could the unattractive female do? She who had been skimming along on life's turning but never-changing periphery had to be ready to be a 'buddy' by day and maybe by night. She was called upon to be generous only if the pretty girls were unavailable.

I believe most plain girls are virtuous because of the scarcity of opportunity to be otherwise. They shield themselves with an aura of unavailableness (for which after a time they begin to take credit) largely as a defense tactic.

In my particular case, I could not hide behind the curtain of voluntary goodness. I was being crushed by two unrelenting forces: the uneasy suspicion that I might not be a normal female and my newly awakening sexual appetite.

I decided to take matters into my own hands. (An unfortunate but apt phrase.)

Up the hill from our house, and on the same side of the street, lived two handsome brothers. They were easily the most eligible young men in the neighborhood. If I was going to venture into sex, I saw no reason why I shouldn't make my experiment with the best of the lot. I didn't really expect to capture either brother on a permanent basis, but I thought if I could hook one temporarily I might be able to work the relationship into something more lasting.

I planned a chart for seduction with surprise as my opening ploy. One evening as I walked up the hill suffering from youth's vague malaise (there was simply nothing to do), the brother I had chosen came walking directly into my trap.

'Hello, Marguerite.' He nearly passed me.

I put the plan into action. 'Hey.' I plunged, 'Would you like to have a sexual intercourse with me?' Things were going according to the chart. His mouth hung open like a garden gate. I had the advantage and so I pressed it.

'Take me somewhere.'

His response lacked dignity, but in fairness to him I admit that I had left him little chance to be suave.

He asked, 'You mean, you're going to give me some trim?'

I assured him that that was exactly what I was about to give him. Even as the scene was being enacted I realized the imbalance in his values. He thought I was giving him something, and the fact of the matter was that it was my intention to take something from him. His good looks and popularity had made him so inordinately conceited that they blinded him to that possibility.

We went to a furnished room occupied by one of his friends, who understood the situation immediately and got his coat and left us alone. The seductee quickly turned off the lights. I would have preferred them left on, but didn't want to appear more aggressive than I had been already. If that was possible.

I was excited rather than nervous, and hopeful instead of frightened. I had not considered how physical an act of seduction would be. I had anticipated long soulful tongued kisses and gentle caresses. But there was no romance in the knee which forced my legs, nor in the rub of hairy skin on my chest.

Unredeemed by shared tenderness, the time was spent in laborious gropings, pullings, yankings and jerkings.

Not one word was spoken.

My partner showed that our experience had reached its climax by getting up abruptly, and my main concern was how to get home quickly. He may have sensed that he had been used, or his disinterest may have been an indication that I was less than gratifying. Neither possibility bothered me.

Outside on the street we left each other with little more than 'Okay, see you around.'

Thanks to Mr Freeman nine years before, I had had no pain of entry to endure, and because of the absence of romantic involvement neither of us felt much had happened.

At home I reviewed the failure and tried to evaluate my new position. I had had a man. I had been had. I not only didn't enjoy it, but my normalcy was still a question.

What happened to the moonlight-on-the-prairie feeling? Was there something so wrong with me that I couldn't share a sensation that made poets gush out rhyme after rhyme, that made Richard Arlen brave the Arctic wastes and Veronica Lake betray the entire free world?

There seemed to be no explanation for my private infirmity, but being a product (is 'victim' a better word?) of the Southern Negro upbringing, I decided that I 'would understand it all better by-and-by.' I went to sleep.

Three weeks later, having thought very little of the strange and strangely empty night, I found myself pregnant.

The world had ended, and I was the only person who knew it. People walked along the streets as if the pavements hadn't all crumbled beneath their feet. They pretended to breathe in and out while all the time I knew the air had been sucked away in a monstrous inhalation from God Himself. I alone was suffocating in the nightmare.

The little pleasure I was able to take from the fact that if I could have a baby I obviously wasn't a lesbian was crowded into my mind's tiniest corner by the massive pushing in of fear, guilt, and self-revulsion.

For eons, it seemed, I had accepted my plight as the hapless, put-upon victim of fate and the Furies, but this time I had to face the fact that I had brought my new catastrophe upon myself. How was I to blame the innocent man whom I had lured into making love to me? In order to be profoundly dishonest, a person must have one of two qualities: either he is unscrupulously ambitious, or he is unswervingly egocentric. He must believe that for his ends to be served all things and people can justifiably be shifted about, or that he is the center not only of his own world but of the worlds which others inhabit. I had neither element in my personality, so I hefted the burden of pregnancy at sixteen onto my own shoulders where it belonged. Admittedly, I staggered under the weight.

I finally sent a letter to Bailey, who was at sea with the merchant marine. He wrote back, and he cautioned me against telling Mother of my condition. We both knew her to be violently opposed to abortions, and she would very likely order me to quit school. Bailey suggested that if I quit school before getting my high school diploma I'd find it nearly impossible to return.

The first three months, while I was adapting myself to the fact of pregnancy (I didn't really link pregnancy to the possibility of my having a baby until weeks before my confinement), were a hazy period in which days seemed to lie just below the water level, never emerging fully.

Fortunately, Mother was tied up tighter than Dick's hatband in the weave of her own life. She noticed me, as usual, out of the corner of her existence. As long as I was healthy, clothed and smiling she felt no need to focus her attention on me. As always, her major concern was to live the life given to her, and her children were expected to do the same. And to do it without too much brouhaha.

Under her loose scrutiny I grew more buxom, and my brown skin smoothed and tight-pored, like pancakes fried on an unoiled skillet. And still she didn't suspect. Some years before, I had established a code which never varied. I didn't lie. It was understood that I didn't lie because I was too proud to be caught and forced to admit that I was capable of a less than Olympian action. Mother must have concluded that since I was above out-and-out lying I was also beyond deceit. She was deceived.

All my motions focalized on pretending to be that guileless schoolgirl who had nothing more wearying to think about than mid-term exams. Strangely enough, I very nearly caught the essence of teenage capriciousness as I played the role. Except that there were times when physically I couldn't deny to myself that something very important was taking place in my body.

Mornings, I never knew if I would have to jump off the streetcar one step ahead of the warm sea of nausea that threatened to sweep me away. On solid ground, away from the ship-motioned vehicle and the smell of hands coated with recent breakfasts, I regained my balance and waited for the next trolley.

School recovered its lost magic. For the first time since Stamps, information was exciting for itself alone. I burrowed myself into caves of facts, and found delight in the logical resolutions of mathematics.

I credit my new reactions (although I didn't know at the time that I had learned anything from them) to the fact that during what surely must have been a critical period I was not dragged down by hope-lessness. Life had a conveyor-belt quality. It went on unpursued and unpursuing, and my only thought was to remain erect, and keep my secret along with my balance.

Midway along to delivery, Bailey came home and brought me a spun-silver bracelet from South America, Thomas Wolfe's *Look Home-ward, Angel*, and a slew of new dirty jokes.

As my sixth month approached, Mother left San Francisco for Alaska. She was to open a night club and planned to stay three or four months until it got on its feet. Daddy Clidell was to look after me but I was more or less left on my own recognizance and under the unsteady gaze of our lady roomers.

Mother left the city amid a happy and cheerful send-off party (after all how many Negroes were in Alaska?), and I felt treacherous allowing her to go without informing her that she was soon to be a grandmother.

Two days after V-Day, I stood with the San Francisco Summer School class at Mission High School and received my diploma. That evening, in the bosom of the now-dear family home I uncoiled my fearful secret and in a brave gesture left a note on Daddy Clidell's bed. It read: *Dear Parents, I am sorry to bring this disgrace on the family, but I am pregnant. Marguerite.*

The confusion that ensued when I explained to my stepfather that I expected to deliver the baby in three weeks, more or less, was reminiscent of a Molière comedy. Except that it was funny only years later. Daddy Clidell told Mother that I was 'three weeks gone.' Mother, regarding me as a woman for the first time, said indignantly, 'She's more than any three weeks.' They both ac-cepted the fact that I was further along than they had first been told but found it nearly impossible to believe that I had carried a baby, eight months and one week, without their being any the wiser.

Mother asked, 'Who is the boy?' I told her. She recalled him, faintly.

'Do you want to marry him?'

'No.'

'Does he want to marry you?' The father had stopped speaking to me during my fourth month.

'No.'

'Well, that's that. No use ruining three lives.' There was no overt or subtle condemnation. She was Vivian Baxter Jackson. Hoping for the best, prepared for the worst, and unsurprised by anything in between.

Daddy Clidell assured me that I had nothing to worry about. That 'women been gittin' pregnant ever since Eve ate that apple.' He sent one of his waitresses to I. Magnin's to buy maternity dresses for me. For the next two weeks I whirled around the city going to doctors, taking vitamin shots and pills, buying clothes for the baby, and except for the rare moments alone, enjoying the imminent blessed event.

After a short labor, and without too much pain (I decided that the pain of delivery was overrated), my son was born. Just as gratefulness was confused in my mind with love, so possession became mixed up with motherhood. I had a baby. He was beautiful and mine. Totally mine. No one had bought him for me. No one had helped me endure the sickly gray months. I had had help in the child's conception, but no one could deny that I had had an immaculate pregnancy.

Totally my possession, and I was afraid to touch him. Home from the hospital, I sat for hours by his bassinet and absorbed his mysterious perfection. His extremities were so dainty they appeared unfinished. Mother handled him easily with the casual confidence of a baby nurse, but I dreaded being forced to change his diapers. Wasn't I famous for awkwardness? Suppose I let him slip, or put my fingers on that throbbing pulse on the top of his head?

Mother came to my bed one night bringing my three-week-old baby. She pulled the cover back and told me to get up and hold him while she put rubber sheets on my bed. She explained that he was going to sleep with me.

I begged in vain. I was sure to roll over and crush out his life or break those fragile bones. She wouldn't hear of it, and within minutes the pretty golden baby was lying on his back in the center of my bed, laughing at me.

I lay on the edge of the bed, stiff with fear, and vowed not to sleep all night long. But the eat-sleep routine I had begun in the hospital, and kept up under Mother's dictatorial command, got the better of me. I dropped off.

My shoulder was shaken gently. Mother whispered, 'Maya, wake up. But don't move.'

I knew immediately that the awakening had to do with the baby. I tensed. 'I'm awake.'

She turned the light on and said, 'Look at the baby.' My fears were so powerful I couldn't move to look at the center of the bed. She said again, 'Look at the baby.' I didn't hear sadness in her voice, and that helped me to break the bonds of terror. The baby was no longer in the center of the bed. At first I thought he had moved. But after closer investigation I found that I was lying on my stomach with my arm bent at a right angle. Under the tent of blanket, which was poled by my elbow and forearm, the baby slept touching my side.

Mother whispered, 'See, you don't have to think about doing the right thing. If you're for the right thing, then you do it without thinking.'

She turned out the light and I patted my son's body lightly and went back to sleep.

Toni Morrison (1931–)

An outstanding figure in twentieth-century literature, Toni Morrison was born Chloe Anthony Wofford in Lorain, Ohio. She was the second of four children born to working-class parents whose families had fled the poverty and racism of the South. During the Depression her father did odd jobs before securing work, like many black immigrants, in the steel mills. Morrison has described her childhood as impoverished but rich in black music, myths and lore. In different circumstances, her mother might have been a great singer (Macdonald 1998: 8). She also told ghost stories and decoded dreams (McKay 1983: 414). Morrison grew up knowing there were different ways of perceiving reality. In her essay, 'Rootedness: the Ancestor as Foundation', she explains: 'We are a very practical people, very down-to-earth, even shrewd people. But within that practicality we also accepted what I suppose could be called superstition and magic, which is another way of knowing things. But to blend those two worlds together at the same time was enhancing, not limiting' (Evans 1984: 342).

Toni Morrison attended Lorain High School, a racially integrated school, from where she graduated with honours in 1949. She went on to study English at the prestigious black university, Howard University, in Washington – at that time a segregated city. She graduated from there in 1953 and in 1955 was awarded a Masters degree at Cornell University. In order to send her daughter money for her studies, her mother took a series of 'humiliating jobs' (McKay 1983: 413).

On graduating, Morrison taught introductory English at Texas Southern University in Houston. In 1957 she returned to Howard to teach, and met Harold Morrison, a Jamaican architect. They were married in 1958 and in 1961 their first son was born. The marriage was unhappy: Morrison continued teaching and joined a writers' group. She left her husband when she was pregnant with her second child and they were later divorced. She raised her two sons Harold and Slade singlehandedly working full time and writing novels in the evenings when the children were asleep. In 1964 she joined Random House as an associate editor in Syracuse. In 1976 she was transferred to New York and became senior editor, a post she held until 1983. She has taught at the State University of New York and between 1976 and 1977 she was visiting lecturer at Yale University. In 1987 she became Robert F. Goheen Professor at Princeton University.

Toni Morrison has published seven novels to date. Her first two, *The Bluest Eye* (1970) and *Sula* (1973), focus on the difficulties of finding one's identity as an African-American woman living in a white racist society. *Beloved*, published in 1987, presents the untold story of the black slave mother whose slavery determines her motherhood. *Beloved* won the Pulitzer Prize and forms part of a trilogy with *Jazz* (1992) and *Paradise* (1998). In 1993 Morrison won the Nobel Prize for Literature, the first time an African-American had been awarded this prize.

Beloved is regarded as one of the most important texts in African-American literature to have been written in recent years. It fulfils Morrison's own description of black writing: 'I think about what black writers do as having a quality of hunger and disturbance that never ends' (McKay 1988: 429).

Primary reading

Morrison, T. 1970/1994 *The Bluest Eye*, Harmondsworth: Penguin.

Morrison, T. 1973/1982 *Sula*, Harmondsworth: Penguin.

Morrison, T. 1987/1988 *Beloved*, London: Picador.

Morrison, T. 1992 *Playing in the Dark: Whiteness and the Literary Imagination*, Cambridge, MA and London: Harvard University Press.

Further reading

Bloom, H. (ed.) 1990 *Toni Morrison*, New York and Philadelphia: Chelsea House.

Christian, B. 1985 *Black Feminist Criticism: Perspectives on Black Women Writers*, New York: Pergamon Press.

Evans, M. (ed.) 1984 *Black Women Writers (1950–1980). A Critical Evaluation*, New York: Doubleday.

Fields, K. 1989 'To Embrace Dead Strangers: Toni Morrison's *Beloved*'. In: *Mother Puzzles: Daughters and Mothers in Contemporary American Literature* M. Pearlman (ed.), New York: Greenwood Press, pp. 159–69.

Horvitz, D. 1989 'Nameless Ghosts: Possession and Dispossession in *Beloved*', *Studies in American Fiction* 17: 157–67.

Keenan, S. 1993 ' "Four Hundred Years of Silence": Myth, History, and Motherhood in Toni Morrison's *Beloved*' in *Recasting the World: Writing after Colonialism* J. White (ed.), Baltimore: Johns Hopkins University Press, pp. 45–81.

Macdonald, M. 1998 'Respect', *Observer* 29 March: 4–8.

McKay, N. 1983 'An Interview with Toni Morrison', *Contemporary Literature* 24 (4): 413–29.

Plasa, C. (ed.) 1998 *Toni Morrison: Beloved*, Cambridge: Icon Books.

Rushdy, A.H.A. 1990 'Rememory: Primal Scenes and Constructions in Toni Morrison's Novels', *Contemporary Literature* 31 (3): 300–23.

Schapiro, B. 1991 'The Bonds of Love and the Boundaries of Self in Toni Morrison's *Beloved*', *Contemporary Literature* 32 (2): 194–210.

Tate, C. (ed.) 1985 *Black Women Writers at Work*, Harpenden: Oldcastle Books.

Beloved

From Toni Morrison, *Beloved*, London: Picador, pp. 250–62.

As Denver's outside life improved, her home life deteriorated. If the whitepeople of Cincinnati had allowed Negroes into their lunatic asylum they could have found candidates in 124. Strengthened by the gifts of food, the source of which neither Sethe nor Beloved questioned, the women had arrived at a doomsday truce designed by the devil. Beloved sat around, ate, went from bed to bed. Sometimes she screamed, 'Rain! Rain!' and clawed her throat until rubies of blood opened there, made brighter by her midnight skin. Then Sethe shouted, 'No!' and knocked over chairs to get to her and wipe the jewels away. Other times Beloved curled up on the floor, her wrists between her knees, and stayed there for hours. Or she would go to the creek, stick her feet in the water and whoosh it up her legs. Afterward she would go to Sethe, run her fingers over the woman's teeth while tears slid from her wide black eyes. Then it seemed to Denver the thing was done: Beloved bending over Sethe looked the mother, Sethe the teething child, for other than those times when Beloved needed her, Sethe confined herself to a corner chair. The bigger Beloved got, the smaller Sethe became; the brighter Beloved's eyes, the more those eyes that used never to look away became slits of sleeplessness. Sethe no longer combed her hair or splashed her face with water. She sat in the chair licking her lips like a chastised child while Beloved ate up her life, took it, swelled up with it, grew taller on it. And the older woman yielded it up without a murmur.

Denver served them both. Washing, cooking, forcing, cajoling her mother to eat a little now and then, providing sweet things for Beloved as often as she could to calm her down. It was hard to know what she would do from minute to minute. When the heat got hot, she might walk around the house naked or wrapped in a sheet, her belly protruding like a winning watermelon.

Denver thought she understood the connection between her mother and Beloved: Sethe was trying to make up for the handsaw; Beloved was making her pay for it. But there would never be an end to that, and seeing her mother diminished shamed and infuriated her. Yet she knew Sethe's greatest fear was the same one Denver had in the beginning – that Beloved might leave. That before Sethe could make her understand what it meant – what it took to drag the teeth of that saw under the little chin; to feel the baby blood pump like oil in her hands; to hold her face so her head would stay on; to squeeze her so she could absorb, still, the death spasms that shot through that adored body, plump and sweet with life – Beloved might leave. Leave before Sethe could make her realize that worse than that – far worse – was what Baby Suggs died of, what Ella knew, what Stamp saw and what made Paul D tremble. That anybody white could take your whole self for anything that came to mind. Not just work, kill, or maim you, but dirty you. Dirty you so bad you couldn't like yourself anymore. Dirty you so bad you forgot who you were and couldn't think it up. And though she and others lived through and got over it, she could never let it happen to her own. The best thing she was, was her children. Whites might dirty *her* all right, but not her best thing, her beautiful, magical best thing – the part of her that was clean. No undreamable dreams about whether the headless, feetless torso hanging in the tree with a sign on it was her husband or Paul A; whether the bubbling-hot girls in the colored-school fire set by patriots included her daughter; whether a gang of whites invaded her daughter's private parts, soiled her daughter's thighs and threw her daughter out of the wagon. *She* might have to work the slaughter-house yard, but not her daughter.

And no one, nobody on this earth, would list her daughter's characteristics on the animal side of the paper. No. Oh no. Maybe Baby Suggs could worry about it, live with the likelihood of it; Sethe had refused – and refused still.

This and much more Denver heard her say from her corner chair, trying to persuade Beloved, the one and only person she felt she had to convince, that what she had done was right because it came from true love.

Beloved, her fat new feet propped on the seat of a chair in front of the one she sat in, her unlined hands resting on her stomach, looked at her. Uncomprehending everything except that Sethe was the woman who took her face away, leaving her crouching in a dark, dark place, forgetting to smile.

Her father's daughter after all, Denver decided to do the necessary. Decided to stop relying on kindness to leave something on the stump. She would hire herself out somewhere, and although she was afraid to leave Sethe and Beloved alone all day not knowing what calamity either one of them would create, she came to realize that her presence in that house had no influence on what either woman did. She kept them alive and they ignored her. Growled when they chose; sulked, explained, demanded, strutted, cowered, cried and provoked each other to the edge of violence, then over. She had begun to notice that even when Beloved was quiet, dreamy, minding her own business, Sethe got her going again. Whispering, muttering some justification, some bit of clarifying information to Beloved to explain what it had been like, and why, and how come. It was as though Sethe didn't really want forgiveness given; she wanted it refused. And Beloved helped her out.

Somebody had to be saved, but unless Denver got work, there would be no one to save, no one to come home to, and no Denver either. It was a new thought, having a self to look out for and preserve, And it might not have occurred to her if she hadn't met Nelson Lord leaving his grandmother's house as Denver entered it to pay a thank you for half a pie. All he did was smile and say, 'Take care of yourself, Denver,' but she heard it as though it were what language was made for. The last time he spoke to her his words blocked up her ears. Now they opened her mind. Weeding the garden, pulling vegetables, cooking, washing, she plotted what to do and how. The Bodwins were most likely to help since they had done it twice. Once for Baby Suggs and once for her mother. Why not the third generation as well?

She got lost so many times in the streets of Cincinnati it was noon before she arrived, though she started out at sunrise. The house sat back from the sidewalk with large windows looking out on a noisy, busy street. The Negro woman who answered the front door said, 'Yes?'

'May I come in?'

'What you want?'

'I want to see Mr. and Mrs. Bodwin.'

'Miss Bodwin. They brother and sister.'

'Oh.'

'What you want em for?'

'I'm looking for work. I was thinking they might know of some.'

'You Baby Suggs' kin, ain't you?'

'Yes, ma'am.'

'Come on in. You letting in flies.' She led Denver toward the kitchen, saying, 'First thing you have to know is what door to knock on.' But Denver only half heard her because she was stepping on something soft and blue. All around her was thick, soft and blue. Glass cases crammed full of glistening things. Books on tables and shelves. Pearl-white lamps with shiny metal bottoms. And a smell like the cologne she poured in the emerald house, only better.

'Sit down,' the woman said. 'You know my name?'

'No, ma'am.'

'Janey. Janey Wagon.'

'How do you do?'

'Fairly. I heard your mother took sick, that so?'

'Yes, ma'am.'

'Who's looking after her?'

'I am. But I have to find work.'

Janey laughed. 'You know what? I've been here since I was four-teen, and I remember like yesterday when Baby Suggs, holy, came here and sat right there where you are. Whiteman brought her. That's how she got that house you all live in. Other things, too.'

'Yes, ma'am.'

'What's the trouble with Sethe?' Janey leaned against an indoor sink and folded her arms.

It was a little thing to pay, but it seemed big to Denver. Nobody was going to help her unless she told it – told all of it. It was clear Janey wouldn't and wouldn't let her see the Bodwins otherwise. So Denver told this stranger what she hadn't told Lady Jones, in return for which Janey admitted the Bodwins needed help, although they didn't know it. She was alone there, and now that her employers were getting older, she couldn't take care of them like she used to. More and more she was required to sleep the night there. Maybe she could talk them into letting Denver do the night shift, come right after supper, say, maybe get the breakfast. That way Denver could care for Sethe in the day and earn a little something at night, how's that?

Denver had explained the girl in her house who plagued her mother as a cousin come to visit, who got sick too and bothered them both. Janey seemed more interested in Sethe's condition, and from what Denver told her it seemed the woman had lost her mind. That wasn't the Sethe she remembered. This Sethe had lost her wits, finally, as Janey knew she would – trying to do it all alone with her nose in the air. Denver squirmed under the criticism of her mother, shifting in the chair and keeping her eyes on the inside sink. Janey Wagon went on about pride until she got to Baby Suggs, for whom she had nothing but sweet words. 'I never went to those woodland services she had, but she was always nice to me. Always. Never be another like her.'

'I miss her too,' said Denver.

'Bet you do. Everybody miss her. That was a good woman.'

Denver didn't say anything else and Janey looked at her face for a while. 'Neither one of your brothers ever come back to see how you all was?'

'No, ma'am.'

'Ever hear from them?'

'No, ma'am. Nothing.'

'Guess they had a rough time in that house. Tell me, this here woman in your house. The cousin. She got any lines in her hands?'

'No,' said Denver.

'Well,' said Janey. 'I guess there's a God after all.'

The interview ended with Janey telling her to come back in a few days. She needed time to convince her employers what they needed: night help because Janey's own family needed her. 'I don't want to quit these people, but they can't have all my days and nights too.'

What did Denver have to do at night?

'Be here. In case.'

In case what?

Janey shrugged. 'In case the house burn down.' She smiled then. 'Or bad weather slop the roads so bad I can't get here early enough for them. Case late guests need serving or cleaning up after. Anything. Don't ask me what whitefolks need at night.'

'They used to be good whitefolks.'

'Oh, yeah. They good. Can't say they ain't good. I wouldn't trade them for another pair, tell you that.'

With those assurances, Denver left, but not before she had seen, sitting on a shelf by the back door, a blackboy's mouth full of money.

His head was thrown back farther than a head could go, his hands were shoved in his pockets. Bulging like moons, two eyes were all the face he had above the gaping red mouth. His hair was a cluster of raised, widely spaced dots made of nail heads. And he was on his knees. His mouth, wide as a cup, held the coins needed to pay for a delivery or some other small service, but could just as well have held buttons, pins or crab-apple jelly. Painted across the pedestal he knelt on were the words 'At Yo Service.'

The news that Janey got hold of she spread among the other coloredwomen. Sethe's dead daughter, the one whose throat she cut, had come back to fix her. Sethe was worn down, speckled, dying, spinning, changing shapes and generally bedeviled. That this daughter beat her, tied her to the bed and pulled out all her hair. It took them days to get the story properly blown up and themselves agitated and then to calm down and assess the situation. They fell into three groups: those that believed the worst; those that believed none of it; and those, like Ella, who thought it through.

'Ella. What's all this I'm hearing about Sethe?'

'Tell me it's in there with her. That's all I know.'

'The daughter? The killed one?'

'That's what they tell me.'

'How they know that's her?'

'It's sitting there. Sleeps, eats and raises hell. Whipping Sethe every day.'

'I'll be. A baby?'

'No. Grown. The age it would have been had it lived.'

'You talking about flesh?'

'I'm talking about flesh.'

'Whipping her?'

'Like she was batter.'

'Guess she had it coming.'

'Nobody got that coming.'

'But, Ella –'

'But nothing. What's fair ain't necessarily right.'

'You can't just up and kill your children.'

'No, and the children can't just up and kill the mama.'

It was Ella more than anyone who convinced the others that rescue was in order. She was a practical woman who believed there was a root either to chew or avoid for every ailment. Cogitation, as she called it, clouded things and prevented action. Nobody loved her and she wouldn't have liked it if they had, for she considered love a serious disability. Her puberty was spent in a house where she was shared by father and son, whom she called 'the lowest yet.' It was 'the lowest yet' who gave her a disgust for sex and against whom she measured all atrocities. A killing, a kidnap, a rape – whatever, she listened and nodded. Nothing compared to 'the lowest yet.' She understood Sethe's rage in the shed twenty years ago, but not her reaction to it, which Ella thought was prideful, misdirected, and Sethe herself too complicated. When she got out of jail and made no gesture toward anybody, and lived as though she were alone, Ella junked her and wouldn't give her the time of day.

The daughter, however, appeared to have some sense after all. At least she had stepped out the door, asked for the help she needed and wanted work. When Ella heard 124 was occupied by some-thing-or-other beating up on Sethe, it infuriated her and gave her another opportunity to measure what could very well be the devil himself against 'the lowest yet.' There was also something very personal in her fury. Whatever Sethe had done, Ella didn't like the idea of past errors taking possession of the present. Sethe's crime was staggering and her pride outstripped even that; but she could not countenance the possibility of sin moving on in the house, unleashed and sassy. Daily life took as much as she had. The future was sunset; the past something to leave behind. And if it didn't stay behind, well, you might have to stomp it out. Slave life; freed life – every day was a test and a trial. Nothing could be counted on in a world where even when you were a solution you were a problem.

'Sufficient unto the day is the evil thereof,' and nobody needed more; nobody needed a grown-up evil sitting at the table with a grudge. As long as the ghost showed out from its ghostly place – shaking stuff, crying, smashing and such – Ella respected it. But if it took flesh and came in her world, well, the shoe was on the other foot. She didn't mind a little communication between the two worlds, but this was an invasion.

'Shall we pray?' asked the women.

'Uh huh,' said Ella. 'First. Then we got to get down to business.'

The day Denver was to spend her first night at the Bodwins', Mr. Bodwin had some business on the edge of the city and told Janey he would pick the new girl up before supper. Denver sat on the porch steps with a bundle in her lap, her carnival dress sun-faded to a quieter rainbow. She was looking to the right, in the direction Mr. Bodwin would be coming from. She did not see the women approaching, accumulating slowly in groups of twos and threes from the left. Denver was looking to the right. She was a little anxious about whether she would prove satisfactory to the Bodwins, and uneasy too because she woke up crying from a dream about a running pair of shoes. The sadness of the dream she hadn't been able to shake, and the heat oppressed her as she went about the chores. Far too early she wrapped a nightdress and hairbrush into a bundle. Nervous, she fidgeted the knot and looked to the right.

Some brought what they could and what they believed would work. Stuffed in apron pockets, strung around their necks, lying in the space between their breasts. Others brought Christian faith – as shield and sword. Most brought a little of both. They had no idea what they would do once they got there. They just started out, walked down Bluestone Road and came together at the agreed-upon time. The heat kept a few women who promised to go at home. Others who believed the story didn't want any part of the confrontation and wouldn't have come no matter what the weather. And there were those like Lady Jones who didn't believe the story and hated the ignorance of those who did. So thirty woman made up that company and walked slowly, slowly toward 124.

It was three in the afternoon on a Friday so wet and hot Cincinnati's stench had traveled to the country: from the canal, from hanging meat and things rotting in jars; from small animals dead in the fields, town sewers and factories. The stench, the heat, the moisture – trust the devil to make his presence known. Otherwise it looked almost like a regular workday. They could have been going to do the laundry at the orphanage or the insane asylum; corn shucking at the mill; or to clean fish, rinse offal, cradle whitebabies, sweep stores, scrape hog skin, press lard, case-pack sausage or hide in tavern kitchens so whitepeople didn't have to see them handle their food.

But not today.

When they caught up with each other, all thirty, and arrived at 124, the first thing they saw was not Denver sitting on the steps, but themselves. Younger, stronger, even as little girls lying in the grass asleep. Catfish was popping grease in the pan and they saw themselves scoop German potato salad onto the plate. Cobbler oozing purple syrup colored their teeth. They sat on the porch, ran down to the creek, teased the men, hoisted children on their hips or, if they were the children, straddled the ankles of old men who held their little hands while giving them a horsey ride. Baby Suggs laughed and skipped among them, urging more. Mothers, dead now, moved their shoulders to mouth harps. The fence they had leaned on and climbed over was gone. The stump of the butternut had split like a fan. But there they were, young and happy, playing in Baby Suggs' yard, not feeling the envy that surfaced the next day.

Denver heard mumbling and looked to the left. She stood when she saw them. They grouped, murmuring and whispering, but did not step foot in the yard. Denver waved. A few waved back but came no closer. Denver sat back down wondering what was going on. A woman dropped to her knees. Half of the others did likewise. Denver saw lowered heads, but could not hear the lead prayer – only the

BELOVED

earnest syllables of agreement that backed it: Yes, yes, yes, oh yes. Hear me. Hear me. Do it, Maker, do it. Yes. Among those not on their knees, who stood holding 124 in a fixed glare, was Ella, trying to see through the walls, behind the door, to what was really in there. Was it true the dead daughter come back? Or a pretend? Was it whipping Sethe? Ella had been beaten every way but down. She remembered the bottom teeth she had lost to the brake and the scars from the bell were thick as rope around her waist. She had delivered, but would not nurse, a hairy white thing, fathered by 'the lowest yet.' It lived five days never making a sound. The idea of that pup coming back to whip her too set her jaw working, and then Ella hollered.

Instantly the kneelers and the standers joined her. They stopped praying and took a step back to the beginning. In the beginning there were no words. In the beginning was the sound, and they all knew what that sound sounded like.

Edward Bodwin drove a cart down Bluestone Road. It displeased him a bit because he preferred his figure astride Princess. Curved over his own hands, holding the reins made him look the age he was. But he had promised his sister a detour to pick up a new girl. He didn't have to think about the way – he was headed for the house he was born in. Perhaps it was his destination that turned his thoughts to time – the way it dripped or ran. He had not seen the house for thirty years. Not the butternut in front, the stream at the rear nor the block house in between. Not even the meadow across the road. Very few of the interior details did he remember because he was three years old when his family moved into town. But he did remember that the cooking was done behind the house, the well was forbidden to play near, and that women died there: his mother, grandmother, an aunt and an older sister before he was born. The men (his father and grandfather) moved with himself and his baby sister to Court Street sixty-seven years ago. The land, of course, eighty acres of it on both sides of Bluestone, was the central thing, but he felt something sweeter and deeper about the house which is why he rented it for a little something if he could get it, but it didn't trouble him to get no rent at all since the tenants at least kept it from the disrepair total abandonment would permit.

There was a time when he buried things there. Precious things he wanted to protect. As a child every item he owned was available and accountable to his family. Privacy was an adult indulgence, but when he got to be one, he seemed not to need it.

The horse trotted along and Edward Bodwin cooled his beautiful mustache with his breath. It was generally agreed upon by the women in the Society that, except for his hands, it was the most attractive feature he had. Dark, velvety, its beauty was enhanced by his strong clean-shaven chin. But his hair was white, like his sister's – and had been since he was a young man. It made him the most visible and memorable person at every gathering, and cartoonists had fastened onto the theatricality of his white hair and big black mustache whenever they depicted local political antagonism. Twenty years ago when the Society was at its height in opposing slavery, it was as though his coloring was itself the heart of the matter. The 'bleached nigger' was what his enemies called him, and on a trip to Arkansas, some Mississippi rivermen, enraged by the Negro boatmen they competed with, had caught him and shoe-blackened his face and his hair. Those heady days were gone now; what remained was the sludge of ill will; dashed hopes and difficulties beyond repair. A tranquil Republic? Well, not in his lifetime.

Even the weather was getting to be too much for him. He was either too hot or freezing, and this day was a blister. He pressed his hat down to keep the sun from his neck, where heatstroke was a real possibility. Such thoughts of mortality were not new to him (he was over seventy now), but they still had the power to annoy. As he drew closer to the old homestead, the place that continued to surface in his dreams, he was even more aware of the way time moved. Measured by the wars he had lived through but not fought in (against the Miami, the Spaniards, the Secessionists), it was slow. But measured by the burial of his private things it was the blink of an eye. Where, exactly, was the box of tin soldiers? The watch chain with no watch? And who was he hiding them from? His father, probably, a deeply religious man who knew what God knew and told everybody what it was. Edward Bodwin thought him an odd man, in so many ways, yet he had one clear directive: human life is holy, all of it. And that his son still believed, although he had less and less reason to. Nothing since was as stimulating as the old days of letters, petitions, meetings, debates, recruitment, quarrels, rescue and downright sedition. Yet it had worked, more or less, and when it had not, he and his sister made themselves available to circumvent obstacles. As they had when a runaway slavewoman lived in his homestead with her mother-in-law and got herself into a world of trouble. The Society managed to turn infanticide and the cry of savagery around, and build a further case for abolishing slavery. Good years, they were, full of spit and conviction. Now he just wanted to know where his soldiers were and his watchless chain. That would be enough for this day of unbearable heat: bring back the new girl and recall exactly where his treasure lay. Then home, supper, and God willing, the sun would drop once more to give him the blessing of a good night's sleep.

The road curved like an elbow, and as he approached it he heard the singers before he saw them.

When the women assembled outside 124, Sethe was breaking a lump of ice into chunks. She dropped the ice pick into her apron pocket to scoop the pieces into a basin of water. When the music entered the window she was wringing a cool cloth to put on Beloved's forehead. Beloved, sweating profusely, was sprawled on the bed in the keeping room, a salt rock in her hand. Both women heard it at the same time and both lifted their heads. As the voices grew louder, Beloved sat up, licked the salt and went into the bigger room. Sethe and she exchanged glances and started toward the window. They saw Denver sitting on the steps and beyond her, where the yard met the road, they saw the rapt faces of thirty neighborhood women. Some had their eyes closed; others looked at the hot, cloudless sky. Sethe opened the door and reached for Beloved's hand. Together they stood in the doorway. For Sethe it was as though the Clearing had come to her with all its heat and simmering leaves, where the voices of women searched for the right combination, the key, the code, the sound that broke the back of words. Building voice upon voice until they found it, and when they did it was a wave of sound wide enough to sound deep water and knock the pods off chestnut trees. It broke over Sethe and she trembled like the baptized in its wash.

The singing women recognized Sethe at once and surprised themselves by their absence of fear when they saw what stood next to her. The devil-child was clever, they thought. And beautiful. It had taken the shape of a pregnant woman, naked and smiling in the heat of the afternoon sun. Thunderblack and glistening, she stood on long straight legs, her belly big and tight. Vines of hair twisted all over her head. Jesus. Her smile was dazzling.

Sethe feels her eyes burn and it may have been to keep them clear that she looks up. The sky is blue and clear. Not one touch of death in the definite green of the leaves. It is when she lowers her eyes to look again at the loving faces before her that she sees him. Guiding the mare, slowing down, his black hat wide-brimmed enough to hide his face but not his purpose. He is coming into her yard and he is coming for her best thing. She hears wings. Little hummingbirds stick needle beaks right through her headcloth into her hair and beat their wings. And if she thinks anything, it is no. No no. Nonono. She flies. The ice pick is not in her hand; it is her hand.

Standing alone on the porch, Beloved is smiling. But now her hand is empty. Sethe is running away from her, running, and she feels the emptiness in the hand Sethe has been holding. Now she is running into the faces of the people out there, joining them and leaving Beloved behind. Alone. Again. Then Denver, running too. Away from her to the pile of people out there. They make a hill. A hill of black people, falling. And above them all, rising from his place with a whip in his hand, the man without skin, looking. He is looking at her.

Eavan Boland (1944–)

Eavan Boland was born in Dublin. At the age of six she moved with her family to England. She describes her feeling of exile from her country and its language in her poems 'An Irish Childhood in England: 1951' and 'Fond Memory' (Boland 1995: 126–8). She was educated in London and New York and has recounted how she began writing poems in boarding school, reading Yeats after lights out. She studied English at Trinity College, Dublin where, she says, she learned to write poems in a style not her own, a hybrid of the Irish lyric and the British Movement (Boland 1987: 19).

Boland married the novelist Kevin Casey, moved out of the city centre to the suburbs and gave birth to two daughters, Sarah and Eavan Frances. With this move away from the literary life of Dublin into a life of domesticity Boland pinpoints a shift in her writing: 'The poems I had been writing no longer seemed necessary or true' (Boland 1987: 20). The ordinary day to day routine lived by women did not feature much in her country's poetry. She explains: 'I had no clear sense of how my womanhood could connect with my life as a poet, or what claims each would make on the other' (Boland 1995: ix).

Boland has written extensively about her struggle to bridge the gap between her life as a woman and the Irish poetic tradition she inherited, in which women are idealised or mythologised. She was entering uncharted territory: 'as an Irish woman poet I have very little precedent' she said in an interview in 1987 (Reizbaum 1989: 475). In *A Kind of Scar: The Woman Poet in a National Tradition* (1989), she writes of the difficulty for women in changing from being the subjects and objects of poetry to authoring their own. Resisting the temptation to easy polemic and outright rejection of the tradition she inherited, she has sought rather to reconstruct that tradition to include the lives of ordinary women, as opposed to the Dark Rosaleens and Cathleen Ni Houlihans of Irish poetry.

In her essay, 'The Woman Poet' (1987), Boland describes finding her inspiration in eighteenth-century French painters, particularly Chardin, whose paintings revealing the beauty of everyday objects provided her with a means of reconciling her woman's life as wife and mother with the life of a poet. Her poem, 'Envoi' (Boland 1995: 123), describes her aim as blessing the ordinary and sanctifying the common.

Eavan Boland's courageous enterprise of restoring the ordinary to Irish poetry has not been without risks. Her collections, *In Her Own Image* (1980) and *Night Feed* (1982), with their subjects of anorexia, mastectomy, menstruation and motherhood, aroused criticism from the largely chauvinist Irish literary establishment. It is a sign of victory that she has become accepted as a major Irish poet by convincing her readers that the ordinary is not synonymous with the unimportant but has its own sort of sacredness. Her poetry has helped modern Irish women in their struggle to articulate a sense of identity for themselves.

Primary reading

Boland, E. 1982 *Night Feed*, Dublin: Arlen House.

Boland, E. 1987 'The Woman Poet: Her Dilemma', *American Poetry Review* vol. 16 (1): 17–20.

Boland, E. 1989 *A Kind of Scar: The Woman Poet in a National Tradition*, Dublin: Attic Press.

Boland, E. 1995 *Collected Poems*, Manchester: Carcanet.

Further reading

Hagen, P. L. and Zelman, T.W. 1991 ' "We Were Never on the Scene of the Crime": Eavan Boland's repossession of History', *Twentieth-Century Literature* 37 (4): 442–53.

Reizbaum, E. 1989 'An Interview with Eavan Boland. Conducted by Marilyn Reizbaum', *Contemporary Literature* 30 (4): 471–79.

Willis, C. 1991 'Contemporary Irish Women Poets: the Privatisation of Myth' in *Diverse Voices. Essays on Twentieth-Century Women Writers in English* H. Devine Jump (ed.), New York and London: Harvester Wheatsheaf, pp. 248–72.

Night Feed

From Eavan Boland, *Collected Poems*, Manchester: Carcanet, 1995, p. 88.

This is dawn.
Believe me
This is your season, little daughter.
The moment daisies open,
The hour mercurial rainwater

Makes a mirror for sparrows.
It's time we drowned our sorrows.

I tiptoe in.
I lift you up
Wriggling
In your rosy, zipped sleeper.
Yes, this is the hour
For the early bird and me
When finder is keeper.

I crook the bottle.
How you suckle!
This is the best I can be.
Housewife
To this nursery
Where you hold on.
Dear life.

A silt of milk.
The last suck.
And now your eyes are open.
Birth-coloured and offended.
Earth wakes.
You go back to sleep.
The feed is ended.

Worms turn.
Stars go in.
Even the moon is losing face.
Poplars stilt for dawn
And we begin
The long fall from grace.
I tuck you in.

Zee Edgell (1940–)

Zee Edgell was born in Belize City and educated in Belize during the 1940s and 50s. She trained as a journalist in England and Jamaica and taught at St Catherine's Academy in Belize between 1966 and 1968. She has travelled widely, living in Afghanistan, Nigeria, Bangladesh and Somalia where she worked with UNICEF. Until 1982 she was Director of the Women's Bureau in Belize. *Beka Lamb*, published in 1982, was her first novel and it won the Fawcett Society Book Prize. It was the first novel by a Belizean to reach an international audience. Her second novel, *In Times Like These*, was published in 1991 and also deals with women's experience of life in pre-independence Belize.

The following extract from *Beka Lamb* shows Beka trying to find her voice in the argument between her Granny Ivy and her mother, Lilla, over the wake for Greatgran Straker. It is an argument that embraces different interpretations of her country's past. Granny Ivy is a nationalist who defends her country's history and values and sees the wake as a vital link with their African roots. Beka's mother, Lilla, focuses more on the future and the necessity for Beka to find her way in the modern world. Lilla, it becomes apparent from this extract, has had her own bad experiences under colonialism and wishes to protect her daughter. Her mothering is shaped by the political situation in which she finds herself. At this stage in the novel Lilla's creativity is still expressed in cultivating, with great difficulty in the Belizean climate, roses like the ones she sees in English magazines. By the end of the novel she has given up on roses and will grow indigenous plants.

There are no easy answers to the argument between Lilla and Granny Ivy, no simple right or wrong. This society, like Beka herself, is at a painful stage of growth. Granny Ivy upholds her country's traditions but she is also a fatalist, believing that in Belize 'tings bruk down' (Edgell 1982: 16) and that it will be impossible for a local black girl like Beka to win the essay prize. Her mother has a nostalgia for England yet it is she who thinks of the future and the importance of Beka's education in helping her escape a life of domestic drudgery. 'If you manage to finish school, your education will help you to reach a clearing' she tells her daughter (Edgell 1982: 10). It is she who at the end of this extract gives Beka the weapon that will help her find her voice. With her pen Beka has the chance to write her way out of marginality and overcome the voicelessness that critics have seen as a crucial concept in any discussion of Caribbean women and literature (Davies and Fido 1990: 3). It is a significant example in women's fiction of a mother aiding her daughter's creativity and developing sense of self.

Primary reading

Edgell, Z. 1982 *Beka Lamb*, Oxford: Heinemann.

Edgell, Z. 1991 *In Times Like These*, Oxford: Heinemann.

Further reading

Abruna, L. Niesen de 1990 'Twentieth-Century Women Writers from the English-Speaking Caribbean' in *Caribbean Women Writers. Essays from the First International Conference* S. R. Cudjoe (ed.), Wellesley: Calaloux, pp. 86–97.

Bromley, R. 1985 'Reaching a Clearing. Gender and Politics in *Beka Lamb*', *Wasafiri* 1 (2): 10–14.

Campbell, E. 1987 'The Dichotomized Heroine in West Indian Fiction', *The Journal of Commonwealth Literature* XXII (1): 137–43.

Davies, C. B. and Fido, E. S. (eds.) 1990 *Out of the Kumbla. Caribbean Women and Literature*, Trenton: Africa World Press.

Flockemann, M. 1992 ' "Not-Quite Insiders and Not-Quite Outsiders": The "Process of Womanhood" in *Beka Lamb*, *Nervous Conditions* and *Daughters of the Twilight*', *The Journal of Commonwealth Literature* XXVII (1): 37–47.

Woodcock, B. 1986 'Post-1975 Caribbean fiction and the challenge to English literature', *Critical Quarterly* 28 (4): 79–95.

Beka Lamb

From Zee Edgell, *Beka Lamb*, Oxford: Heinemann, 1982, pp. 66–71.

On the ninth morning after Greatgran Straker died, Granny Ivy returned from Bridge Foot market with her everyday straw basket bulging.

'I bring fish for today and some tough beef to stew for tomorrow, Lilla, since we'll sleep late because of the wake tonight. You going to wake, Beka?'

'Mama says no, Gran. I have to study anyhow.'

'Why not, Lilla? Beka over fourteen now and it's holiday time. No harm in it.'

'I don't believe in it, Miss Ivy. How Aunt Tama could plan a thing like this, knowing how I feel and then ask Bill to help pay for it, I don't know. My Grandmother was Christian, and she had a Christian burial. We don't need to protect ourselves from my Granny Straker.'

'Well, whatever else I may say 'bout Tama, I must tell you that she at least don't give up *all* the old ways.'

'That's just a bunch of superstition, Miss Ivy. When a person dies, that's it. No amount of bramming can do a thing more. Granny Straker's spirit isn't roaming around trying to hurt a single soul.'

'It's only a get-together to remember and pay respect to the dead, Lilla. Tama is cooking, and getting the musicians. You should be glad to hear people talking about the days when your Grandmother was young. Moreover, a lot of people over on that side could do with a boil-up from those that have it to give. It's a help to the living.'

'It's not the money to feed people that worry me, Miss Ivy. I know all about the old days when Granny Straker was young. I know it by heart, and I don't need a wake to remind me. I am fed up with it. I don't want to remember. The old ways will poison the new. I don't want Beka getting into the habit of those things. She's having enough trouble right now with school.'

'Lawd, Lill, you actin' like the wake is obeah.'

'It's all connected, Miss Ivy. It's all connected.'

'All connected to what, Mama?'

Ignoring the question, Lilla continued,

'Granny Straker wouldn't have wanted a wake. She was trying to progress. And that's what Bill and I are trying to do with this family. You and Tama as bad that way as the Caribs in Stann Creek that you associate with.'

'Miss Benguche in elementary school says Caribs have a lot of traditions that creoles give up, Mama. She thinks keeping them is a good thing if they don't do any harm.'

'Stay out of this, Beka,' Lilla said. 'Here, start scaling this fish. Start from the tail and go down. You might as well learn kitchen work, because it seems like that's all you'll be good for.'

'You don't know a thing 'bout Carib people, Lilla,' Granny Ivy said, bumping yams, oranges and plantains onto the counter.

'After '31 hurricane, families in Stann Creek sent food to feed lots of people up here, and we were glad to take from their hands then. After service, I don't close my church door. And anyhow, when you get right down to it, Carib and creole are branches of the same African tree, although I am not saying I could marry a Carib man . . .'

'Miss Ivy, let me tell you something,' Lilla interrupted, pointing the butcher knife covered with scales at Miss Ivy. 'Tama practises a lot of things she learnt down there. She even frighten Beka one time when I sent Beka with her for a few days to Stann Creek. All Beka did was take two johnny cakes from the pile she left to cool, but she lied to Tama about it. Tama took Beka to her bedroom with the other children of the house, closed the curtains and set a table. She filled a glass with water. Took a hair from her head, tied it to a wedding ring, and held it in the glass over the water, and then she pretended that the ring bumped against the glass by itself when Beka's name was called. All the time chanting I don't know what all. To this day, Beka believes that ring bumped against the glass by itself!'

'Anyhow,' Granny Ivy continued just as if Lilla hadn't been talking, 'I don't believe Carib people sacrifice children and I don't believe that if they put a doll with pins and a bottle of fowl blood under the stairs . . .'

'Miss Benguche says,' Beka interrupted, wiping the scales off her cheek with her frock tail,

'Shut your mouth, Beka.' Granny Ivy said.

'But, Gran, Miss says . . . Miss says . . .'

'I'll clothespin your mouth as well as your flat nose if you don't shut up, Beka! Miss, Miss, all I hear from you is Miss. Keep quiet for a change.'

Flinging the knife down onto the floor, Beka shouted,

'When I grow up I am going to marry a Carib!' The slap across her face came with such swiftness and strength that Beka staggered back against the stove.

'Don't you ever speak to your Gran like that again!'

In agony, Beka rushed up the attic stairs and flung herself across her bed weeping in confusion, guilt and shame. Why couldn't she be good to her family? Why couldn't she learn to say and do the right thing? 'Why am I so horrible?' Beka whispered. 'What is wrong with me?'

Every year, after Christmas, Caribs wearing masks, painted black and red, and dressed in colourful costumes decorated with jingling shells, danced to drums at street corners, and in yards, for gifts of money. The excitement generated by the drumbeats drew the children of the town in swarms. One year the children in Beka's class returned to school, tumbling all over themselves in their eagerness to tell 'teacher' what they had seen, in whose yard, or at which street corner, the drumming or dancing had been best. To quiet the class, Miss Benguche, a Carib, explained that the Caribs were descendants of African slaves who escaped from West Indian plantations by paddling their way to St Vincent. There, they mingled with the Caribans, originally from South America, adopting much of their language and some of their ways, but keeping many of their African traditions. The British wanted the land the Caribs occupied after a while, and so they were shunted to Roatan, in the Republic of Honduras, and quite a number, over the years, paddled to Stann Creek, and other towns along the Belizean coast, where they established towns and villages.

Lilla climbed the stairs slowly and walked over to Beka's attic space to sit on the edge of the bed. She touched Beka's back with a hand smelled of fish and limes, but Beka kept her face to the window.

'Beka, please look at me.' Beka turned her head around, eyes swollen and rebellious. Her mother's face looked frightened and contrite.

'You can come to the wake with us if you still want to, Beka. Why I am trying to keep you away from the things I experienced as a child, I don't rightly know. But sometimes your Mama have bad worries that she can't explain to herself, let alone begin to tell you. But if you like, I'll try to tell you a little about when I was young.' Beka nodded, turning completely around.

'Remember when you came home from school last year and was so angry to find my father sitting at the table? Well, you shouldn't have been. Granny Ivy used to tell me that after my mother died, and for a long time afterwards, he took good care of me. My mother wanted me to go to the convent, so he used to pay for me to go. I was the blackest and poorest one in my class.'

'But your skin is light, and your hair almost straight.'

'Yes, but in those days most black children used to go to the Protestant schools. The majority of the girls at the convent were white skinned, either mestizos, bakras, or children of foreigners. Nobody's fault, just the way it was. Sometimes my shoes had holes. I couldn't sport gold bangles or golden earrings, my clothes didn't look like theirs did. And although I used to invite a few of them to my house, they wouldn't come, excepting once or twice, because my house was in a poor area and it was almost flat on the ground like Toycie's. I felt out of place many times. Well, one day, I said more or less what I am saying to you to my father and he said,

"Well, Lilla, if those things are more important to you than your education, you'd better leave. My skin looks white, but I am a poor man.' He refused to pay to let me finish school. I never spoke very much to him again until last year when you came home from school and found him sitting at the table. So I had two years of high school. Your Dad never went to high school at all." '

Beka was quiet for a while, watching her mother smooth out the wrinkled sheet and trace the red roses she'd embroidered on the edge of Beka's pillow slip.

'Mama?'

'Mmm?'

'Mama, is it the obeah why creole and Carib don't mix too much?'
Her mother's eyes grew puzzled. Then she said,

'To tell you the truth, Beka, I don't rightly know. I doubt if many
creoles could tell you. Nobody really remembers the reasons. We
creoles are so different, one from the other, that it's hard for us to mix
properly amongst ourselves, let alone among Carib people who have
a lot more things in common. Maybe it's because Carib people
remind us of what we lost trying to get up in the world. See, in the old
days, according to Granny Straker, the more you left behind the old
ways, the more acceptable you were to the powerful people in the
government and the churches who had the power to change a black
person's life. Mind you, many of the old ways were harmful, health-
wise and so on. Anyhow, when slavery was over in fact, a lot of
people only went to the bush to cut mahogany when they absolutely
had to do so. The bush maybe reminded them of the cruelties and
forced labour, for little or nothing, which they had endured. Living in
town became a habit. Some did want to buy land, but the law didn't
encourage it. Things are changing though.'

'Is that why you don't like to go up to Sibun for holidays like
Daddy Bill and Granny Ivy would prefer us to do?'

Her mother laughed high, long and joyously like Beka had not
heard since the day she failed first form.

'That may be true, Beky Beky. You've maybe put your finger on
something. Maybe we'll spend our holiday up Sibun River next year.
You'd like that wouldn't you?'

Beka nodded, smiling at her mother's happy face.

'Daddy would come with us then, I think.'

'We'll see, Beka. We'll see. Did you find your present yet?'

'No,' Beka answered, startled. 'Which present?'

'Go look in your drawer.'

Beka crossed over to her work table, and pulled hard at the drawer
which always stuck. Today it came out so smoothly she stumbled a

little. Lying on top of her jumble of papers was a package wrapped in green kite paper and tied with a bright red ribbon twirled into a fancy bow. She opened the package carefully, and there was the new exercise book from Gordillo's. She picked it up, flicking through the pages.

'What's it for, Mama? I have plenty of empty blanks.'

Something dropped with a clink and Beka picked from the floor a beautiful grey-blue fountain pen which she knew her mother must have purchased from St Ignatius Press on Queen Street. Carrying everything to the bed she asked again,

'Why did you give them to me?'

'Well, the pen *was* to be a present for passing. The exercise book I thought about later.'

'Am I going back to school?'

'Your Dad still has not decided. But that pen and that exercise book are only for at home.'

'To do what?'

'Well, everytime you feel like telling a lie, I want you to write it down in there and pretend you are writing a story. That way, you can tell the truth and save the lie for this notebook. And when we tell you stories about before time, you can write them down in there, too, for your children to read.'

'I'm never going to get married,' Beka said.

'Then you'll have it for yourself, then.'

'It's a *nice* pen,' Beka said, uncapping it, gently checking to see if the nib had been damaged by its fall.

'Shall I give you a different hairstyle for the wake tonight?'

'Nope,' Beka said. 'I am going to sit right here and write down what you said.'

Pleased that her gift was a success, Lilla's laugh pealed out again, 'Just don't exaggerate, Beka!'

'I'll try not to, Mama love,' Beka laughed in return, opening her brand new exercise book.

Amy Tan (1952–)

Amy Tan was born in Oakland, California to Chinese immigrant parents. Her name 'An-mei' means 'blessing from America'. Her father was a Beijing-educated electrical engineer and Baptist minister. Her parents emigrated to America in 1949, leaving behind Tan's three half-sisters (Ling 1990: 137). The Communist Revolution meant that they lost contact with these daughters and it was not until Tan was twelve that she learnt of their existence (ibid.).

In 1967 Tan's elder brother died of a brain tumour and the following year her father too died of the same illness. Tan moved with her mother and younger brother to Europe and attended school in Switzerland. She received her Master's degree in linguistics from San Jose State University and worked as a freelance business writer. In 1974 she married Louis De Mattei, a tax attorney: they live in California. A few years ago Tan met her half-sisters in China for the first time.

It is Tan's mother who is a major inspiration for her novels. In *The Joy Luck Club* (1989) Tan draws on traditional Chinese storytelling and her own family history to interweave stories of Chinese immigrant mothers and their American-born daughters. As their mothers tell of their struggles to find happiness, their daughters recount their fight to be themselves in the face of overpowering maternal love and a different cultural conditioning. They may resist their mothers' attempts to draw them back into their Chinese heritage but at the end of the novel when one of the daughters, Jing-Mei Woo, visits China she realises that she can't help but be Chinese (Tan 1989/1994: 267). It was a realisation that Tan herself had when she visited China for the first time in 1987. Indeed *The Joy Luck Club* is a very personal book – in an interview she gave to *The New York Times* in 1989 Tan said of her novel: 'When I was writing, it was so much for my mother and myself . . . I wanted her to know what I thought about China and what I thought about growing up in this country' (Heung 1993: 598–9).

'Scar' is An-Mei's story of her life in China. The mother-daughter lineage has been disrupted through rape. An-Mei's mother has been forced to become the concubine of a wealthy merchant and is no longer permitted to see her daughter or her mother, Popo. Yet when Popo is dying An-Mei's mother returns to affirm, through an ancient ritual, the mother-daughter bond. In a society where females are regarded as disposable property and given early lessons in silence and self-denial, the affirmation of the mother-daughter bond is a consolation and also an act of subversion.

Primary reading

Tan, A. 1989/1994 *The Joy Luck Club*, London: Minerva.

Tan, A. 1991 *The Kitchen God's Wife*, London: HarperCollins.

Tan, A. 1996 *The Hundred Secret Senses*, London: HarperCollins.

Further reading

Heung, M. 1993 'Daughter-Text/Mother-Text: Matrilineage in Amy Tan's *Joy Luck Club*', *Feminist Studies* 19 (3): 597–616.

Jung, C. and Kerenyi, C. 1963 *Essays on a Science of Mythology*, New York: Harper & Row.

Kingston, M. 1976/1981 *The Woman Warrior: Memoirs of a Girlhood Among Ghosts*, London: Picador.

Ling, A. 1990 *Between Worlds. Women Writers of Chinese Ancestry*, New York: Pergamon Press.

Wong, S. C. 1993 *Reading Asian American Literature. From Necessity to Extravagance*, Princeton: Princeton University Press.

The Joy Luck Club

From Amy Tan, *The Joy Luck Club*, London: Minerva, 1994, pp. 42–8.

When I was a young girl in China, my grandmother told me my mother was a ghost. This did not mean my mother was dead. In those days, a ghost was anything we were forbidden to talk about. So I knew Popo wanted me to forget my mother on purpose, and this is how I came to remember nothing of her. The life that I knew began in the large house in Ningpo with the cold hallways and tall stairs. This was my uncle and auntie's family house, where I lived with Popo and my little brother.

But I often heard stories of a ghost who tried to take children away, especially strong-willed little girls who were disobedient. Many times Popo said aloud to all who could hear that my brother and I had fallen out of the bowels of a stupid goose, two eggs that nobody wanted, not even good enough to crack over rice porridge. She said this so that the ghosts would not steal us away. So you see, to Popo we were also very precious.

All my life, Popo scared me. I became even more scared when she grew sick. This was in 1923, when I was nine years old. Popo had swollen up like an overripe squash, so full her flesh had gone soft and rotten with a bad smell. She would call me into her room with the terrible stink and tell me stories. 'An-mei,' she said, calling me by my school name. 'Listen carefully.' She told me stories I could not understand.

One was about a greedy girl whose belly grew fatter and fatter. This girl poisoned herself after refusing to say whose child she carried. When the monks cut open her body, they found inside a large white winter melon.

'If you are greedy, what is inside you is what makes you always hungry,' said Popo.

Another time, Popo told me about a girl who refused to listen to her elders. One day this bad girl shook her head so vigorously to refuse her auntie's simple request that a little white ball fell from her ear and out poured all her brains, as clear as chicken broth.

'Your own thoughts are so busy swimming inside that everything else gets pushed out,' Popo told me.

Right before Popo became so sick she could no longer speak, she pulled me close and talked to me about my mother. 'Never say her name,' she warned. 'To say her name is to spit on your father's grave.'

The only father I knew was a big painting that hung in the main hall. He was a large, unsmiling man, unhappy to be so still on the wall. His restless eyes followed me around the house. Even from my room at the end of the hall, I could see my father's watching eyes. Popo said he watched me for any signs of disrespect. So sometimes, when I had thrown pebbles at other children at school, or had lost a book through carelessness, I would quickly walk by my father with a know-nothing look and hide in a corner of my room where he could not see my face.

I felt our house was so unhappy, but my little brother did not seem to think so. He rode his bicycle through the courtyard, chasing chickens and other children, laughing over which ones shrieked the loudest. Inside the quiet house, he jumped up and down on Uncle and Auntie's best feather sofas when they were away visiting village friends.

But even my brother's happiness went away. One hot summer day when Popo was already very sick, we stood outside watching a village funeral procession marching by our courtyard. Just as it passed our gate, the heavy framed picture of the dead man toppled from its stand and fell to the dusty ground. An old lady screamed and fainted. My brother laughed and Auntie slapped him.

My auntie, who had a very bad temper with children, told him he had no *shou*, no respect for ancestors or family, just like our mother. Auntie had a tongue like hungry scissors eating silk cloth. So when my brother gave her a sour look, Auntie said our mother was so thoughtless she had fled north in a big hurry, without taking the dowry furniture from her marriage to my father, without bringing her ten pairs of silver chopsticks, without paying respect to my father's grave and those of our ancestors. When my brother accused Auntie of frightening our mother away, Auntie shouted that our mother had married a man named Wu Tsing who already had a wife, two concubines, and other bad children.

And when my brother shouted that Auntie was a talking chicken without a head, she pushed my brother against the gate and spat on his face.

'You throw strong words at me, but you are nothing,' Auntie said. 'You are the son of a mother who has so little respect she has become *ni*, a traitor to our ancestors. She is so beneath others that even the devil must look down to see her.'

That is when I began to understand the stories Popo taught me, the lessons I had to learn for my mother. 'When you lose your face, An-mei,' Popo often said, 'it is like dropping your necklace down a well. The only way you can get it back is to fall in after it.'

Now I could imagine my mother, a thoughtless woman who laughed and shook her head, who dipped her chopsticks many times to eat another piece of sweet fruit, happy to be free of Popo, her unhappy husband on the wall, and her two disobedient children. I felt unlucky that she was my mother and unlucky that she had left us. These were the thoughts I had while hiding in the corner of my room where my father could not watch me.

I was sitting at the top of the stairs when she arrived. I knew it was my mother even though I had not seen her in all my memory. She stood just inside the doorway so that her face became a dark shadow. She was much taller than my auntie, almost as tall as my uncle. She looked strange, too, like the missionary ladies at our school who were insolent and bossy in their too-tall shoes, foreign clothes, and short hair.

My auntie quickly looked away and did not call her by name or offer her tea. An old servant hurried away with a displeased look. I tried to keep very still, but my heart felt like crickets scratching to get out of a cage. My mother must have heard, because she looked up. And when she did, I saw my own face looking back at me. Eyes that stayed wide open and saw too much.

In Popo's room my auntie protested, 'Too late, too late,' as my mother approached the bed. But this did not stop my mother.

'Come back, stay here,' murmured my mother to Popo. '*Nuyer* is here. Your daughter is back.' Popo's eyes were open, but now her mind ran in many different directions, not staying long enough to see anything. If Popo's mind had been clear she would have raised her two arms and flung my mother out of the room.

I watched my mother, seeing her for the first time, this pretty woman with her white skin and oval face, not too round like Auntie's or sharp like Popo's. I saw that she had a long white neck, just like the goose that had laid me. That she seemed to float back and forth like a ghost, dipping cool cloths to lay on Popo's bloated face. As she peered into Popo's eyes, she clucked soft worried sounds. I watched her carefully, yet it was her voice that confused me, a familiar sound from a forgotten dream.

When I returned to my room later that afternoon, she was there, standing tall. And because I remember Popo told me not to speak her name, I stood there, mute. She took my hand and led me to the settee. And then she also sat down as though we had done this every day.

My mother began to loosen my braids and brush my hair with long sweeping strokes.

'An-mei, you have been a good daughter?' she asked, smiling a secret look.

I looked at her with my know-nothing face, but inside I was trembling. I was the girl whose belly held a colorless winter melon.

'An-mei, you know who I am,' she said with a small scold in her voice. This time I did not look for fear my head would burst and my brains would dribble out of my ears.

She stopped brushing. And then I could feel her long smooth fingers rubbing and searching under my chin, finding the spot that was my smooth-neck scar. As she rubbed this spot, I became very still. It was as though she were rubbing the memory back into my skin. And then her hand dropped and she began to cry, wrapping her hands around her own neck. She cried with a wailing voice that was so sad. And then I remembered the dream with my mother's voice.

I was four years old. My chin was just above the dinner table, and I could see my baby brother sitting on Popo's lap, crying with an angry face. I could hear voices praising a steaming dark soup brought to the table, voices murmuring politely, '*Ching! Ching!*' – Please, eat!

And then the talking stopped. My uncle rose from his chair. Everyone turned to look at the door, where a tall woman stood. I was the only one who spoke.

'Ma,' I had cried, rushing off my chair, but my auntie slapped my face and pushed me back down. Now everyone was standing up and

shouting, and I heard my mother's voice crying, 'An-mei! An-mei!'
Above this noise, Popo's shrill voice spoke.

'Who is this ghost? Not an honored widow. Just a number-three
concubine. If you take your daughter, she will become like you. No
face. Never able to lift up her head.'

Still my mother shouted for me to come. I remember her voice so
clearly now. An-mei! An-mei! I could see my mother's face across the
table. Between us stood the soup pot on its heavy chimney-pot stand
– rocking slowly, back and forth. And then with one shout this dark
boiling soup spilled forward and fell all over my neck. It was as
though everyone's anger were pouring all over me.

This was the kind of pain so terrible that a little child should never
remember it. But it is still in my skin's memory. I cried out loud only a
little, because soon my flesh began to burst inside and out and cut off
my breathing air.

I could not speak because of this terrible choking feeling. I could
not see because of all the tears that poured out to wash away the pain.
But I could hear my mother's crying voice. Popo and Auntie were
shouting. And then my mother's voice went away.

Later that night Popo's voice came to me.

'An-mei, listen carefully.' Her voice had the same scolding tone she
used when I ran up and down the hallway. 'An-mei, we have made
your dying clothes and shoes for you. They are all white cotton.'

I listened, scared.

'An-mei,' she murmured, now more gently. 'Your dying clothes are
very plain. They are not fancy, because you are still a child. If you die,
you will have a short life and you will still owe your family a debt.
Your funeral will be very small. Our mourning time for you will be
very short.'

And then Popo said something that was worse than the burning on
my neck.

'Even your mother has used up her tears and left. If you do not get
well soon, she will forget you.'

Popo was very smart. I came hurrying back from the other world to find my mother.

Every night I cried so that both my eyes and my neck burned. Next to my bed sat Popo. She would pour cool water over my neck from the hollowed cup of a large grapefruit. She would pour and pour until my breathing became soft and I could fall asleep. In the morning, Popo would use her sharp fingernails like tweezers and peel off the dead membranes.

In two years' time, my scar became pale and shiny and I had no memory of my mother. That is the way it is with a wound. The wound begins to close in on itself, to protect what is hurting so much. And once it is closed, you no longer see what is underneath, what started the pain.

I worshipped this mother from my dream. But the woman standing by Popo's bed was not the mother of my memory. Yet I came to love this mother as well. Not because she came to me and begged me to forgive her. She did not. She did not need to explain that Popo chased her out of the house when I was dying. This I knew. She did not need to tell me she married Wu Tsing to exchange one unhappiness for another. I knew this as well.

Here is how I came to love my mother. How I saw in her my own true nature. What was beneath my skin. Inside my bones.

It was late at night when I went to Popo's room. My auntie said it was Popo's dying time and I must show respect. I put on a clean dress and stood between my auntie and uncle at the foot of Popo's bed. I cried a little, not too loud.

I saw my mother on the other side of the room. Quiet and sad. She was cooking a soup, pouring herbs and medicines into the steaming pot. And then I saw her pull up her sleeve and pull out a sharp knife. She put this knife on the softest part of her arm. I tried to close my eyes, but could not.

And then my mother cut a piece of meat from her arm. Tears poured from her face and blood spilled to the floor.

My mother took her flesh and put it in the soup. She cooked magic in the ancient tradition to try to cure her mother this one last time. She opened Popo's mouth, already too tight from trying to keep her spirit in. She fed her this soup, but that night Popo flew away with her illness.

Even though I was young, I could see the pain of the flesh and the worth of the pain.

This is how a daughter honors her mother. It is *shou* so deep it is in your bones. The pain of the flesh is nothing. The pain you must forget. Because sometimes that is the only way to remember what is in your bones. You must peel off your skin, and that of your mother, and her mother before her. Until there is nothing. No scar, no skin, no flesh.

Angela Carter (1940–1992)

Angela Carter was born Angela Stalker in Eastbourne. She spent the war years in Yorkshire with her maternal grandmother, a Northern working-class, larger than life character whom Lorna Sage sees as the source of Carter's 'tough as old boots' matriarchs (Sage 1994a: 5–7). Carter wrote of her grandmother: 'She came from a community where women rule the roost and she effortlessly imparted a sense of my sex's ascendancy in the scheme of things' (Carter 1982: 8).

By contrast, Carter's mother was genteel and fragile. She had won a scholarship to a young ladies' grammar school, married early and had given up work in accordance with the prevailing convention. Carter's wry memories of her mother in her essay, 'The Mother Lode' (1976), are curiously vague and generalised, being more about the general atmosphere of her home rather than about her mother as a person. She does wish, though, that she had protected her mother more against her 'harridan' of a grandmother. All the same, it seems in keeping that the little girl in 'The Werewolf' does not go home to mother and safety; instead she stays in her grandmother's house and prospers.

After the war, Carter returned to London. A beneficiary of the welfare state, she was educated at a direct grant school in Balham. Tall and large-boned, she went through a teenage period of anorexia. In 1959 she followed her father's profession in working as a reporter for the *Croydon Advertiser*. In 1960 she married Paul Carter from whom she was divorced in 1972. Between 1962 and 1965 she read English at Bristol University, specialising in medieval literature. In 1966 her first novel, *Shadow Dance*, was published and in 1967 she won the John Llewellyn Rhys prize for her second novel, *The Magic Toyshop*.

Carter was awarded a Somerset Maugham Travel Award and for two years she lived in Japan, an experience which profoundly affected her thinking about sexuality: 'In Japan, I learnt what it was to be a woman and became radicalised' she wrote later (Carter 1982: 28). As a girl she felt she had suffered 'a degree of colonialisation of the mind' (Wandor 1983: 71) as far as femininity was concerned. She began to explore the notion of gender as performance.

In 1977 Carter settled in South London with Mark Pearce though she spent extensive periods teaching abroad, notably in the US and in Australia. Their son, Alexander, was born in 1983. Carter's account in the *New Statesman* of her experiences on the maternity ward as an elderly primigravida would make anyone's hair stand on end: at one point the (female) consultant suggested she give up her baby for adoption (Carter 1983: 25), an interesting example of what Adrienne Rich has termed the institutionalisation of motherhood. In an interview in 1987, Carter described herself as 'not proud of myself as a mother' but proud of her child (Watts 1987: 163). She denied that motherhood had changed her image of herself though in a perceptive and illuminating essay on Carter, 'Mother is a Figure of Speech . . .', Nicole Ward Jouve detects a change of attitude towards motherhood in Carter's last two novels, *Nights at the Circus* and *Wise Children*, published after she had become a mother (Sage 1994b: 163, 168).

From the mid-1960s onwards Carter, fairy godmother and witch, fabulist and realist, a dazzling spinner of tales, was at the forefront of contemporary writing with her flamboyant, often outrageous explorations of Western sexuality. After a period in the 1970s when her work was not well understood, her reputation really took off with her move to Virago and the publication of *The Bloody Chamber* (1979), later made into a film, *Company of Wolves* (1984), for which she co-wrote the screenplay with Neil Jordan. She published nine novels and four collections of stories as well as reviews, essays and radio plays. She died in London of lung cancer at the tragically early age of fifty-one.

Primary reading

Carter, A. 1979 *The Sadeian Woman. An Exercise in Cultural History*, London: Virago.

Carter, A. 1982 *Nothing Sacred. Selected Writings*, London: Virago.

Carter, A. 1983 'Notes from a maternity ward', *New Statesman* 16/23; December.

Carter, A. (ed.) 1990 *The Virago Book of Fairytales*, London: Virago.

Carter, A. 1996 *Burning your Boats. Collected Short Stories*, London: Vintage.

Further reading

Duncker, P. 1984 'Re-Imagining the Fairy Tales: Angela Carter's Bloody Chambers', *Literature and History* 10 (1): 3–14.

Jordan, E. 1992 'The Dangers of Angela Carter' in *New Feminist Discourses* I. Armstrong (ed.), London and New York: Routledge.

Rose, E. C. 1983 'Through the Looking Glass: When Women Tell Fairytales', *The Voyage In: Fictions of Female Development* E. Abel, M. Hirsch, E. Langland (eds.), Hanover and London: University Press of New England, pp. 209–27.

Sage, L. 1994a *Angela Carter*, Plymouth: Northcote House.

Sage, L. (ed.) 1994b *Flesh and the Mirror. Essays on the Art of Angela Carter*, London: Virago.

Wandor, M. 1983 *On Gender and Writing*, London: Pandora.

Watts, H. C. 1987 'Angela Carter: an interview', *Bête Noire* Spring: 161–76.

Ashputtle *or* The Mother's Ghost

From Angela Carter, *Burning Your Boats. Collected Short Stories*, London: Vintage, 1996, pp. 390–96.

1 The Mutilated Girls

But although you could easily take the story away from Ashputtle and centre it on the mutilated sisters – indeed, it would be easy to think of it as a story about cutting bits off women, so that they will *fit in*, some sort of circumcision-like ritual chop, nevertheless, the story always begins not with Ashputtle or her stepsisters but with Ashputtle's mother, as though it is really always the story of her mother even if, at the beginning of the story, the mother herself is just about to exit the narrative because she is at death's door: 'A rich man's wife fell sick, and, feeling that her end was near, she called her only daughter to her bedside.'

Note the absence of the husband/father. Although the woman is defined by her relation to him ('a rich man's wife') the daughter is unambiguously hers, as if hers alone, and the entire drama concerns only women, takes place almost exclusively among women, is a fight between two groups of women – in the right-hand corner, Ashputtle and her mother; in the left-hand corner, the stepmother and *her* daughters, of whom the father is unacknowledged but all the same is predicated by both textual and biological necessity.

In the drama between two female families in opposition to one another because of their rivalry over men (husband/father, husband/ son), the men seem no more than passive victims of their fancy, yet their significance is absolute because it is ('a rich man', 'a king's son') economic.

Ashputtle's father, the old man, is the first object of their desire and their dissension; the stepmother snatches him from the dead mother before her corpse is cold, as soon as her grip loosens. Then there is the young man, the potential bridegroom, the hypothetical son-in-law, for whose possession the mothers fight, using their daughters as instruments of war or as surrogates in the business of mating.

If the men, and the bank balances for which they stand, are the passive victims of the two grown women, then the girls, all three, are animated solely by the wills of their mothers. Even if Ashputtle's mother dies at the beginning of the story, her status as one of the dead only makes her position more authoritative. The mother's ghost dominates the narrative and is, in a real sense, the motive centre, the event that makes all the other events happen.

On her death bed, the mother assures the daughter: 'I shall always look after you and always be with you.' The story tells you how she does it.

At this point, when her mother makes her promise, Ashputtle is nameless. She is her mother's daughter. That is all we know. It is the stepmother who names her Ashputtle, as a joke, and, in doing so, wipes out her real name, whatever that is, banishes her from the family, exiles her from the shared table to the lonely hearth among the cinders, removes her contingent but honourable status as daughter and gives her, instead, the contingent but disreputable status of servant.

Her mother told Ashputtle she would always look after her, but then she died and the father married again and gave Ashputtle an imitation mother with daughters of her own whom she loves with the same fierce passion as Ashputtle's mother did and still, posthumously, does, as we shall find out.

With the second marriage comes the vexed question: who shall be the daughters of the house? Mine! declares the stepmother and sets the freshly named, non-daughter Ashputtle to sweep and scrub and sleep on the hearth while her daughters lie between clean sheets in Ashputtle's bed. Ashputtle, no longer known as the daughter of her mother, nor of her father either, goes by a dry, dirty, cindery nickname for everything has turned to dust and ashes.

Meanwhile, the false mother sleeps on the bed where the real mother died and is, presumably, pleasured by the husband/father in that bed, unless there is no pleasure in it for her. We are not told what the husband/father does as regards domestic or marital function, but we can surely make the assumption that he and the stepmother share a bed, because that is what married people do.

And what can the real mother/wife do about it? Burn as she might with love, anger and jealousy, she is dead and buried.

The father, in this story, is a mystery to me. Is he so besotted with his new wife that he cannot see how his daughter is soiled with kitchen refuse and filthy from her ashy bed and always hard at work? If he sensed there was a drama in hand, he was content to leave the entire production to the women for, absent as he might be, always remember that it is in *his* house where Ashputtle sleeps on the cinders, and he is the invisible link that binds both sets of mothers and daughters in their violent equation. He is the unmoved mover, the unseen organising principle, like God, and, like God, up he pops in person, one fine day, to introduce the essential plot device.

Besides, without the absent father there would be no story because there would have been no conflict.

If they had been able to put aside their differences and discuss everything amicably, they'd have combined to expel the father. Then all the women could have slept in one bed. If they'd kept the father on, he could have done the housework.

This is the essential plot device introduced by the father: he says, 'I am about to take a business trip. What presents would my three girls like me to bring back for them?'

Note that: his *three* girls.

It occurs to me that perhaps the stepmother's daughters were really, all the time, his own daughters, just as much his own daughters as Ashputtle, his 'natural' daughters, as they say, as though there is something inherently unnatural about legitimacy. *That* would realign the forces in the story. It would make his connivance with the ascendancy of the other girls more plausible. It would make the speedy marriage, the stepmother's hostility more probable.

But it would also transform the story into something else, because it would provide motivation, and so on; it would mean I'd have to provide a past for all these people, that I would have to equip them with three dimensions, with tastes and memories, and I would have to think of things for them to eat and wear and say. It would transform 'Ashputtle' from the bare necessity of fairy tale, with its characteristic copula formula, 'and then', to the emotional and technical complexity of bourgeois realism. They would have to learn to think. Everything would change.

I will stick with what I know.

What presents do his three girls want?

'Bring me a silk dress,' said his eldest girl. 'Bring me a string of pearls,' said the middle one. What about the third one, the forgotten one, called out of the kitchen on a charitable impulse and drying her hands, raw with housework, on her apron, bringing with her the smell of old fire?

'Bring me the first branch that knocks against your hat on the way home,' said Ashputtle.

Why did she ask for that? Did she make an informed guess at how little he valued her? Or had a dream told her to use this random formula of unacknowledged desire, to allow blind chance to choose her present for her? Unless it was her mother's ghost, awake and restlessly looking for a way home, that came into the girl's mouth and spoke the request for her.

He brought her back a hazel twig. She planted it on her mother's grave and watered it with tears. It grew into a hazel tree. When Ashputtle came out to weep upon her mother's grave, the turtle dove crooned: 'I'll never leave you, I'll always protect you.'

Then Ashputtle knew that the turtle dove was her mother's ghost and she herself was still her mother's daughter, and although she had wept and wailed and longed to have her mother back again, now her heart sank a little to find out that her mother, though dead, was no longer gone and henceforward she must do her mother's bidding.

Came the time for that curious fair they used to hold in that country, when all the resident virgins went to dance in front of the king's son so that he could pick out the girl he wanted to marry.

The turtle dove was mad for that, for her daughter to marry the prince. You might have thought her own experience of marriage might have taught her to be wary, but no, needs must, what else is a girl to do? The turtle dove was mad for her daughter to marry so she flew in and picked up the new silk dress with her beak, dragged it to the open window, threw it down to Ashputtle. She did the same with the string of pearls. Ashputtle had a good wash under the pump in the yard, put on her stolen finery and crept out the back way, secretly, to the dancing grounds, but the stepsisters had to stay home and sulk because they had nothing to wear.

The turtle dove stayed close to Ashputtle, pecking her ears to make her dance vivaciously, so that the prince would see her, so that the prince would love her, so that he would follow her and find the clue of the fallen slipper, for the story is not complete without the ritual humiliation of the other woman and the mutilation of her daughters.

The search for the foot that fits the slipper is essential to the enactment of this ritual humiliation.

The other woman wants that young man desperately. She would do anything to catch him. Not losing a daughter, but gaining a son. She wants a son so badly she is prepared to cripple her daughters. She takes up a carving knife and chops off her elder daughter's big toe, so that her foot will fit the little shoe.

Imagine.

Brandishing the carving knife, the woman bears down on her child, who is as distraught as if she had not been a girl but a boy and the old woman was after a more essential portion than a toe. 'No!' she screams. 'Mother! No! Not the knife! No!' But off it comes, all the same, and she throws it in the fire, among the ashes, where Ashputtle finds it, wonders at it, and feels both awe and fear at the phenomenon of mother love.

Mother love, which winds about these daughters like a shroud.

The prince saw nothing familiar in the face of the tearful young woman, one shoe off, one shoe on, displayed to him in triumph by her mother, but he said: 'I promised I would marry whoever the shoe fitted so I will marry you,' and they rode off together.

The turtle dove came flying round and did not croon or coo to the bridal pair but sang a horrid song: 'Look! Look! There's blood in the shoe!'

The prince returned the ersatz ex-fiancée at once, angry at the trick, but the stepmother hastily lopped off her other daughter's heel and pushed *that* poor foot into the bloody shoe as soon as it was vacant so, nothing for it, a man of his word, the prince helped up the new girl and once again he rode away.

Back came the nagging turtle dove: 'Look!' And, sure enough, the shoe was full of blood again.

'Let Ashputtle try,' said the eager turtle dove.

So now Ashputtle must put her foot into the hideous receptacle, this open wound, still slick and warm as it is, for nothing in any of the many texts of this tale suggests the prince washed the shoe out between the fittings. It was an ordeal in itself to put a naked foot into the bloody shoe, but her mother, the turtle dove, urged her to do so in a soft, cooing croon that could not be denied.

If she does not plunge without revulsion into this open wound, she won't be fit to marry. That is the song of the turtle dove, while the other mad mother stood impotently by.

Ashputtle's foot, the size of the bound foot of a Chinese woman, a stump. Almost an amputee already, she put her tiny foot in it.

'Look! Look!' cried the turtle dove in triumph, even while the bird betrayed its ghostly nature by becoming progressively more and more immaterial as Ashputtle stood up in the shoe and commenced to walk around. Squelch, went the stump of the foot in the shoe. Squelch. 'Look!' sang out the turtle dove. 'Her foot fits the shoe like a corpse fits the coffin!

'See how well I look after you, my darling!'

2 The Burned Child

A burned child lived in the ashes. No, not really burned – more charred, a little bit charred, like a stick half-burned and picked off the fire. She looked like charcoal and ashes because she lived in the ashes since her mother died and the hot ashes burned her so she was scabbed and scarred. The burned child lived on the hearth, covered in ashes, as if she were still mourning.

After her mother died and was buried, her father forgot the mother and forgot the child and married the woman who used to rake the ashes, and that was why the child lived in the unraked ashes, and there was nobody to brush her hair, so it stuck out like a mat, nor to wipe the dirt off her scabbed face, and she had no heart to do it for herself, but she raked the ashes and slept beside the little cat and got the burned bits from the bottom of the pot to eat, scraping them out, squatting on the floor, by herself in front of the fire, not as if she were human, because she was still mourning.

Her mother was dead and buried, but felt perfect exquisite pain of love when she looked up through the earth and saw the burned child covered in ashes.

'Milk the cow, burned child, and bring back all the milk,' said the stepmother, who used to rake the ashes and milk the cow, once upon a time, but the burned child did all that, now.

The ghost of the mother went into the cow.

'Drink milk, grow fat,' said the mother's ghost.

The burned child pulled on the udder and drank enough milk before she took the bucket back and nobody saw, and time passed, she drank milk every day, she grew fat, she grew breasts, she grew up.

There was a man the stepmother wanted and she asked him into the kitchen to get his dinner, but she made the burned child cook it, although the stepmother did all the cooking before. After the burned child cooked the dinner the stepmother sent her off to milk the cow.

'I want that man for myself,' said the burned child to the cow.

The cow let down more milk, and more, and more, enough for the girl to have a drink and wash her face and wash her hands. When she washed her face, she washed the scabs off and now she was not burned at all, but the cow was empty.

'Give your own milk, next time,' said the ghost of the mother inside the cow. 'You've milked me dry.'

The little cat came by. The ghost of the mother went into the cat.

'Your hair wants doing,' said the cat. 'Lie down.'

The little cat unpicked her raggy lugs with its clever paws until the burned child's hair hung down nicely, but it had been so snagged and tangled that the cat's claws were all pulled out before it was finished.

'Comb your own hair, next time,' said the cat. 'You've maimed me.'

The burned child was clean and combed, but stark naked.

There was a bird sitting in the apple tree. The ghost of the mother left the cat and went into the bird. The bird struck its own breast with its beak. Blood poured down on to the burned child under the tree. It ran over her shoulders and covered her front and covered her back. When the bird had no more blood, the burned child got a red silk dress.

'Make your own dress, next time,' said the bird. 'I'm through with that bloody business.'

The burned child went into the kitchen to show herself to the man. She was not burned any more, but lovely. The man left off looking at the stepmother and looked at the girl.

'Come home with me and let your stepmother stay and rake the ashes,' he said to her and off they went. He gave her a house and money. She did all right.

'Now I can go to sleep,' said the ghost of the mother. 'Now everything is all right.'

3 Travelling Clothes

The stepmother took the red-hot poker and burned the orphan's face with it because she had not raked the ashes. The girl went to her mother's grave. In the earth her mother said: 'It must be raining. Or else it is snowing. Unless there is a heavy dew tonight.'

'It isn't raining, it isn't snowing, it's too early for the dew. My tears are falling on your grave, mother.'

The dead woman waited until night came. Then she climbed out and went to the house. The stepmother slept on a feather bed, but the burned child slept on the hearth among the ashes. When the dead woman kissed her, the scar vanished. The girl woke up. The dead woman gave her a red dress.

'I had it when I was your age.'

The girl put the red dress on. The dead woman took worms from her eyesockets; they turned into jewels. The girl put on a diamond ring.

'I had it when I was your age.'

They went together to the grave.

'Step into my coffin.'

'No,' said the girl. She shuddered.

'I stepped into *my* mother's coffin when I was your age.'

The girl stepped into the coffin although she thought it would be the death of her. It turned into a coach and horses. The horses stamped, eager to be gone.

'Go and seek your fortune, darling.'

Margaret Atwood (1939–)

Margaret Atwood was born in Ottawa, the second of three children. Her father was an entomologist and until she was twelve, Atwood spent six to eight months of the year in the bush. When not at school, the children were taught by their mother, a resourceful woman who could use a gun, shoot bows and arrows and survive on her own in the bush with small children for long periods of time.

In 1946 the family moved to Toronto where Atwood attended high school and then the University of Toronto where she studied English (1957–61). She became a graduate student at Harvard,

---

253

receiving her MA in 1962. She began a doctorate on English metaphysical romance but interrupted her studies to teach English at the University of British Columbia while working on her first novel, *The Edible Woman*.

Atwood's first volume of poems was published in 1961 and since then she has had a prolific career as poet, novelist, short story writer and critic, winning many prizes and establishing her reputation as Canada's most important contemporary writer. In 1967 she married James Polk. In 1973 they were divorced and she moved to Ontario with the writer, Graeme Gibson. They have one daughter, Jess, born in 1976. 'Giving Birth' was published a year later in Atwood's collection, *Dancing Girls* (1977). In 1980, Atwood and her family moved to Toronto where she now lives.

The theme of motherhood and its links with creativity runs through much of Atwood's work. She has said that though many women writers in the past have remained childless, she doesn't believe being a mother and being a writer are incompatible (Ingersoll 1992: 226). Many of her heroines are in fact failed artists and thwarted mothers, for example, the protagonist of *Surfacing* (1972) who has to undo the psychological effect of an abortion and acknowledge her debt to her mother or Marian in *The Edible Woman* (1969) who rejects all female roles, including that of maternity. *The Handmaid's Tale* (1985), perhaps Atwood's best-known work, deals with the themes of fertility and childbirth in the futurist state of Gilead, a right-wing dystopia based on Old Testament patriarchy.

'Giving Birth' may be read in conjunction with Atwood's poems to her daughter, such as 'Solstice Poem' and 'A Red Shirt' in *Two-Headed Poems* (1978). In 'Five Poems for Grandmothers' in the same volume, Atwood writes of the maternal legacy in terms of fluidity of identity: 'Sons branch out, but/one woman leads to another' (Atwood 1987: 14). Her short story, 'Significant Moments in the Life of my Mother' (in *Bluebeard's Egg*, 1988) is a brilliantly funny and unsentimental portrayal of her mother.

Primary reading

Atwood, M. 1969/1980 *The Edible Woman*, London: Virago.

Atwood, M. 1972/1979 *Surfacing*, London: Virago.

Atwood, M. 1977/1984 *Dancing Girls and Other Stories*, London: Virago.

Atwood, M. 1985/1987 *The Handmaid's Tale*, London: Virago.

Atwood, M. 1987 *Selected Poems II: Poems Selected and New 1976–1986*, Boston: Houghton Mifflin.

Atwood, M. 1988 *Bluebeard's Egg*, London: Virago.

Further reading

Ingersoll, E. G. (ed.) 1992 *Margaret Atwood: Conversations*, London: Virago.

Nicholson, C. (ed.) 1994 *Margaret Atwood: Writing and Subjectivity*, New York: St Martin's Press.

Rigney, B. H. 1987 *Margaret Atwood*, London: Macmillan.

Rosenberg, J. H. 1984 *Margaret Atwood*, Boston: Twayne.

Giving Birth

From Margaret Atwood, *Dancing Girls*, London: Virago, 1984, pp. 225–40.

But who gives it? And to whom is it given? Certainly it doesn't feel like giving, which implies a flow, a gentle handing over, no coercion. But there is scant gentleness here, it's too strenuous, the belly like a knotted fist, squeezing, the heavy trudge of the heart, every muscle in the body tight and moving, as in a slow-motion shot of a high-jump, the faceless body sailing up, turning, hanging for a moment in the air, and then – back to real time again – the plunge, the rush down, the result. Maybe the phrase was made by someone viewing the result only: in this case, the rows of babies to whom birth has occurred, lying like neat packages in their expertly wrapped blankets, pink or blue, with their labels Scotch Taped to their clear plastic cots, behind the plate-glass window.

No one ever says *giving death*, although they are in some ways the same, events, not things. And *delivering*, that act the doctor is generally believed to perform: who delivers what? Is it the mother who is delivered, like a prisoner being released? Surely not; nor is the child delivered to the mother like a letter through a slot. How can you be both the sender and the receiver at once? Was someone in bondage, is someone made free? Thus language, muttering in its archaic tongues of something, yet one more thing, that needs to be re-named.

It won't be by me, though. These are the only words I have, I'm stuck with them, stuck in them. (That image of the tar sands, old tableau in the Royal Ontario Museum, second floor north, how persistent it is. Will I break free, or will I be sucked down, fossilized, a sabre-toothed tiger or lumbering brontosaurus who ventured out too far? Words ripple at my feet, black, sluggish, lethal. Let me try once more, before the sun gets me, before I starve or drown, while I can. It's only a tableau after all, it's only a metaphor. See, I can speak, I am not trapped, and you on your part can understand. So we will go ahead as if there were no problem about language.)

This story about giving birth is not about me. In order to convince you of that I should tell you what I did this morning, before I sat down at this desk – a door on top of two filing cabinets, radio to the left, calendar to the right, these devices by which I place myself in time. I got up at twenty-to-seven, and, halfway down the stairs, met my daughter, who was ascending, autonomously she thought, actually in the arms of her father. We greeted each other with hugs and smiles; we then played with the alarm clock and the hot water bottle, a ritual we go through only on the days her father has to leave the house early to drive into the city. This ritual exists to give me the illusion that I am sleeping in. When she finally decided it was time for me to get up, she began pulling my hair. I got dressed while she explored the bathroom scales and the mysterious white altar of the toilet. I took her downstairs and we had the usual struggle over her clothes. Already she is wearing miniature jeans, miniature T-shirts. After this she fed herself: orange, banana, muffin, porridge.

We then went out to the sun porch, where we recognized anew, and by their names, the dog, the cats and the birds, blue jays and goldfinches at this time of year, which is winter. She puts her fingers on my lips as I pronounce these words; she hasn't yet learned the secret of making them. I am waiting for her first word: surely it will be miraculous, something that has never yet been said. But if so, perhaps she's already said it and I, in my entrapment, my addiction to the usual, have not heard it.

In her playpen I discovered the first alarming thing of the day. It was a small naked woman, made of that soft plastic from which jiggly spiders and lizards and the other things people hang in their car windows are also made. She was given to my daughter by a friend, a woman who does props for movies, she was supposed to have been a prop but she wasn't used. The baby loved her and would crawl around the floor holding her in her mouth like a dog carrying a bone, with the head sticking out one side and the feet out the other. She seemed chewy and harmless, but the other day I noticed that the baby had managed to make a tear in the body with her new teeth. I put the woman into the cardboard box I use for toy storage.

But this morning she was back in the playpen and the feet were gone. The baby must have eaten them, and I worried about whether or not the plastic would dissolve in her stomach, whether it was toxic. Sooner or later, in the contents of her diaper, which I examine with the usual amount of maternal brooding, I knew I would find two small pink plastic feet. I removed the doll and later, while she was still singing to the dog outside the window, dropped it into the garbage. I am not up to finding tiny female arms, breasts, a head, in my daughter's disposable diapers, partially covered by undigested carrots and the husks of raisins, like the relics of some gruesome and demented murder.

Now she's having her nap and I am writing this story. From what I have said, you can see that my life (despite these occasional surprises, reminders of another world) is calm and orderly, suffused with that warm, reddish light, those well-placed blue highlights and reflecting surfaces (mirrors, plates, oblong window-panes) you think of as belonging to Dutch genre paintings; and like them it is realistic in detail and slightly sentimental. Or at least it has an aura of sentiment. (Already I'm having moments of muted grief over those of my daughter's baby clothes which are too small for her to wear any more. I will be a keeper of hair, I will store things in trunks, I will weep over photos.) But above all it's solid, everything here has solidity. No more of those washes of light, those shifts, nebulous effects of cloud, Turner sunsets, vague fears, the impalpables Jeanie used to concern herself with.

I call this woman Jeanie after the song. I can't remember any more of the song, only the title. The point (for in language there are always these 'points,' these reflections; this is what makes it so rich and sticky, this is why so many have disappeared beneath its dark and shining surface, why you should never try to see your own reflection in it; you will lean over too far, a strand of your hair will fall in and come out gold, and, thinking it is gold all the way down, you yourself will follow, sliding into those outstretched arms, towards the mouth you think is opening to pronounce your name but instead, just before your ears fill with pure sound, will form a word you have never heard before . . .)

The point, for me, is in the hair. My own hair is not light brown, but Jeanie's was. This is one difference between us. The other point is the dreaming; for Jeanie isn't real in the same way that I am real. But by now, and I mean your time, both of us will have the same degree of reality, we will be equal: wraiths, echoes, reverberations in your own brain. At the moment though Jeanie is to me as I will someday be to you. So she is real enough.

Jeanie is on her way to the hospital, to give birth, to be delivered. She is not quibbling over these terms. She's sitting in the back seat of the car, with her eyes closed and her coat spread over her like a blanket. She is doing her breathing exercises and timing her contractions with a stopwatch. She has been up since two-thirty in the morning, when she took a bath and ate some lime Jell-O, and it's now almost ten. She has learned to count, during the slow breathing, in numbers (from one to ten while breathing in, from ten to one while breathing out) which she can actually see while she is silently pronouncing them. Each number is a different colour and, if she's concentrating very hard, a different typeface. They range from plain roman to ornamented circus numbers, red with gold filigree and dots. This is a refinement not mentioned in any of the numerous books she's read on the subject. Jeanie is a devotee of handbooks. She has at least two shelves of books that cover everything from building kitchen cabinets to auto repairs to smoking your own hams. She doesn't do many of these things, but she does some of them, and in her suitcase, along with a washcloth, a package of lemon Life Savers, a pair of glasses, a hot water bottle, some talcum powder and a paper bag, is the book that suggested she take along all of these things.

(By this time you may be thinking that I've invented Jeanie in order to distance myself from these experiences. Nothing could be further from the truth. I am, in fact, trying to bring myself closer to something that time has already made distant. As for Jeanie, my intention is simple: I am bringing her back to life.)

There are two other people in the car with Jeanie. One is a man, whom I will call A., for convenience. A. is driving. When Jeanie opens her eyes, at the end of every contraction, she can see the back of his slightly balding head and his reassuring shoulders. A. drives well and not too quickly. From time to time he asks her how she is, and she tells him how long the contractions are lasting and how long there is between them. When they stop for gas he buys them each a Styrofoam container of coffee. For months he has helped her with the breathing exercises, pressing on her knee as recommended by the book, and he will be present at the delivery. (Perhaps it's to him that

the birth will be given, in the same sense that one gives a performance.) Together they have toured the hospital maternity ward, in
company with a small group of other pairs like them: one thin
solicitous person, one slow bulbous person. They have been shown
the rooms, shared and private, the sitz-baths, the delivery room itself,
which gave the impression of being white. The nurse was light-
brown, with limber hips and elbows; she laughed a lot as she
answered questions.

'First they'll give you an enema. You know what it is? They take a
tube of water and put it up your behind. Now, the gentlemen must
put on this – and these, over your shoes. And these hats, this one for
those with long hair, this for those with short hair.'

'What about those with no hair?' says A.

The nurse looks up at his head and laughs. 'Oh, you still have
some,' she says. 'If you have a question, do not be afraid to ask.'

They have also seen the film made by the hospital, a full-colour
film of a woman giving birth to, can it be a baby? 'Not all babies will
be this large at birth,' the Australian nurse who introduces the movie
says. Still, the audience, half of which is pregnant, doesn't look very
relaxed when the lights go on. ('If you don't like the visuals,' a friend
of Jeanie's has told her, 'you can always close your eyes.') It isn't the
blood so much as the brownish-red disinfectant that bothers her. 'I've
decided to call this whole thing off,' she says to A., smiling to show
it's a joke. He gives her a hug and says, 'Everything's going to be fine.'

And she knows it is. Everything will be fine. But there is another
woman in the car. She's sitting in the front seat, and she hasn't turned
or acknowledged Jeanie in any way. She, like Jeanie, is going to the
hospital. She too is pregnant. She is not going to the hospital to give
birth, however, because the words, the words, are too alien to her
experience, the experience she is about to have, to be used about it at
all. She's wearing a cloth coat with checks in maroon and brown, and
she has a kerchief tied over her hair. Jeanie has seen her before, but
she knows little about her except that she is a woman who did not

wish to become pregnant, who did not choose to divide herself like this, who did not choose any of these ordeals, these initiations. It would be no use telling her that everything is going to be fine. The word in English for unwanted intercourse is rape. But there is no word in the language for what is about to happen to this woman.

Jeanie has seen this woman from time to time throughout her pregnancy, always in the same coat, always with the same kerchief. Naturally, being pregnant herself has made her more aware of other pregnant women, and she has watched them, examined them covertly, every time she has seen one. But not every other pregnant woman is this woman. She did not, for instance, attend Jeanie's prenatal classes at the hospital, where the women were all young, younger than Jeanie.

'How many will be breast-feeding?' asks the Australian nurse with the hefty shoulders.

All hands but one shoot up. A modern group, the new generation, and the one lone bottle-feeder, who might have (who knows?) something wrong with her breasts, is ashamed of herself. The others look politely away from her. What they want most to discuss, it seems, are the differences between one kind of disposable diaper and another. Sometimes they lie on mats and squeeze each other's hands, simulating contractions and counting breaths. It's all very hopeful. The Australian nurse tells them not to get in and out of the bathtub by themselves. At the end of an hour they are each given a glass of apple juice.

There is only one woman in the class who has already given birth. She's there, she says, to make sure they give her a shot this time. They delayed it last time and she went through hell. The others look at her with mild disapproval. *They* are not clamouring for shots, they do not intend to go through hell. Hell comes from the wrong attitude, they feel. The books talk about *discomfort*.

'It's not discomfort, it's pain, baby,' the woman says.

The others smile uneasily and the conversation slides back to disposable diapers.

Vitaminized, conscientious, well-read Jeanie, who has managed to avoid morning sickness, varicose veins, stretch marks, toxemia and depression, who has had no aberrations of appetite, no blurrings of vision – why is she followed, then, by this other? At first it was only a glimpse now and then, at the infants' clothing section in Simpson's Basement, in the supermarket lineup, on street corners as she herself slid by in A.'s car: the haggard face, the bloated torso, the kerchief holding back the too-sparse hair. In any case, it was Jeanie who saw her, not the other way around. If she knew she was following Jeanie she gave no sign.

As Jeanie has come closer and closer to this day, the unknown day on which she will give birth, as time has thickened around her so that it has become something she must propel herself through, a kind of slush, wet earth underfoot, she has seen this woman more and more often, though always from a distance. Depending on the light, she has appeared by turns as a young girl of perhaps twenty to an older woman of forty or forty-five, but there was never any doubt in Jeanie's mind that it was the same woman. In fact it did not occur to her that the woman was not real in the usual sense (and perhaps she was, originally, on the first or second sighting, as the voice that causes an echo is real), until A. stopped for a red light during this drive to the hospital and the woman, who had been standing on the corner with a brown paper bag in her arms, simply opened the front door of the car and got in. A. didn't react, and Jeanie knows better than to say anything to him. She is aware that the woman is not really there: Jeanie is not crazy. She could even make the woman disappear by opening her eyes wider, by staring, but it is only the shape that would go away, not the feeling. Jeanie isn't exactly afraid of this woman. She is afraid for her.

When they reach the hospital, the woman gets out of the car and is through the door by the time A. has come around to help Jeanie out of the back seat. In the lobby she is nowhere to be seen. Jeanie goes through Admission in the usual way, unshadowed.

GIVING BIRTH

There has been an epidemic of babies during the night and the maternity ward is overcrowded. Jeanie waits for her room behind a dividing screen. Nearby someone is screaming, screaming and mumbling between screams in what sounds like a foreign language. Portuguese, Jeanie thinks. She tells herself that for them it is different, you're supposed to scream, you're regarded as queer if you don't scream, it's a required part of giving birth. Nevertheless she knows that the woman screaming is the other woman and she is screaming from pain. Jeanie listens to the other voice, also a woman's, comforting, reassuring: her mother? A nurse?

A. arrives and they sit uneasily, listening to the screams. Finally Jeanie is sent for and she goes for her prep. Prep school, she thinks. She takes off her clothes – when will she see them again? – and puts on the hospital gown. She is examined, labelled around the wrist and given an enema. She tells the nurse she can't take Demerol because she's allergic to it, and the nurse writes this down. Jeanie doesn't know whether this is true or not but she doesn't want Demerol, she has read the books. She intends to put up a struggle over her pubic hair – surely she will lose her strength if it is all shaved off – but it turns out the nurse doesn't have very strong feelings about it. She is told her contractions are not far enough along to be taken seriously, she can even have lunch. She puts on her dressing gown and rejoins A., in the freshly vacated room, eats some tomato soup and a veal cutlet, and decides to take a nap while A. goes out for supplies.

Jeanie wakes up when A. comes back. He has brought a paper, some detective novels for Jeanie and a bottle of Scotch for himself. A. reads the paper and drinks Scotch, and Jeanie reads *Poirot's Early Cases*. There is no connection between Poirot and her labour, which is now intensifying, unless it is the egg-shape of Poirot's head and the vegetable marrows he is known to cultivate with strands of wet wool (placentae? umbilical cords?). She is glad the stories are short; she is walking around the room now, between contractions. Lunch was definitely a mistake.

'I think I have back labour,' she says to A. They get out the handbook and look up the instructions for this. It's useful that everything has a name. Jeanie kneels on the bed and rests her forehead on her arms while A. rubs her back. A. pours himself another Scotch, in the hospital glass. The nurse, in pink, comes, looks, asks about the timing, and goes away again. Jeanie is beginning to sweat. She can only manage half a page or so of Poirot before she has to clamber back up on the bed again and begin breathing and running through the coloured numbers.

When the nurse comes back, she has a wheelchair. It's time to go down to the labour room, she says. Jeanie feels stupid sitting in the wheelchair. She tells herself about peasant women having babies in the fields, Indian women having them on portages with hardly a second thought. She feels effete. But the hospital wants her to ride, and considering the fact that the nurse is tiny, perhaps it's just as well. What if Jeanie were to collapse, after all? After all her courageous talk. An image of the tiny pink nurse, antlike, trundling large Jeanie through the corridors, rolling her along like a heavy beach ball.

As they go by the check-in desk a woman is wheeled past on a table, covered by a sheet. Her eyes are closed and there's a bottle feeding into her arm through a tube. Something is wrong. Jeanie looks back – she thinks it was the other woman – but the sheeted table is hidden now behind the counter.

In the dim labour room Jeanie takes off her dressing gown and is helped up onto the bed by the nurse. A. brings her suitcase, which is not a suitcase actually but a small flight bag, the significance of this has not been lost on Jeanie, and in fact she now has some of the apprehensive feelings she associates with planes, including the fear of a crash. She takes out her Life Savers, her glasses, her washcloth and the other things she thinks she will need. She removes her contact lenses and places them in their case, reminding A. that they must not be lost. Now she is purblind.

There is something else in her bag that she doesn't remove. It's a talisman, given to her several years ago as a souvenir by a travelling friend of hers. It's a rounded oblong of opaque blue glass, with four yellow-and-white eye shapes on it. In Turkey, her friend has told her, they hang them on mules to protect against the Evil Eye. Jeanie knows this talisman probably won't work for her, she is not Turkish and she isn't a mule, but it makes her feel safer to have it in the room with her. She had planned to hold it in her hand during the most difficult part of labour but somehow there is no longer any time for carrying out plans like this.

An old woman, a fat old woman dressed all in green, comes into the room and sits beside Jeanie. She says to A., who is sitting on the other side of Jeanie, 'That is a good watch. They don't make watches like that any more.' She is referring to his gold pocket watch, one of his few extravagances, which is on the night table. Then she places her hand on Jeanie's belly to feel the contraction. 'This is good,' she says, her accent is Swedish or German. 'This, I call a contraction. Before, it was nothing.' Jeanie can no longer remember having seen her before. 'Good. Good.'

'When will I have it?' Jeanie asks, when she can talk, when she is no longer counting.

The old woman laughs. Surely that laugh, those tribal hands, have presided over a thousand beds, a thousand kitchen tables . . . 'A long time yet,' she says. 'Eight, ten hours.'

'But I've been *doing* this for twelve hours already,' Jeanie says.

'Not hard labour,' the woman says. 'Not good, like this.'

Jeanie settles into herself for the long wait. At the moment she can't remember why she wanted to have a baby in the first place. That decision was made by someone else, whose motives are now unclear. She remembers the way women who had babies used to smile at one another, mysteriously, as if there was something they knew that she didn't, the way they would casually exclude her from their frame of reference. What was the knowledge, the mystery, or was having a baby really no more inexplicable than having a car accident or an orgasm? (But these too were indescribable, events of the body, all of them; why should the mind distress itself trying to find a language for them?) She has sworn she will never do that to any woman without children, engage in those passwords and exclusions. She's old enough, she's been put through enough years of it to find it tiresome and cruel.

But – and this is the part of Jeanie that goes with the talisman hidden in her bag, not with the part that longs to build kitchen cabinets and smoke hams – she is, secretly, hoping for a mystery. Something more than this, something else, a vision. After all she is risking her life, though it's not too likely she will die. Still, some women do. Internal bleeding, shock, heart failure, a mistake on the part of someone, a nurse, a doctor. She deserves a vision, she deserves to be allowed to bring something back with her from this dark place into which she is now rapidly descending.

She thinks momentarily about the other woman. Her motives, too, are unclear. Why doesn't she want to have a baby? Has she been raped, does she have ten other children, is she starving? Why hasn't she had an abortion? Jeanie doesn't know, and in fact it no longer matters why. *Uncross your fingers*, Jeanie thinks to her. Her face, distorted with pain and terror, floats briefly behind Jeanie's eyes before it too drifts away.

Jeanie tries to reach down to the baby, as she has many times before, sending waves of love, colour, music, down through her arteries to it, but she finds she can no longer do this. She can no longer feel the baby as a baby, its arms and legs poking, kicking, turning. It has collected itself together, it's a hard sphere, it does not have time right now to listen to her. She's grateful for this because she isn't sure anyway how good the message would be. She no longer has control of the numbers either, she can no longer see them, although she continues mechanically to count. She realizes she has practised for the wrong thing, A. squeezing her knee was nothing, she should have practised for this, whatever it is.

'Slow down,' A. says. She's on her side now, he's holding her hand. 'Slow it right down.'

'I can't. I can't do it, I can't do this.'

'Yes, you can.'

'Will I sound like that?'

'Like what?' A. says. Perhaps he can't hear it: it's the other woman, in the room next door or the room next door to that. She's screaming and crying, screaming and crying. While she cries she is saying, over and over, 'It hurts. It hurts.'

'No, you won't,' he says. So there is someone, after all.

A doctor comes in, not her own doctor. They want her to turn over on her back.

'I can't,' she says. 'I don't like it that way.' Sounds have receded, she has trouble hearing them. She turns over and the doctor gropes with her rubber-gloved hand. Something wet and hot flows over her thighs.

'It was just ready to break,' the doctor says. 'All I had to do was touch it. Four centimetres,' she says to A.

'Only *four*?' Jeanie says. She feels cheated; they must be wrong. The doctor says her own doctor will be called in time. Jeanie is outraged at them. They have not understood, but it's too late to say this and she slips back into the dark place, which is not hell, which is more like being inside, trying to get out. *Out*, she says or thinks. Then she is floating, the numbers are gone, if anyone told her to get up, go out of the room, stand on her head, she would do it. From minute to minute she comes up again, grabs for air.

'You're hyperventilating,' A. says. 'Slow it down.' He is rubbing her back now, hard, and she takes his hand and shoves it viciously further down, to the right place, which is not the right place as soon as his hand is there. She remembers a story she read once, about the Nazis tying the legs of Jewish women together during labour. She never really understood before how that could kill you.

A nurse appears with a needle. 'I don't want it,' Jeanie says.

'Don't be hard on yourself,' the nurse says. 'You don't have to go through pain like that.' What pain? Jeanie thinks. When there is no pain she feels nothing, when there is pain, she feels nothing because there is no *she*. This, finally, is the disappearance of language. *You don't remember afterwards*, she has been told by almost everyone.

Jeanie comes out of a contraction, gropes for control. 'Will it hurt the baby?' she says.

'It's a mild analgesic,' the doctor says. 'We wouldn't allow anything that would hurt the baby.' Jeanie doesn't believe this. Nevertheless she is jabbed, and the doctor is right, it is very mild, because it doesn't seem to do a thing for Jeanie, though A. later tells her she has slept briefly between contractions.

Suddenly she sits bolt upright. She is wide awake and lucid. 'You have to ring that bell right now,' she says. 'This baby is being born.'

A. clearly doesn't believe her. 'I can feel it, I can feel the head,' she says. A. pushes the button for the call bell. A nurse appears and checks, and now everything is happening too soon, nobody is ready. They set off down the hall, the nurse wheeling. Jeanie feels fine. She watches the corridors, the edges of everything shadowy because she doesn't have her glasses on. She hopes A. will remember to bring them. They pass another doctor.

'Need me?' she asks.

'Oh no,' the nurse answers breezily. 'Natural childbirth.'

Jeanie realizes that this woman must have been the anaesthetist. 'What?' she says, but it's too late now, they are in the room itself, all those glossy surfaces, tubular strange apparatus like a science-fiction movie, and the nurse is telling her to get onto the delivery table. No one else is in the room.

'You must be crazy,' Jeanie says.

'Don't push,' the nurse says.

'What do you mean?' Jeanie says. This is absurd. Why should she wait, why should the baby wait for them because they're late?

'Breathe through your mouth,' the nurse says. 'Pant,' and Jeanie finally remembers how. When the contraction is over she uses the nurse's arm as a lever and hauls herself across onto the table.

From somewhere her own doctor materializes, in her doctor suit already, looking even more like Mary Poppins than usual, and Jeanie says, 'Bet you weren't expecting to see me so soon!' The baby is being born when Jeanie said it would, though just three days ago the doctor said it would be at least another week, and this makes Jeanie feel jubilant and smug. Not that she knew, she'd believed the doctor.

She's being covered with a green tablecloth, they are taking far too long, she feels like pushing the baby out now, before they are ready. A. is there by her head, swathed in robes, hats, masks. He has forgotten her glasses. 'Push now,' the doctor says. Jeanie grips with her hands, grits her teeth, face, her whole body together, a snarl, a fierce smile, the baby is enormous, a stone, a boulder, her bones unlock, and, once, twice, the third time, she opens like a birdcage turning slowly inside out.

A pause; a wet kitten slithers between her legs. 'Why don't you look?' says the doctor, but Jeanie still has her eyes closed. No glasses, she couldn't have seen a thing anyway. 'Why don't you look?' the doctor says again.

Jeanie opens her eyes. She can see the baby, who has been wheeled up beside her and is fading already from the alarming birth purple. A good baby, she thinks, meaning it as the old woman did: *a good watch*, well-made, substantial. The baby isn't crying; she squints in the new light. Birth isn't something that has been given to her, nor has she taken it. It was just something that has happened so they could greet each other like this. The nurse is stringing beads for her name. When the baby is bundled and tucked beside Jeanie, she goes to sleep.

As for the vision, there wasn't one. Jeanie is conscious of no special knowledge; already she's forgetting what it was like. She's tired and very cold; she is shaking, and asks for another blanket. A. comes back to the room with her; her clothes are still there. Everything is quiet, the other woman is no longer screaming. Something has happened to her, Jeanie knows. Is she dead? Is the baby dead? Perhaps she is one of those casualties (and how can Jeanie herself be sure, yet, that she will not be among them) who will go into postpartum depression and never come out. 'You see, there was nothing to be afraid of,' A. says before he leaves, but he was wrong.

The next morning Jeanie wakes up when it's light. She's been warned about getting out of bed the first time without the help of a nurse, but she decides to do it anyway (peasant in the field! Indian on the portage!). She's still running adrenaline, she's also weaker than she thought, but she wants very much to look out the window. She feels she's been inside too long, she wants to see the sun come up. Being awake this early always makes her feel a little unreal, a little insubstantial, as if she's partly transparent, partly dead.

(It was to me, after all, that the birth was given, Jeanie gave it, I am the result. What would she make of me? Would she be pleased?)

The window is two panes with a venetian blind sandwiched between them; it turns by a knob at the side. Jeanie has never seen a window like this before. She closes and opens the blind several times. Then she leaves it open and looks out.

All she can see from the window is a building. It's an old stone building, heavy and Victorian, with a copper roof oxidized to green. It's solid, hard, darkened by soot, dour, leaden. But as she looks at this building, so old and seemingly immutable, she sees that it's made of water. Water, and some tenuous jelly-like substance. Light flows through it from behind (the sun is coming up), the building is so thin, so fragile, that it quivers in the slight dawn wind. Jeanie sees that if the building is this way (a touch could destroy it, a ripple of the earth, why has no one noticed, guarded it against accidents?) then the rest of the world must be like this too, the entire earth, the rocks, people, trees, everything needs to be protected, cared for, tended. The enormity of this task defeats her; she will never be up to it, and what will happen then?

Jeanie hears footsteps in the hall outside her door. She thinks it must be the other woman, in her brown-and-maroon-checked coat, carrying her paper bag, leaving the hospital now that her job is done. She has seen Jeanie safely through, she must go now to hunt through the streets of the city for her next case. But the door opens, it's nurse, who is just in time to catch Jeanie as she sinks to the floor, holding on to the edge of the air-conditioning unit. The nurse scolds her for getting up too soon.

After that the baby is carried in, solid, substantial, packed together like an apple, Jeanie examines her, she is complete, and in the days that follow Jeanie herself becomes drifted over with new words, her hair slowly darkens, she ceases to be what she was and is replaced, gradually, by someone else.

Michèle Roberts (1949–)

M ichèle Roberts was born in London to an English Protestant father and a French Catholic mother. She was one of twin sisters and also had an elder sister and a younger brother. Roberts was brought up bilingual, spending summer holidays with her mother's family in France, a country which figures largely in her writing. 'Une Glossaire/A Glossary' published in her collection *During Mother's Absence* portrays her childhood recollections of France.

Michèle Roberts was educated at a convent in England before going on to Oxford to read English. After Oxford, she went as a librarian with the British Council to Bangkok, South Vietnam and

Cambodia. When she returned to England she spent time living in a women's commune in London. Her first writing grew out of collaborative work with other feminist writers such as Sara Maitland, Zoë Fairburns and Michelene Wandor.

Michèle Roberts is both a poet and a novelist. From 1975 to 1977 she was poetry editor of *Spare Rib* and from 1981–83 of *City Limits*. Her first novel, *A Piece of the Night* (1978), with its themes of female sexuality and sensuous nature descriptions has been compared to the work of Colette. In it the heroine rejects the patriarchalism of Catholicism, comes to an uneasy reconciliation with her mother, and finds her identity through loving other women. Her next novel, *The Visitation* (1983), again features a woman's difficult relationship with her mother as she comes to terms with the lost masculine part of herself. Her third novel, *The Wild Girl* (1984), makes a plea for a spirituality that would embrace the mother as well as the father.

The mother-daughter theme runs through Roberts's poetry as well, in particular her Demeter-Persephone poems in *The Mirror of the Mother* (1986). In 'A psalm for Easter' in *Psyche and the hurricane* (1991) attendance at a birth prompts memories of the poet's own mother and a wish for reconciliation with her. Roberts has said: 'I catch myself writing, or wanting to write, about a woman achieving wholeness, being reunited with her mother . . . healing the splits inside herself,' (Roberts 1986: 229; ellipsis mine). In this context Michèle Roberts's work, with its theme of the quest for the lost mother, can be seen as the polar opposite of Angela Carter's determination to demolish idealisations of motherhood in her writing.

Primary reading
Roberts, M. 1978 *A Piece of the Night*, London: The Women's Press.
Roberts, M. 1983 *The Visitation*, London: The Women's Press.
Roberts, M. 1984 *The Wild Girl*, London: Methuen.
Roberts, M. 1986 'Write, she said' in *The Progress of Romance: the Politics*

of Popular Fiction J. Radford (ed.), London and New York: Routledge & Kegan Paul.

Roberts, M. 1987 *The Book of Mrs Noah*, London: Methuen.

Roberts, M. 1990 *In the Red Kitchen*, London: Methuen.

Roberts, M. 1990 'Musing Over Power', *The New Statesman* 16 March: 31–3.

Roberts, M. 1994 *During Mother's Absence*, London: Virago.

Roberts, M. 1995 *All the Selves I Was. New and Selected Poems*, London: Virago.

Roberts, M. 1998 *Food, Sex and God. On Inspiration and Writing*, London: Virago.

Further reading

Wandor, M. 1983 *On Gender and Writing*, London: Pandora.

White, R. 1993 'Essay: the Novels of Michèle Roberts', *Bête Noire* 14/15: 144–57.

White, R. 1993 'An Interview with Michèle Roberts', *Bête Noire* 14/15: 125–40.

God's House

From Michèle Roberts, *During Mother's Absence*, London: Virago, 1994, pp. 99–119.

Inside the priest's house it was very dark. I flattened my palms against the invisible air then advanced step by tiptoeing step. I smelt dust and the dregs of wine. I'd left the heat outside. The curved edge of a stone doorway was cold, grazed my cheek. Groping forwards, I encountered glass, a metal catch. With a rattle and squeak of iron bars I undid the shutters, pushed them open. Light drowned me. I saw that I was in a kitchen, bare except for a cooker and oilcloth-covered table. Sunlight fell across glistening brown paint on to my hands. I turned around and leaned back against the windowsill.

I was a burglar. My first break and entry. I wasn't sure what I wanted to steal.

I was back with you, in our old house where I'd been born twelve years before. Now a veranda had been added on at the front, bellying forwards into the garden, and your bed had been put there under the dome of glass. Half in and half out. You sat up when you saw me come in, and held out your arms.

– You haven't left yet then, I said.

The room behind us was full of relatives, a sort of party going on. You gestured towards me to come closer. You held all my attention: your lashless monkey eyes that were very bright, your translucent skin, your full, blistered lips, the outline of your head under its fuzz of curls. Everything that there was between us concentrated into that look we exchanged. Above the glass roof was the red sky, the break of dawn.

For a while the road ran through the plain, along the poplar-lined Canal du Midi, and then it rose, as the land lifted itself and became hillier. A straight road, running between golden-green plane trees, towards Spain. The rounded hills, brown and dark yellow, took us up, and up. We swung off the main road on to a smaller one, and one yet smaller.

Our village was called Beauregard-du-Perdu. We turned, as instructed, by the wash-house and fountain, and drove up the main street lined with plane trees. A green tunnel pierced with bits of dancing light. At its top I saw the stone bulk of the church, a rounded doorway decorated with zigzags. To the right, behind low gates of grey metal, was the house my aunt and uncle were renting from some French friends. We recognised it straight away from the photographs. I got out of the car and saw the other house, opposite. No. What I saw was the high wall enclosing it, the steps up to the padlocked wooden door in the wall, worn steps that curved sideways then went up to the church behind. A notice tacked to the door, just above the padlock, said A VENDRE. As I stared, the church bells began to clang out the hour and I started back from their dull, flat noise.

My aunt bent towards me.

– Lily. Would you like to be the one to knock on the neighbour's door and ask for the keys? Show us how well you speak French.

I inspected the gravel under my new shoes that I'd bought for the funeral. The gravel was grey like the metal gates, loose chips under my stiff toes. I lifted a foot and scraped it along the ground.

– No point, my uncle said: here she is anyway.

Our letter of introduction named her as Madame Cabazou, a widow. She came out of the alleyway opposite our house, below the wall with its wooden door and its FOR SALE notice. A blue enamel sign proclaimed that the alley was called Impasse des Saints. Madame Cabazou was as quick as one of the lizards on the hot wall nearby. Small and skinny, eyes black as olives in her brown face, grey hair cut short. Gold daisies in her pierced ears. Her marriage earrings, she told me later on: that she wore every day. Flick flick went her tongue in her mouth as she exclaimed and shook hands and pulled the key from her housecoat pocket and ushered us in. She darted off again with a wave of her hand, a promise to bring us a bowl of plums picked that morning from the trees in her field.

Our holiday home was a little house on three floors, its walls painted a cool blue-grey. Red speckled tiles underfoot downstairs, unpolished wooden floorboards in the two bedrooms. Up here the windows had white shutters that creased up like concertinas and let in long arms of brambles laden with roses, and tiny balconies, no bigger than windowsills, in white-painted wrought iron. The bed in my room was narrow and high, with a white cover. The chairs were old-fashioned, with curvy backs. They broke when you sat on them; they were just for show.

The garden was large considering it was in the middle of a village, my aunt said. It was mainly grass, with flowerbeds and tangly shrubs dotted about in it. The solid privet hedge surrounding it was such a dark green it was almost black. Over it reared the plane trees that lined the village street outside. Sage green, almond green, sea green, bottle green, those were the colours of the bushes and plants. The flowers were so bright with the light in them, mauve and pink. The sun dazzling down on the garden at midday made it white. Too hot to sit in without a hat. I felt scorched. I preferred the coolness of the broken-down barn with its earth floor, where swallows flashed in and out, quick blue streaks. On the first morning the swallows flew into my room when I was still in bed and I felt welcomed.

I was puzzled when the telephone rang. I hadn't seen one the night before. There it was, by the bed. I lifted the receiver and said hello.

Your voice sounded exactly as it always did.

– Hello, you said back to me: how are you getting on?

– D'you mean to say, I asked: that they've got telephones up there? You laughed.

– Of course we have. How else could we get in touch? Now come on, I haven't much time, how's your father managing, and how are you?

– Oh he's doing fine, I said: more or less. You know. He's being extra careful when he drives the car.

Why did I say that? I don't know. Just then the church bells began to ring, battering the windowpanes, and your voice faded away under their onslaught.

My aunt and uncle were welded to their white plastic lounging chairs. Turned towards each other, they held hands and chatted. They were pink-faced, melting in the heat. I strolled past them with a wave, went out to explore the village.

The church door seemed locked. I shoved it with my shoulder but its resistance didn't yield. I wandered on past it, paused at an open pair of tall wrought-iron gates, went in.

I was in the cemetery. The village within the village. The houses of the dead neatly arranged side by side. The path ran all the way round, tombs on both sides. Some of the graves were just mounds of earth, with fragile, blackened crosses in crumbling iron at their heads. Others were doors laid down on the ground, thick polished stone bearing pots of pink and red porcelain roses, open porcelain books with gilt letters spelling out the names of the dead. Whole families seemed to be crammed into small tight plots. Some of the graves had photographs in black metal frames. Some had stone angels. One had a crucifix made of tiny black beads.

Madame Cabazou knelt by a shiny slab of white granite. She inserted mauve flowers, like the ones in our garden, into a black vase on top of it. I looked over her shoulder to read her husband's name carved into the stone. Emile.

– He died three months ago, Madame Cabazou said: I'm not used to it yet.

She stood up and clasped my arm. Then she held my hand in hers. Water shone in her eyes, tipped over, flowed down her cheeks.

Just behind the graves the hills began, high and round, crusted with yellow sunflowers. The landscape crackled with their dark gold and black. The earth was a rich brown. We were high up in a wild and lonely place. From here you could see the Pyrenees, misty blue shapes against the blue sky.

Madame Cabazou wore a black housecoat printed with pink roses. She let go of me and fished a handkerchief out of her pocket. She mopped her eyes.

– The village is dying, she said: we used to have vineyards up there but not any more. Only sunflowers now round here. So all the young ones have gone. Just us old people left. It's good your family has come to stay. You'll liven us up.

– They're not my parents, I told her: they're my uncle and aunt.

Madame Cabazou whistled. An ancient beagle bitch trundled out of the bushes, panting, and followed us down the path. I winced away from her in case she snapped or bit.

– Betty, Betty, good dog, said Madame Cabazou: oh she's a good dog my Betty, all the dogs in the village are good, none of them will harm you, they don't bite.

– My mother's just died, I said in the loudest voice I could manage: so they've brought me away on holiday to be nice to me.

Madame Cabazou stood stock still in the centre of the path and cried some more.

– Oh poor child poor child poor little one.

She hung on to my hand again as she wept. Then she blew her nose and shut the tall gates behind us. The church bells began to clamour out the Angelus. Bash, bash, bash.

– Electronic, said Madame Cabazou: the old lady who used to ring the Angelus, because her father did before her, she died this spring. No village priest any longer, either. Just one who serves all the villages in turn. The presbytery's been empty for a long time.

She fingered the little silver crucifix slung round her neck on a silver chain and sighed.

– The presbytery? I asked.

– The priest's house, she said: there.

We were going down the stone steps from the side of the church, down into the well of green light under the plane trees. She waved her hand at the high wall beside us, the wooden door let into it. We paused there, on the corner of the alleyway, to say goodbye.

– Oh this heat, she said: I do love it. And it's so good for my arthritis.

She tapped me on the cheek.

– You must have faith. Your mother is with God. We must believe that. She's up there in heaven. She's alive for all eternity.

She hurried off. The old dog lurched along after her, slack-bellied, velvety nose in the dust.

You grasped my hand. We took off together with a swift kick, we whirred into the night sky. Holding on to you I was drawn along, buoyant, an effortless progress under the stars above the wheeling earth.

We flew into the mouth of a dark tunnel. I could see nothing, I gripped your hand, felt cold air stream over my eyelids. You knew your way. You carried us both along, our arms were wings.

– I wanted to show you what dying was like, you said: I wanted you to know. Open your eyes. Look.

Below us, in the tunnel, were hospital beds crowded with sick people. They lay still and silent, faces upturned as we flew past. Then they dwindled behind us, and we burst out of the tunnel back into the soft blackness of the night.

– That was dying, you said: we've gone past death now.

Our curving flight traced the shape of the earth below. We swooped sideways, down. Another opening loomed. Another tunnel? I wasn't sure. The silvery stars rolled past. We were carried on the shoulders of the wind.

– There's a lot more I've got to find out about, you explained: I've got a lot more to explore. Come on, let's go in here next.

A mosquito whined in my ear. I cursed and sat up. You were no longer there.

We ate lunch in the garden, beside the hedge, under the shade of a big white umbrella. Onion tart and tomato salad, bread and cheese, a plate of dark blue figs. My aunt and uncle drank a lot of wine. They went indoors for a siesta.

I sat on, idly looking at the bushes, the flowerbeds. All sun-drenched, glittering. The shutters of the rooms upstairs were only half closed. I heard my aunt call out and laugh. Her noise rattled against my skin.

The dog Betty appeared in the farthest corner of the garden. She emerged from under the fig tree which grew there, began to toddle across the grass. She pursued her sedate, determined way as though it were marked out for her, pushing aside tall clumps of weeds that blocked her path, stepping delicately over the empty wine bottle my uncle had let fall. She didn't bother looking at me. I decided she must be on some private dog-road, some sort of dogs' short-cut via holes in our hedge we hadn't seen.

She flattened herself by the gate and tried to wriggle under. She was too fat to manage it. She whined and thumped her tail. I got up and opened the gate. She trotted through, then paused. She was waiting for me. I thought I would follow her to find out where she'd go.

She crossed the road and turned into the alley. Madame Cabazou's house, I knew, was the first one along. On the opposite side, on the corner with the street, was the priest's house behind its high wall. Betty didn't go home to her mistress. She nosed at a low wicker gate set into the wall near the end of the alley.

I tore aside the rusty wire netting stretched across the top of the gate and peered over it. A short path, overhung with creepers, led steeply upwards to a stone facade half obscured by leaves. I understood. This was a back way into the priest's house, one not protected by padlocks and keys. In a moment I'd climbed through the netting and over the gate and dropped down on the other side. The branches of trees brushed my face and arms. Soft debris of dead leaves under my feet. I stood still and listened. The entire village seemed to be asleep. No sharp voice, no tap on my shoulder, pulled me back. I crept up the path. I forgot Betty: she'd gone.

The house rose up before me, wide, three solid storeys of cream-coloured stone under a red-tiled roof. Blank-faced, its brown shutters closed. Three steps led up to its double wooden door. On either side of this were stone benches with claw feet, and tall bushes of oleander spilling worn pink flowers along the ground. I didn't hurry working out how to enter the house because the garden laid insistent hands on me and made me want to stay in it for ever.

From the outside you couldn't see that there was a garden at all. It was hidden. A secret place. It was small and square and overgrown, completely enclosed by the towering walls that surrounded it: the house on one side, the neighbour's barn on a second, and the walls of the street and the alleyway on the other two.

Inside these walls the garden was further enclosed by a luxuriant green vine trained on to wires. What must once have been a tidy green plot edged by the vine, by bushes and trees, was now a thicket you had to push your way into. I crept into a little sweet-smelling box of wilderness. Just big enough to hold me. Just the right size. In its green heart I stood upright in the long grass and counted two cherry trees, an apple tree laden with fruit, more oleanders, a lofty bush of bamboo plumes and several of blackcurrant. I picked a leaf and rubbed it to release the harsh scent. There was an ancient well in one corner, fenced about with cobwebs and black iron spikes. I lifted its wooden lid, peered down at its black mirror, threw a pebble in and heard the far splash.

I was frightened of going into the house all by myself, so I dared myself to do it as soon as the church bells began to strike the hour. The doors were clasped together merely by a loop of thin wire. I twisted a stick in it, broke it. Then I pushed the doors open and entered the house.

Once I'd wrestled with the shutters in the kitchen and flung them wide, screeching on their unoiled hinges, I could see. The red-tiled floor, the white fireplace with columns on either side and a white carving of scrolls and flowers above, the stone arch I'd come through from the hall, the cooker black with grease, the yellow oilcloth on the table.

A corridor wound around the ground floor. I passed a store-room full of old furniture and carpentry things, a wine cellar lined with empty metal racks, a poky lavatory with decorated blue tiles going up the wall. I picked my way up an open wooden staircase, like a ladder, to the salon and the bedrooms above. The salon was empty, grand as a ballroom but desolate. Striped blue and gold wallpaper hung down in curly strips, exposing the plaster and laths behind. The floor was bendy when I walked on it. The bedrooms were dusty and dark, falls of soot piled in their fireplaces. Old stained mattresses rested on broken-down springs, old books, parched covers stiff with dirt, sprawled face down on the lino, old chairs with cracked backs and seats were mixed up anyhow with rolls of lino, split satin cushions.

I put out my hands and touched these things in the half-dark. I draped my shoulders with a torn bedspread of scarlet chenille, then passed my hands over the wounded furniture. I blessed it, I told it to be healed now, and that it was forgiven. Then I departed from those sad rooms, closing their doors behind me one by one.

I crawled up a second wooden stair, to the attic. Bright spears of light tore gaps in the walls and roof, pointed at a floor littered with feathers and droppings. A headless plaster statue leaned in the far corner. His hands clasped a missal. He wore a surplice and cassock. I recognised him, even without his head, as St John Vianney, the curé of Ars. We'd done him at school. I looked for his head among the dusty junk surrounding him but couldn't find it. So I went back downstairs, into the garden again.

My bed in our old house was in the corner of the room. Shadows fingered the wall next to me and lay down on me like blankets. You'd draped a shadow over your face like a mantilla. You advanced, carrying a night-light. I was afraid of the dark but not of you, even though a grey cobwebby mask clung to your eyes and mouth and hid them.

You bent over me and spoke.

– What a mess you've left everything in. Bits and pieces all over the place. Silly girl.

You whispered in my ear.

– One day I'll tell you all the secrets I've ever known.

My aunt ladled cold cucumber soup from the white china tureen into white soup plates. We pushed our spoons across the pale green ponds, to and fro like swimmers. My spoon was big, silver-plated; I liked its heaviness in my hand. My uncle drank his soup heartily, stuffed in mouthfuls of bread, called for a second helping. My aunt waved the ladle at the moths butting the glass dome of the lamp she'd set on the table. It threw just enough light for us to eat by. The rest of the garden was swallowed by black night. From Madame Cabazou's house across the street came the sound of a man's voice reading the news on TV.

My aunt and uncle spoke to each other and left me in peace. I could lean against their chat like a pillow while I searched my memory.

– No, my father said on the morning of the funeral: I don't believe in the afterlife. Though your mother tried to. Bound to, wasn't she, being a Catholic. We just conk out I think. That's the end of it. The end of consciousness.

My uncle's red cheeks bulged with bread. He caught my eye and lifted his glass to me. My aunt collected our empty soup plates and stacked them on one side of the table. My uncle swallowed his faceful of bread and fetched the next course. Stuffed red peppers. I lifted mine out of the dish on to my plate, inserted my knife, slit the red skin. The pepper fell apart easily, like a bag of thin red silk. Rice and mushrooms tumbled out, a strip of anchovy.

– Overcooked, frowned my aunt: your fault, Lily, for coming back so late. Whatever were you up to?

I shrugged and smiled.

– Oh we understand, she said: you're young, you don't want to hang around all the time with us middle-aged folks! And we trust you to be sensible. Not to do anything silly.

She began to toss green salad in a clear plastic bowl, moving the wooden spoons delicately between the oily leaves that gave off the fragrance of tarragon.

– Of course you need some time by yourself, she said: especially just now. You want to amuse yourself, spend time by yourself, that's fine. Of course we understand.

It was early evening when I arrived at the house. Climbing the hill had taken me several hours. Now the sky at the horizon was green, as sharp as apples. The moon rose. A single silver star burned high above the lavender-blue sea.

The house was built into the cliff, at the very top, where the chalky ground levelled out, became turf dotted with gorse, sea-pinks, scabious. The front door stood open so I went in.

The whole place smelt of freshly sawn wood. Fragrance of resin, of cedar. Large rooms, airy and light. The walls and ceilings were painted a clear glowing blue. Beds were dotted about, manuscripts spilled across them. I wondered who they were, the people who lived here and strewed their papers over their beds. Then I saw the figure of a woman in the far doorway, leaning against the frame of the door, with her back to me. The owner of the house. Would she mind my presence? I was uninvited. A trespasser.

She turned round.

I'd forgotten that you'd ever looked like this. Young, with thick curly brown hair, amused hazel eyes, fresh unlined skin. Not a trace of sorrow or of pain. You were healthy. You were fully alive.

– I'm living here now, you explained with a smile and a wave of the hand: in Brahma's house.

You walked me about the spacious blue rooms, up and down the wide, ladder-like staircases of golden wood.

– Tell your father, you said: the cure for grief is, you have to sit by an open window and look out of it.

Your face was calm. No fear in it. You weren't suffering any more.

– You look so well, I blurted out: and all your hair's grown back!

– It's time for you to go, you told me.

You stood on the front steps and waved me off. My eyes measured the width of the doorway. I thought I'd slip through, stay with you.

You shook your head, slammed the door shut on my efforts to break back in.

At eight o'clock prompt each day a siren wailed along the main road. That second morning, Madame Cabazou leaned over our gates and called.

– The bread van. Hurry up, girl. It doesn't wait long.

I stumbled after her, half-asleep. She dashed along on nimble slippered feet, a thick cardigan thrust on over her white nightdress. The dog Betty trailed us, folds of fat swaying.

Down by the fountain we joined a queue of old people who all smiled and exclaimed. Madame Cabazou introduced me, made me shake hands all round. Once I was part of them they went on swapping bits of news. Madame Cabazou was the lively one. Her chatter was staccato, her hands flew about like the swallows that zigzagged between our house and barn.

– My wretched grandchildren, she cried: they hardly ever come and see me. Children these days. Oh they don't care.

I bought a bag of croissants and a thick loaf, one up from a baguette, that was called simply a *pain*. I walked slowly back up the street to the house. The voices of the old people rose and fell behind me, bubbles of sound, like the splash of water in the fountain. They were recalling the funeral they'd been to the week before. A young girl, from a farm over by the lake, had been trapped by her hair in her father's baling machine and strangled. The voices grew high and excited, like the worrying of dogs.

After breakfast my aunt and uncle drove off in the car to visit the castle at Montségur. I waved them goodbye, then prowled about the kitchen, collecting the things I needed and packing them into a basket. I shut the grey metal gates behind me and crossed the road into the alleyway.

Madame Cabazou was working in the little vegetable patch in front of her house. Her thin body was bent double as she tugged weeds from the earth. Today she had on a blue housecoat, and she'd tied her straw hat on like a bonnet, the strings knotted under her chin. I slunk past while her stooped back was turned and hoisted myself over the wicker gate.

Once inside the priest's kitchen I opened the shutters and the windows to let in light and air. I swept the floor with the dustpan and brush I'd brought, dusted the table and the fireplace and the window-sills. I laid a fire, with sticks and bits of wood from the store-room. I'd brought a small saucepan to cook in. I had a metal fish-slice and one wooden spoon. For lunch I might have stewed apples, using the fruit from the tree outside. I might try mixing up some grape juice. I had three plastic bottles of mineral water in my basket, a croissant saved from breakfast, a blue and white checked teacloth, and a couple of books. I left all this equipment on the table in the kitchen, and went outside.

I dropped into the garden like a stone or a plant, taking up my place. The garden had been waiting for me. I belonged in it. I had discovered it and in that act had been accepted by it. Now I was part of it. Hidden, invisible. The long grass closed over my head, green water. The bushes stretched wide their flowering branches around me. The bright green vine walled me in with its jagged leaves, curling tendrils, heavy bunches of grapes. Around the edges of the garden rustled the tops of the trees.

I had plenty of time to get to know the garden. I had seven whole days in which to stare at the ants and beetles balanced on the blades of grass next to my face, to finger the different textures of stems, to listen to the crickets and birds. I rolled over on to my back, put my hands under my head, and stared at the sky through branches and leaves. My hammock. I swung in it upside down. It dandled me. I fell asleep and didn't wake for hours.

Over supper my aunt and uncle told me about the castle of Montségur, perched on top of a steep mountain. They'd climbed up the slippery rocks. They'd eaten their picnic in the lofty stronghold where the Cathars had held out against St Dominic's armies come to smash them and drag them down to the waiting pyre.

– God how I loathe the Catholic Church, cried my aunt: God how I loathe all priests!

My uncle poured red wine into tumblers.

– Nice day, Lily? he asked.

I nodded. My mouth was full of cream-laden spaghetti scented with rosemary and sage. I had the idea that if I kept on eating the memory of my mother wouldn't be able to climb out of my silence, out of the long gaps between my words, and disturb me. So I held out my plate for a second helping and bent my head over it. I concentrated on the pleasures of biting, of chewing and swallowing, the pleasure of feeling full.

I was in bed but I wasn't asleep. The room was dark, and very warm. Gold glow of a lamp in one corner. Rain beat against the window, I heard it shush-shush through the curtains. Around me was folded the softest and lightest of quilts. Like being tucked up in a cloud. Or held in your arms. For you were there, a dim presence by the lamp, humming to yourself while you read a book about gardening. Peace was the physical knowledge of warmth, of your familiar profile, your sleeve of dark pink silk resting on the plump arm of your chair, the dim blue and gold pattern of the wallpaper.

You repeated to me: you're safe now. Safe now. Safe now.

– Our last day, Lily, smiled my aunt: are you sure you don't want to come out with us for a drive? I can't think what you find to do on your own here day after day.

I shook my head.

– Well, she said: if you don't, you don't, I suppose. You could make a start on your packing, in that case.

Her words jolted me. For seven days I'd been in retreat, in my

private green world. I'd ceased to hear the church bells banging out
the hours overhead. Hunger was my only clock. A week, in which I'd
lain on the grass reading or daydreaming, had flowed past without my
knowing or caring what day it was. Back home my schoolbooks
waited, and a timetable ruled into squares.

I had an ache inside me. A sort of yawn that hurt. A voice in my
stomach that wanted to scream. I felt stretched, and that I might
topple over and break in two.

Back home I'd enter an empty house. My mother was dead. If only
that could be a fact that was well past, something I'd dealt with and
got over. Recovered from. I didn't want to embark on a life in which
she'd go on and on being dead, on and on not being there. I didn't
want to let it catch up with me. I shut the grey metal gates and hurried
across the road.

Madame Cabazou was sitting on her front step, picking fleas out of
Betty's coat. She nipped them between her fingernails until their little
black backs cracked. Crack! Crack! She brushed the fleas from her
fingertips like grains of black sand.

— Do you want some melons? she asked: I've got far too many. Even
with this tiny patch I've grown more, this year, than I can use.

She waved her hand at the tidy rows of tomatoes, melons and
courgettes. The earth between them was spotless, fine as sieved flour.
She scowled at it.

— We used to have proper fields of crops, and the vineyard. Not
like this. This pocket handkerchief of a garden. Oh I do miss all that, I
can't tell you how much.

— Perhaps one melon? I suggested: we're leaving tomorrow morning early. We could have melon tonight.

— Come and fetch it later on, she sang out: I'll pick you one that's
really ripe.

She shoved Betty's nose off her lap, and got up. She put her hands
in her pockets and gazed at me.

She jerked her head towards the wicker gate in the wall.

– Some German people coming to view the house this afternoon, she remarked: with a lady from the agency.

I tried to sound indifferent.

– Oh really?

– The man who drives the bread-van told me, she said: this morning. His brother-in-law works in the café next door to the agency in Carcassonne, he heard them talking about it when they came in for a beer. Didn't you hear him say so down at the van this morning? You were off in some dream.

Coldness clutched me inside. I stared at Madame Cabazou.

– If I were you, she said: I'd come and fetch that melon this afternoon. You dream too much, it's not good. Better wake up. Otherwise you can be sure you'll be in trouble. Too much time by yourself, that's your problem.

Her words hurt me like slaps on the face. I swung away without saying anything. Tears burned my eyes but I wouldn't cry while she was watching me. I heard her front door close, then her voice drifted through the window, scolding Betty, breaking into song. She was cold-hearted. She didn't care how much she'd upset me. She didn't know how it felt to be told I'd got to leave this house and this garden for good.

I'd believed for a whole week that it was my house, my garden. I'd hardly believed it even. I just knew it. I'd just been part of it. The garden had seemed to know me, had taken me in without fuss. Leaving it, going outside and not coming back, would be like having my skin peeled off. I might die. Something was tearing me apart inside. It frightened me. I was a piece of paper being slowly ripped in two. I staggered, and fell on to the little patch of tangled grass under the vine. I started crying and could not stop. The crying went on and on, and the pain. It twisted me up, it sawed me, it squeezed my heart so I could hardly breathe. The worst thing was feeling so lonely, and knowing I always would.

Just before my mother died, the night before, I was with her. It wasn't her any more, this tiny person so thin under her nightie I couldn't bear to look at her, with clawlike hands and a head that was a skull. Her eyes were the same, that was the only part of her left that I knew. She looked out of the darkness she was in and recognised me. For a couple of minutes she fought her way up from the morphine and tried to speak. She looked at me so trustfully. My father had said I should say goodbye to her but I couldn't.

— You're not going to die just yet are you, I said loudly: you're not going to die just yet.

Her cracked lips tried to smile.

— Oh yes I am, she whispered: oh yes I think I am.

That night I dreamed of her bed in the glass conservatory, half in and half out of the house. I woke up at dawn and saw the sky like red glass. My father came in and said my mother had just died.

I could think of her being alive. I could think of her being dead. What I could not bear to think of was that moment when she died, was dying, died. When she crossed over from being alive to being dead. I couldn't join the two things up, I couldn't connect them, because at the point where they met and changed into each other was pain, my body caught in a vice, my bones twisted and wrenched, my guts torn apart. I gave birth to her dying. Violently she was pulled out of me. I felt I was dying too. I could hear an animal howling. It was me.

I lay on the grass exhausted. I felt empty. Nothing left in me. I was an old sack used then thrown away. Now I was low as the grass, low as the ground. Flattened. I was worn out. As though a mountain had stamped on me.

A yawn possessed me and I looked up. My eyelids felt swollen like car tyres, and my nose too, and my mouth. I licked the salt tears off the corners of my lips, blew my nose.

I lay staring at the gnarled trunk of the vine, the weeds and grasses stirring about its root, the yellow flowers mixed in with them whose name I didn't know.

Then it stopped being me looking at the vine, because I dissolved into it, became it. I left me behind. Human was the same as plant. This corner of the garden, the earth: one great warm breathing body that was all of us, that lived strongly, whose life I felt coursing inside me, sap blood juices of grass. Love was the force that made things grow. Love grew the vine, the weeds, me. I started crying again because of the joy. It swept through me. The knowledge of love. Such sweetness and warmth inside me and the vine and the grass under the light of the sun.

Madame Cabazou whistled for me as though I were Betty. We both came running. I carried a melon home under each arm. She kissed me on both cheeks to say goodbye, instructed me, if I wished to be well thought of, to write to her. She snatched me out of my garden, shook me, set me upright, told me to go home now. She pushed me off.

Next morning I slumped in the back seat of the car as we drove out of the village and headed for the motorway. I wanted to take the road back, to go the other way, to stay. I cried as we left the high golden hills and descended on to the plain. The wind from the sea, that Madame Cabazou called the *marin*, blew strongly. It meant the end of summer. It sang an elegy for my mother. She was dead she was gone I had lost her she would never come back and live with us again.

Every cell in every leaf had had a voice, which spoke to me.

– *Of course I am here. Where else should I be but here. Where else could I possibly be.*

BIBLIOGRAPHY

Primary reading

Angelou, M. 1969/1984 *I Know Why the Caged Bird Sings*, London: Virago.

Angelou, M. 1974/1985 *Gather Together in My Name*, London: Virago.

Angelou, M. 1976 *Singin' and Swingin' and Getting' Merry Like Christmas*, New York: Random House.

Angelou, M. 1981 *The Heart of a Woman*, New York: Random House.

Angelou, M. 1986 *All God's Children Need Travelling Shoes*, New York: Random House.

Atwood, M. 1969/1980 *The Edible Woman*, London: Virago.

Atwood, M. 1972/1979 *Surfacing*, London: Virago.

Atwood, M. 1977/1984 *Dancing Girls and Other Stories*, London: Virago.

Atwood, M. 1985/1987 *The Handmaid's Tale*, London: Virago.

Atwood, M. 1987 *Selected Poems II: Poems Selected and New 1976–1986*, Boston: Houghton Mifflin.

Atwood, M. 1988 *Bluebeard's Egg*, London: Virago.

Boland, E. 1982 *Night Feed*, Dublin: Arlen House.

Boland, E. 1987 'The Woman Poet: Her Dilemma', *American Poetry Review* 16 (1): 17–20.

Boland, E. 1989 *A Kind of Scar: The Woman Poet in a National Tradition*, Dublin: Attic Press.

Boland, E. 1995 *Collected Poems*, Manchester: Carcanet.

Carter, A. 1977/1982 *The Passion of New Eve*, London: Virago.

Carter, A. 1979 *The Sadeian Woman. An Exercise in Cultural History*, London: Virago.

Carter, A. 1982 *Nothing Sacred. Selected Writings*, London: Virago.

Carter, A. 1983 'Notes from a maternity ward', *New Statesman* 16/23: December.

Carter, A. (ed.) 1990 *The Virago Book of Fairytales*, London: Virago.

Carter, A. 1996 *Burning your Boats. Collected Short Stories*, London: Vintage.

Drabble, M. 1964/1966 *The Garrick Year*, Harmondsworth: Penguin.

Drabble, M. 1965/1968 *The Millstone*, Harmondsworth: Penguin.

Drabble, M. 1967/1969 *Jerusalem the Golden*, Harmondsworth: Penguin.

Drabble, M. 1969/1971 *The Waterfall*, Harmondsworth: Penguin.

Drabble, M. 1975/1977 *The Realms of Gold*, Harmondsworth: Penguin.

Edgell, Z. 1982 *Beka Lamb*, Oxford: Heinemann.

Holtby, W. 1924/1981 *The Crowded Street*, London: Virago.

Holtby, W. 1936/1988 *South Riding*, London: Virago.

Jameson, S. 1934/1982 *Company Parade*, London: Virago.

Jameson, S. 1969/1984 *Journey from the North*. Vol. 1, London: Virago.

Jameson, S. 1970/1984 *Journey from the North*. Vol. 2, London: Virago.

Mew, C. 1953 *Collected Poems of Charlotte Mew*, with a memoir by Alida Monro, London: Duckworth.

Mew, C. 1981 *Collected Poems and Prose* V. Warner (ed.), Manchester: Carcanet.

Morrison, T. 1970/1994 *The Bluest Eye*, Harmondsworth: Penguin.

Morrison, T. 1973/1982 *Sula*, Harmondsworth: Penguin.

Morrison, T. 1987/1988 *Beloved*, London: Picador.

Morrison, T. 1992 *Playing in the Dark: Whiteness and the Literary Imagination*, Cambridge, MA and London: Harvard University Press.

Olsen, T. 1978/1980 *Silences*, London: Virago.

Olsen, T. 1990 *Tell Me A Riddle and Yonnondio*, London: Virago.

Plath, S. 1963/1966 *The Bell Jar*, London: Faber & Faber.

Plath, S. 1975 *Letters Home: Correspondence 1950–1963* Aurelia Schober Plath (ed.), London: Faber & Faber.

Plath, S. 1977/1979 *Johnny Panic and the Bible of Dreams and Other Prose Writings*, London: Faber & Faber.

Plath, S. 1981 *Collected Poems*, edited with an introduction by Ted Hughes, London: Faber & Faber.

Raine, K. 1973 *Farewell Happy Fields. Memories of Childhood*, London: Hamish Hamilton.

Raine, K. 1975 *The Land Unknown*, London: Hamish Hamilton.

Raine, K. 1977 *The Lion's Mouth. Concluding Chapters of Autobiography*, London: Hamish Hamilton.

Raine, K. 1981 *Collected Poems 1935–1980*, London: Allen & Unwin.

Rhys, J. 1928/1973 *Quartet*, Harmondsworth: Penguin.

Rhys, J. 1930/1971 *After Leaving Mr Mackenzie*, Harmondsworth: Penguin.

Rhys, J. 1934/1969 *Voyage in the Dark*, Harmondsworth: Penguin.

Rhys, J. 1939/1969 *Good Morning, Midnight*, Harmondsworth: Penguin.

Rhys, J. 1966/1968 *Wide Sargasso Sea*, Harmondsworth: Penguin.

Rhys, J. 1979/1981 *Smile Please*, Harmondsworth: Penguin.

Rhys, J. 1984 *Jean Rhys. Letters 1931–1966* selected and edited by F. Wyndham and D. Melly, London: André Deutsch.

Rich, A. 1976/1977 *Of Woman Born. Motherhood as Experience and Institution*, London: Virago.

Rich, A. 1979/1980 *On Lies, Secrets and Silence. Selected Prose 1966–1978*, London: Virago.

Rich, A. 1980 *The Dream of a Common Language*, New York and London: W.W. Norton.

Rich, A. 1981 *A Wild Patience Has Taken Me This Far. Poems 1978–1981*, New York and London: W.W. Norton.

Rich, A. 1984 *The Fact of a Doorframe. Poems Selected and New 1950–1984*, New York and London: W.W. Norton.

Rich, A. 1987 *Blood, Bread, and Poetry. Selected Prose 1979–1985*, London: Virago.

Rich, A. 1989 *Time's Power. Poems 1985–1988*, New York and London: W.W. Norton.

Roberts, M. 1978 *A Piece of the Night*, London: The Women's Press.

Roberts, M. 1983 *The Visitation*, London: The Women's Press.

Roberts, M. 1984 *The Wild Girl*, London: Methuen.

Roberts, M. 1986 'Write, she said' in *The Progress of Romance: the Politics of Popular Fiction* J. Radford (ed.), London and New York: Routledge & Kegan Paul.

Roberts, M. 1987 *The Book of Mrs Noah*, London: Methuen.

Roberts, M. 1990 *In the Red Kitchen*, London: Methuen.

Roberts, M. 1990 'Musing Over Power', *The New Statesman* 16 March: 31–3.

Roberts, M. 1994 *During Mother's Absence*, London: Virago.

Roberts, M. 1995 *All the Selves I Was. New and Selected Poems*, London: Virago.

Roberts, M. 1998 *Food, Sex and God. On Inspiration and Writing*, London: Virago.

Sinclair, M. 1917a *The Tree of Heaven*, London: Cassell.

Sinclair, M. 1917b *A Defence of Idealism. Some Questions and Conclusions*, London: Macmillan.

Sinclair, M. 1919/1980 *Mary Olivier: A Life*, London: Virago.

Sinclair, M. 1922/1980 *The Life and Death of Harriett Frean*, London: Virago.

Tan, A. 1989/1994 *The Joy Luck Club*, London: Minerva.

Tan, A. 1991 *The Kitchen God's Wife*, London: HarperCollins.

Tan, A. 1996 *The Hundred Secret Senses*, London: HarperCollins.

Walker, A. 1976/1982 *Meridian*, London: The Women's Press.

Walker, A. 1983a *In Search of Our Mothers' Gardens. Womanist Prose*, New York and London: Harcourt Brace.

Walker, A. 1983b *The Color Purple*, London: The Women's Press.

Walker, A. 1989/1990 *The Temple of My Familiar*, Harmondsworth: Penguin.

Walker, A. 1992/1993 *Possessing the Secret of Joy*, New York: Simon & Schuster.

Walker, A. 1994 *The Complete Stories*, London: The Women's Press.

Wickham, A. 1971 *Selected Poems* D. Garnett (ed.), London: Chatto & Windus.

Wickham, A. 1984 *The Writings of Anna Wickham, Free Woman and Poet* edited and introduced by R. D. Smith, London: Virago.

Winterson, J. 1985 *Oranges are Not the Only Fruit*, London: Pandora.

Woolf, V. 1915/1981 *The Voyage Out*, London: Granada.

Woolf, V. 1925/1981 *Mrs Dalloway*, London: Granada.

Woolf, V. 1927/1988 *To the Lighthouse*, London: Granada.

Woolf, V. 1931/1980 *The Waves*, London: Granada.

Woolf, V. 1990 *Moments of Being* J. Schulkind (ed.), London: Grafton.

Woolf, V. 1992 *A Room of One's Own* [1929] *Three Guineas* [1938] M. Shiach (ed.), Oxford: Oxford University Press.

BIBLIOGRAPHY

Yezierska, A. 1925/1975 *Bread Givers*, New York: Persea Books.

Yezierska, A. 1950/1987 *Red Ribbon on a White Horse. My Story*, London: Virago.

Yezierska, A. 1987 *Hungry Hearts and Other Stories*, London: Virago.

Further reading

Aarons, V. 1987 'The Outsider Within: Women in Contemporary Jewish-American Fiction', *Contemporary Literature* 28 (3): 378–93.

Aidoo, A. 1987 *The Dilemma of a Ghost* and *Anowa*, Harlow: Longman.

Angier, C. 1990 *Jean Rhys: Life and Work*, Harmondsworth: Penguin.

Beauvoir, S. de 1953/1972 *The Second Sex*, Harmondsworth: Penguin.

Benjamin, J. 1990 *The Bonds of Love. Psychoanalysis, Feminism and the Problem of Domination*, London: Virago.

Berry, P. and Bishop, A. (eds.) 1985 *Testament of a Generation. The Journalism of Vera Brittain and Winifred Holtby*, London: Virago.

Bloom, H. (ed.) 1990 *Toni Morrison*, New York and Philadelphia: Chelsea House.

Boll, T. E. M. 1973 *Miss May Sinclair: Novelist. A Biographical and Critical Introduction*, Rutherford: Fairleigh Dickinson University Press.

Bowlby, J. 1965 *Child Care and the Growth of Love*, Harmondsworth: Penguin. Abridged version of *Maternal Care and Mental Health*, Geneva, WHO, 1951.

Brittain, V. 1940/1989 *Testament of Friendship*, London: Virago.

Bromley, R. 1985 'Reaching a Clearing. Gender and Politics in *Beka Lamb*', *Wasafiri* 1 (2): 10–14.

Brown, L. W. 1981 *Women Writers in Black Africa*, Westport: Greenwood Press.

Brown, R.M. 1973/1977 *Rubyfruit Jungle*, New York: Bantam.

Burstein, J. H. 1996 *Writing Mothers, Writing Daughters. Tracing the Maternal in Stories by American Jewish Women*, Urbana and Chicago: University of Illinois Press.

Campbell, E. 1987 'The Dichotomized Heroine in West Indian Fiction', *The Journal of Commonwealth Literature* XXII (1): 137–43.

Chang, J. 1991/1993 *Wild Swans. Three Daughters of China*, HarperCollins: London.

Chevigny, B. G. 1983 'Daughters Writing. Toward a Theory of Women's Biography', *Feminist Studies* 9 (1): 79–102.

Chitty, S. (ed.) 1983 *As Once in May. The Early Autobiography of Antonia White and Other Writings*, London: Virago.

Chitty, S. (ed.) 1991 *Antonia White. Diaries 1926–1957*, London: Constable.

Chitty, S. (ed.) 1992 *Antonia White. Diaries 1958–1979*, London: Constable.

Chitty, S. 1985 *Now To My Mother*, London: Weidenfeld.

Chodorow, N. 1978 *The Reproduction of Mothering. Psychoanalysis and the Sociology of Gender*, Berkeley and Los Angeles: University of California Press.

Christian, B. 1985 *Black Feminist Criticism: Perspectives on Black Women Writers*, New York: Pergamon Press.

Coiner, C. 1992 ' "No One's Private Ground": A Bakhtinian Reading of Tillie Olsen's *Tell Me A Riddle*', *Feminist Studies* 18 (2): 257–81.

Cudjoe, S. R. (ed.) 1990 *Caribbean Women Writers. Essays from the First International Conference*, Wellesley: Calaloux.

Cunningham, G. 1982 'Women and Children First: the Novels of Margaret Drabble', *Twentieth-Century Women Novelists* T.F. Staley (ed.), London: Macmillan, pp. 130–52.

Dance, D. C. (ed.) 1986 *Fifty Caribbean Writers*, New York: Greenwood Press.

Davidson, C. N. and Broner, E. M. (eds.) 1980 *The Lost Tradition. Mothers and Daughters in Literature*, New York: Frederick Ungar.

Davies, C. B. and Graves, A. A. (eds.) 1986 *Ngambika. Studies of Women in African Literature*, Trenton: Africa World Press.

Davies, C. B. and Fido, E. S. (eds.) 1990 *Out of the Kumbla. Caribbean Women and Literature*, Trenton: Africa World Press.

Delafield, E. M. 1927/1988 *The Way Things Are*, London: Virago.

Deutsch, H. 1945 *The Psychology of Women*, Vol. 2; *Motherhood*, New York: Grune & Stratton.

Dinnerstein, D. 1978 *The Rocking of the Cradle and the Ruling of the World*, London: Souvenir Press; published in the USA as *The Mermaid and the Minotaur: Sexual Arrangements and Human Malaise*, New York: Harper & Row, 1976.

Duncker, P. 1984 'Re-Imagining the Fairy Tales: Angela Carter's Bloody Chambers', *Literature and History* 10 (1): 3–14.

Elliot, J.M. (ed.) 1989 *Conversations with Maya Angelou*, Mississippi: University Press of Mississippi.

Emecheta, B. 1979/1994 *The Joys of Motherhood*, Oxford: Heinemann.

Evans, M. (ed.) 1984 *Black Women Writers (1950–1980). A Critical Evaluation*, New York: Doubleday.

Ferguson, M. 1994 *Jamaica Kincaid: Where the Land Meets the Body*, Charlottesville and London: University Press of Virginia.

BIBLIOGRAPHY

Fields K. 1989 'To Embrace Dead Strangers: Toni Morrison's *Beloved*'. In: *Mother Puzzles: Daughters and Mothers in Contemporary American Literature* M. Pearlman (ed.), New York: Greenwood Press, pp. 159–69.

Fitzgerald, P. 1984 *Charlotte Mew and Her Friends*, London: Collins.

Flax, J. 1978 'The Conflict between Nurturance and Autonomy in Mother-Daughter Relationships and within Feminism', *Feminist Studies* 4 (2): 171–89.

Flockemann, M. 1992 ' "Not-Quite Insiders and Not-Quite Outsiders": The "Process of Womanhood" in *Beka Lamb*, *Nervous Conditions* and *Daughters of the Twilight*', *The Journal of Commonwealth Literature* XXVII (1): 37–47.

Forster, M. 1995 *Hidden Lives. A Family Memoir*, London: Viking.

Freud, E. 1992 *Hideous Kinky*, London: Hamish Hamilton.

Freud, S. 1961 *The Standard Edition of the Complete Psychological Works of Sigmund Freud* vol. XVII, London: Hogarth Press.

Friedan, B. 1963/1965 *The Feminine Mystique*, Harmondsworth: Penguin.

Frye, J. S. 1981 ' "I Stand Here Ironing": Motherhood as Experience and Metaphor', *Studies in Short Fiction* 18 (3): 287–92.

Gardiner, J. K. 1985 'Mind Mother: Psychoananlysis and Feminism' in *Making a Difference: Feminist Literary Criticism* G. Greene and C. Kahn (eds), London and New York: Methuen.

Gordon, L. 1984 *Virginia Woolf. A Writer's Life*, Oxford: Oxford University Press.

Hagen, P.L. and Zelman, T.W. 1991 ' "We Were Never on the Scene of the Crime": Eavan Boland's Repossession of History', *Twentieth-Century Literature* 37 (4): 442–53.

Hall, R. 1924/1981 *The Unlit Lamp*, London: Virago.

Hall, R. 1928/1982 *The Well of Loneliness*, London: Virago.

Hannay, J. 1987 'Margaret Drabble: An Interview', *Twentieth-Century Literature* 33 (1): 129–49.

Hardin, N.S. 1973a 'An Interview with Margaret Drabble', *Contemporary Literature* 14 (3): 273–95.

Hardin, N.S. 1973b 'Drabble's *The Millstone*: A Fable for our Times', *Critique* 15 (1): 22–34.

Harper, M. F. 1982 'Margaret Drabble and the Resurrection of the English Novel', *Contemporary Literature* 23 (1): 145–68.

Harrison, J. 1903 *Prolegomena to the Study of Greek Religion*, Cambridge: Cambridge University Press.

Harrison, J. 1924 *Mythology*, New York: Longman, Green.

Hedges, E. and Fishkin, S. F. 1994 *Listening to Silences. New Essays in Feminist Criticism*, Oxford: Oxford University Press.

Heilbrun, C. 1991 '*To the Lighthouse*: The New Story of Mother and Daughter' in *Hamlet's Mother*, London: The Women's Press.

Henriksen, L. 1988 *Anzia Yezierska. A Writer's Life*, New Brunswick and London: Rutgers University Press.

Heung, M. 1993 'Daughter-Text/Mother-Text: Matrilineage in Amy Tan's *Joy Luck Club*', *Feminist Studies* 19 (3): 597–616.

Hirsch, M. 'Mothers and Daughters', *Signs* 7 (1): 200–22.

Hirsch, M. 1989 *The Mother/Daughter Plot. Narrative, Psychoanalysis, Feminism*, Bloomington and Indianapolis: Indiana University Press.

Hopkinson, L. P. 1988 *Nothing to Forgive: A Daughter's Life of Antonia White*, London: Chatto & Windus.

Horney, K. 1967 *Feminine Psychology* H. Kelman (ed.), New York: W.W. Norton.

Horvitz, D. 1989 'Nameless Ghosts: Possession and Dispossession in *Beloved*', *Studies in American Fiction* 17: 157–67.

Hughes, F. 1999 *Wooroloo*, Newcastle: Bloodaxe Books.

Hughes, T. 1998 *Birthday Letters*, London: Faber & Faber.

Humm, M. 1994 'Jean Rhys: Race, Gender and History, in *It's My Party: Reading Twentieth-Century Women's Writing* G. Wisker (ed), London: Pluto.

Ingersoll, E. G. (ed.) 1992 *Margaret Atwood: Conversations*, London: Virago.

Ingman, H. 1998 *Women's Fiction Between the Wars. Mothers, Daughters and Writing*, Edinburgh: Edinburgh University Press.

Irigaray, L. 1979/1981 '*Et l'une ne bouge pas sans l'autre*', 'And the One doesn't stir without the Other', transl. H. V. Wenzel *Signs* 7 (1): 607.

James, A. (ed.) 1990 *In Their Own Voices. African Women Writers Talk*, London: James Currey.

Jordan, E. 1992 'The Dangers of Angela Carter' in *New Feminist Discourses* I. Armstrong (ed.), London and New York: Routledge.

Jump H. D. (ed.) 1991 *Diverse Voices. Essays on Twentieth-Century Women Writers in English*, London: Harvester Wheatsheaf.

Jung, C. and Kerenyi, C. 1963 *Essays on a Science of Mythology*, New York: Harper & Row.

Keenan, S. 1993 ' "Four Hundred Years of Silence": Myth, History, and Motherhood in Toni Morrison's *Beloved*' in *Recasting the World: Writing after Colonialism* J. White (ed.), Baltimore: Johns Hopkins University Press, pp. 45–81.

Kenyon, O. 1988 *Women Novelists Today: A Survey of English Writing in the Seventies and Eighties*, Brighton: Harvester Press.

Kincaid, J. 1983 *At the Bottom of the River* New York: Farrar, Straus & Giroux.

Kincaid, J. 1983/1997 *Annie John*, London: Vintage.

Kincaid, J. 1988 *A Small Place*, London: Vintage.

Kincaid, J. 1990/1991 *Lucy*, London: Jonathan Cape.

Kincaid, J. 1996/1997 *The Autobiography of My Mother*, Harmondsworth: Penguin.

Kingston, M. 1976/1981 *The Woman Warrior: Memoirs of a Girlhood Among Ghosts*, London: Picador.

Klein, M. 1948 *Contributions to Psycho-Analysis 1921–1945*, London: Hogarth Press.

Kloepfer, D. K. 1989 *The Unspeakable Mother: Forbidden Discourse in Jean Rhys and H. D.*, Ithaca and London: Cornell University Press.

Lee, H. 1996 *Virginia Woolf*, London: Chatto & Windus.

Lehmann, R. 1930/1982 *A Note in Music*, London: Virago.

Leigh, N. J. 1985 'Mirror, Mirror: the Development of Female Identity in Jean Rhys's Fiction', *World Literature Written in English* 25 (2): 270–85

Leighton, A. 1992 *Victorian Women Poets: Writing Against the Heart*, New York and London: Harvester Wheatsheaf.

Lidoff, J. 1986 'Virginia Woolf's Feminine Sentence', *Literature and Psychology* 32 (3): 43–59.

Lilienfield, J. 1977 ' "The Deceptiveness of Beauty": Mother Love and Mother Hate in *To the Lighthouse*', *Twentieth Century Literature* 23: 345–76.

Ling, A. 1990 *Between Worlds. Women Writers of Chinese Ancestry*, New York: Pergamon Press.

McLuskie, K. and Innes, L. 1988 'Women and African Literature', *Wasafiri* 8, Spring: 3–7.

McKay, N. 1983 'An Interview with Toni Morrison', *Contemporary Literature* 24 (4): 413–29.

Macaulay, R. 1921 *Dangerous Ages*, London: Collins.

Macdonald, M. 1998 'Respect', *Observer* 29 March: 4–8.

Mah, A. Yen 1997 *Falling Leaves. The True Story of an Unwanted Chinese Daughter*, Penguin: Harmondsworth.

Marks, E. and de Courtivron, I. (eds) 1981 *New French Feminisms*, Hemel Hempstead: Harvester Wheatsheaf.

Marshall, P. 1959/1982 *Brown Girl. Brownstones*, London: Virago.

Minow-Pinkney, M. 1987 *Virginia Woolf and the Problem of the Subject*, Brighton: Harvester Press.

Mitchell, J. (ed.) 1991 *The Selected Melanie Klein*, Harmondsworth: Penguin.

Mitchell, J. and Rose, J. (eds.) 1982 *Feminine Sexuality. Jacques Lacan and the Ecole Freudienne*, London: Macmillan.

Moi, T. (ed.) 1986 *The Kristeva Reader*, Oxford: Basil Blackwell.

Morgan, R. (ed.) 1984 *Sisterhood is Global. The International Women's Movement Anthology*, New York: Anchor Books.

Myer, V. G. 1974 *Margaret Drabble: Puritanism and Permissiveness*, London: Vision Press.

Nasta, S. (ed.) 1991 *Motherlands. Black Women's Writing from Africa, the Caribbean and South Asia*, London: The Women's Press.

Newman C. (ed.) 1971 *The Art of Sylvia Plath*, Bloomington and London: Indiana University Press.

Ngcobo, L. (ed.) 1987 *Let it be told. Essays by Black Women in Britain*, London: Pluto.

Nice, V. 1992 *Mothers and Daughters. The Distortion of a Relationship*, London: Macmillan.

Nicholson, C. (ed.) 1994 *Margaret Atwood: Writing and Subjectivity*, New York: St Martin's Press.

Ogunyemi, C. O. 1985 'Womanism: The Dynamics of the Contemporary Black Female Novel in English', *Signs* 11 (Autumn): 63–80.

Olivier, C. 1989 *Jocasta's Children. The Imprint of the Mother*, London and New York: Routledge.

Ostriker, A. 1983 *Writing Like A Woman*, Michigan: University of Michigan Press.

Ostriker, A. 1987 *Stealing the Language. The Emergence of Women's Poetry in America*, London: The Women's Press.

Pearlman, M. and Werlock, A. H. P. 1991 *Tillie Olsen*, Boston: Twayne.

Plasa, C. (ed.) 1998 *Toni Morrison: Beloved*, Cambridge: Icon Books.

Reizbaum, E. 1989 'An Interview with Eavan Boland. Conducted by Marilyn Reizbaum', *Contemporary Literature* 30 (4): 471–9.

Richardson, D. 1993 *Women, Motherhood and Childrearing*, London: Macmillan.

Rigney, B. H. 1987 *Margaret Atwood*, London: Macmillan.

Rose, E. C. 1980 *The Novels of Margaret Drabble*, London: Macmillan.

Rose, E. C. 1983 'Through the Looking Glass: When Women Tell Fairytales' in *The Voyage In: Fictions of Female Development* E. Abel, M. Hirsch, E. Langland (eds), Hanover and London: University Press of New England, pp. 209–27.

Rose, J. 1991 *The Haunting of Sylvia Plath*, London: Virago.

Rosenberg, J. H. 1984 *Margaret Atwood*, Boston: Twayne.

Rosenfelt, D. 1981 'From the Thirties: Tillie Olsen and the Radical Tradition', *Feminist Studies* 7 (3): 371–406.

Rosenman, E. 1986 *The Invisible Presence. Virginia Woolf and the Mother-Daughter Relationship*, Baton Rouge and London: Louisiana State University Press.

Ruddick, S. 1990 *Maternal Thinking. Towards a Politics of Peace*, London: The Women's Press.

Rushdy, A. H. A. 1990 'Rememory: Primal Scenes and Constructions in Toni Morrison's Novels', *Contemporary Literature* 31 (3): 300–23.

Sage, L. 1994a *Angela Carter*, Plymouth: Northcote House.

Sage, L. (ed.) 1994b *Flesh and the Mirror. Essays on the Art of Angela Carter*, London: Virago.

Sayers, J. 1991 *Mothering Psychoanalysis*, London: Hamish Hamilton.

Schapiro, B. 1991 'The Bonds of Love and the Boundaries of Self in Toni Morrison's *Beloved*', *Contemporary Literature* 32 (2): 194–210.

Scharfmann, R. 1982 'Mirroring and Mothering in Simone Schwarz-Bart's *Pluie et vent sur Télumée Miracle* and Jean Rhys's *Wide Sargasso Sea*', *Yale French Studies* 62: 88–106.

Stern, D. 1976 *The First Relationship: Infant and Mother*, Cambridge, MA: Harvard University Press.

Stevenson, A. 1989 *Bitter Fame. A Life of Sylvia Plath*, Harmondsworth: Penguin.

Tate, C. (ed.) 1985 *Black Women Writers at Work*, Harpenden: Oldcastle Books.

Wagner-Martin, L. 1987 *Sylvia Plath. A Biography*, New York: Simon & Schuster.

Wandor, M. 1983 *On Gender and Writing*, London: Pandora.

Warner, M. 1985 *Alone of All Her Sex. The Myth and the Cult of the Virgin Mary*, London: Picador.

Watts, H. C. 1987 'Angela Carter: an interview', *Bête Noire* Spring: 161–76.

White, A. 1933/1978 *Frost in May*, London: Virago.

White, A. 1950/1979 *The Lost Traveller*, London: Virago.

White, A. 1952/1979 *The Sugar House*, London: Virago.

White, A. 1954/1979 *Beyond the Glass*, London: Virago.

White, E. C. 1998 'Alice Walker on Finding Your Bliss', *MS* IX (2): 42–50.

White, R. 1993 'Essay: the Novels of Michèle Roberts', *Bête Noire* 14/15: 144–57.

White, R. 1993 'An Interview with Michèle Roberts', *Bête Noire* 14/15: 125–40.

Whitford, M. (ed.) 1991a *The Irigaray Reader*, Oxford: Basil Blackwell.

Whitford, M. 1991b *Luce Irigaray. Philosophy in the Feminine*, London and New York: Routledge.

Willis, C. 1991 'Contemporary Irish Women Poets: the Privatisation of Myth'. In: *Diverse Voices. Essays on Twentieth-Century Women Writers in English* H. Devine Jump (ed.), New York and London: Harvester Wheatsheaf, pp. 248–72.

Willis, S. 1987 *Specifying. Black Women Writing the American Experience*, London: Routledge.

Winnicott, D. 1971 'Mirror-Role of Mother and Family', *Playing and Reality*, New York: Basic Books.

Wong, S. C. 1993 *Reading Asian American Literature. From Necessity to Extravagance*, Princeton: Princeton University Press.

Woodcock, B. 1986 'Post-1975 Caribbean fiction and the challenge to English literature', *Critical Quarterly* 28 (4): 79–95.